MONUMENTS OF THE
BRITISH NEOLITHIC

5

The Roots of Architecture

For Mum and Dad,
Delia and Justin

Wiltshire 1973 – France 1984,
where this book really began

Cover image: Stonehenge at dusk Phil Rowley

MILES RUSSELL

MONUMENTS OF THE BRITISH NEOLITHIC

The Roots of Architecture

TEMPUS

First published 2002

PUBLISHED IN THE UNITED KINGDOM BY:

Tempus Publishing Ltd
The Mill, Brimscombe Port
Stroud, Gloucestershire GL5 2QG
www.tempus-publishing.com

PUBLISHED IN THE UNITED STATES OF AMERICA BY:

Tempus Publishing Inc.
2 Cumberland Street
Charleston, SC 29401
1-888-313-2665
www.tempuspublishing.com

British Library Cataloguing in Publication Data.
A catalogue record for this book is available from the British Library.

ISBN 0 7524 1953 6

Typesetting and origination by Tempus Publishing.
PRINTED AND BOUND IN GREAT BRITAIN

Contents

List of illustrations

Text figures

Colour Plates

Acknowledgements

The work has its origins in a doctoral thesis conducted at Bournemouth University into the Neolithic monuments of south eastern England. Following discussion with my internal supervisors, Tim Darvill, Kevin Andrews and Roger Doonan, and external examiners Alasdair Whittle and Colin Richards, it became clear that the theories set out in the thesis on the nature and origins of the earliest architecture required greater application. As a result, this text has evolved. I doubt that my supervisors and examiners would now recognise much of what follows (and I certainly do not claim that they agree with any of the comments made hereafter), but I would nevertheless like to thank them for setting me on this particular course of research and investigation.

My thought processes have been greatly helped in the course of my writing by discussion with, and advice from, fellow colleagues, friends and students here in Bournemouth University (most of whom are probably now heartily sick of 'linear structured mounds' and 'vertical land cuts'). A much deserved thank you must go to Vanessa Constant and Ehren Milner: Vanessa for producing all the line drawings presented here and for coping so well with obscure instructions, misinformation (none of it intentional) and poorly photocopied scraps of paper; Ehren for dealing with strange computer software, complex north arrows and the endless conversion of imperial measurements to metrics.

I also owe a huge debt of gratitude to Emma Young and Barbara Alcock of the Sussex Archaeological Society for allowing me access to, and for reproducing, images from the excellent archive that is the Society's photographic collection. Thank you to Gareth Talbot, Tim Darvill, Bronwen Russell and Phil Rowley of Bournemouth University, Derek and Jane Russell, and Sally White of Worthing Museum for allowing me to reproduce some of their excellent photographs here. Thanks also to Louise Pearson, Linda Fransen, Jeff Chartrand and all at I.T. Services at Bournemouth University for resolving the (many) complex issues surrounding technology. I am grateful, as always, to Peter Kemmis Betty and all at Tempus publishing for their help and advice and also for their unswerving belief that the book would be delivered on time. Not even I believed this.

A number of people read and commented upon various chapters and were able to correct errors in both spelling and thinking. Particular thanks here to Roger Doonan, John Gale, Tim Darvill and Glynis Laughlin. Any mistakes, inaccuracies or strange idiosyncrasies that remain are solely my responsibility. The Research Committee of the Archaeology Group at Bournemouth University made a number of generous grants in order to facilitate photographic reproduction, data collection and travel, something which I am particularly grateful of considering this book was written through a time of countryside, motorway and railway shut down (resulting from outbreaks of Foot and Mouth, various fuel protests and industrial action). Special thanks must go to my wife Bronwen for her inexhaustible patience in the face of my obsession with prehistoric architecture (and reluctance to deal with the real world) and apologies to my daughter Megan, who wanted *The Cat in the Hat*, but instead got *The Social Foundations of Prehistoric Britain*.

This book is dedicated to my parents, for first encouraging my love of the past and for permitting countless detours whilst on family holiday to view obscure Roman marching camps and overgrown portal dolmens, and also to my sister and brother for coping with 'yet another trek through a muddy field' between the years 1973 and 1984. Hopefully this goes some way to explaining why I think it was all worth while.

Bournemouth, June 2001

1 Introduction: the Neolithic and 'us'

The Neolithic or 'New Stone Age' was a revolution in every sense of the word. It represents the most fundamental period of change ever to occur within the history of human society. It marks the end of human reliance upon solely the hunting and gathering of foodstuffs and the origins of farming. It is characterised by the first major pieces of land clearance and the demarcation of distinct territories; fixed settlements and major building projects. It marks the end of the natural order of things. It marks the origin of the modern world.

Much of human society is today dominated by two discrete, if heavily interlinked, elements: a dependence on intensive food production and a reliance upon the built environment in which to live and work. Britain, at the beginning of the twenty-first century, is a place where agriculture and architecture increasingly serve to define, and indeed divide, the human community. City development, urban regeneration, crime, traffic congestion and pollution, continue to keep issues surrounding town life at the fore of modern political debate. More recently, however, fuel prices, government subsidies, the decline of the rural economy, fox hunting, public access and epidemics such as B.S.E. and Foot and Mouth, have served to highlight specific rural demands, issues and concerns.

The divide between town and country, between the agricultural world and the architectural, is of course nothing new. Although most people's idea of paradise seems to be a pastoral one, there is a solid tradition of hostility between urbanites and agriculturalists. Sometimes the friction explodes into open conflict. Plague, pestilence, famine and war: the traditional four horseman of the apocalypse, together with their lesser known saddle-mate taxation, have throughout history regularly stirred up social unrest between town and country. From the first Civitas towns of Roman Britain, through the black death, numerous peasant revolts, land enclosures, costly foreign wars, economic recessions and the industrial revolution, history has taught those who live in the countryside to mistrust those who live in cities, whilst those who work in the towns are often deeply suspicious of the rural community. 'Townie' and 'Yokel'; the gulf would today appear insurmountable.

Yet it has not always been like this. The classic social divide is actual a very recent phenomenon within the complex history of human cultural development. There was no 'countryside' to speak of 10,000 years ago in Britain, precisely because there were no towns. There were no farms, nor major pieces of land development. There were no great pieces of architecture. In fact, 10,000 years ago there was no significant human impact upon the land other than the casual bit of species extinction or the occasional piece of deforestation. Generally speaking humankind had not made its presence felt. At some stage this whole situation changed, and human society was set upon the path to global industrialisation and total dependence on agricultural production.

Why?

Why did society switch from a lifestyle of hunting and gathering food, a comparatively easy way of life when compared to farming, to one of intensive food production? Why did they carve up the land so dramatically with ditches, banks, fences and hedges? Why did they start to create such immense monuments to themselves and their dead? Why did they start killing each other in rather large numbers? Why did they want to control the natural order of things so emphatically? What on earth were our ancestors thinking of?

There is no easy answer to any of these questions, though it is clear that, at the very heart of the dilemma, is a great and pivotal divide, not just between town and country, but between more fundamental issues: namely between hunter-gatherer and agriculturalist.

The vast majority of the world's population today depends upon the fruits of agriculture and industry. They do not actively hunt, trap, ensnare, kill, skin and dismember their food; neither do they plant seeds, protect and control their growth then harvest the end product. Instead, they buy their food ready packed (or sometimes even ready cooked) from supermarket shelves. The gulf between those that depend upon natural resources, and their own skill in locating and collecting enough of these resources to survive on, and those who work, eat, sleep and play in a world of brick, glass, steel and concrete is immense. It is almost as if the two forms of lifestyle reflect two very different species of human: on the one hand the industrialised agriculturalist who largely dominates the planet; on the other the hunter-gatherer who is clearly dying out.

There is an advertisement playing on British television at the present time (2001), which shows a bemused, fur-clad Inuit male arriving at a major European airport (why is unfortunately never explained). The piece relates the poor man's exploits as he struggles to cope with the customs and lifestyle of the modern European. The hunter-gatherer does not understand modern forms of transport, such as the internal combustion engine, or communication, such as the television, fax and mobile phone. He does not comprehend European customs and conventions. He is an anachronism. The advert may have been intended as another take on the theme of the 'innocent abroad' in a strange and wholly foreign land, but I cannot help feeling that, in reality, it is just another example of the casual bigotry directed towards those who pursue a hunter-gatherer lifestyle on the fringes of the modern developed world. The agriculturalist/architecturalist does not understand the hunter-gatherer lifestyle and views it with curiosity, or worse with ridicule and contempt.

The theme of the culturally naïve let loose within modern society (inevitably with 'hilarious' consequences), is not new; it recurs in countless cinematic, televisual and literary outings throughout the eighteenth, nineteenth and twentieth centuries. The only real difference is that today, the innocent savage of films such as *Crocodile Dundee* or *George of the Jungle* is used as much to highlight the alien, idiosyncratic, bizarre and sometimes stupid nature of western, urbanised society, as much as to provoke a laugh at 'our less civilised human cousin'. Earlier cinematic references to those existing beyond the limits of the civilised world were unfortunately far more damning. One only has to see how Native African society was portrayed within the first pieces of twentieth-century cinema (such as is evident in any of the early *Tarzan* movies), to realise that bigotry and racism were endemic in the movie business.

Before the British accent became the necessary prerequisite for a Hollywood villain, celluloid evil was usually personified by the 'alien', the native, the tribal. Nowhere is this clearer than in the movie genre known as the Western, where the Native American gets a particularly raw deal. Not even the child-friendly world of the Disney corporation was immune to this syndrome, the 1953 *Peter Pan* movie containing some frankly incredible scenes of casual bigotry, particularly in the less than charming song 'What Made the Red Man Red?' (with its chorus line: 'When did he first say ugh?'). Thankfully, the world-view that inspired and directed such perspectives has today been largely consigned to the cultural dustbin. It is nevertheless a sobering thought that for many people around the globe, first contact with the indigenous societies of the 'New World' was through celluloid, a medium that delighted in showing native groups as culturally impoverished, warlike and savage, with only the basic rudiments of a language. The unswerving Euro-American perspective, evident in pretty much every Western made until the mid-1970s, was that the civilising influence of white society brought peace to the cruel and barbaric native hunter-gatherer. History, of course, is written by the victors, and the reality of the Native American lifestyle, both before and after contact with Europe, is very different.

Despite these subtle shifts in outlook, it is evident that a large percentage of today's western, industrialised society still views members of the non-urban, non-agricultural world as second or third-class citizens. Civilisation is equated with towns, farms and a settled lifestyle, from which high art, science and literature is deemed to evolve. Barbarism is equated with hunting, nomadism and seemingly crude levels of art or architecture. Societies on the fringe of the developing world have been, and continue to be, thought of as peoples whose right to exist is compromised by their opposition to change. The relationship between 'civilisation' and 'barbarism', or those who base their subsistence upon agricultural production and those who rely primarily on hunting and gathering, has been recently well summarised by Hugh Brody, in his book *The Other Side of Eden*:

> Agricultural peoples, especially in the world's rich nation-states, are numerous, immensely rich, well armed and domineering. Hunter-gatherers are few in number, poor, self-effacing and possessed of little military strength. The farmers have it in their power to overwhelm hunter-gatherers, and they continue to do so in the few regions of the world where this domination is not already complete.

The citizens of the modern world, be they farmer or city dweller, are shapers of the natural order, seeking to control all things. They are builders. They are domesticators. They are control freaks at the top of the food chain. The hunter-gatherers, in contrast, do not seek to change, control or reorder the natural world, but just want to survive within it. To do this successfully, they must maintain a form of balance between themselves and other forms of life. They are not automatically at the top of the food chain and they do not seek to permanently alter the land around them. The land provides a way of life, within which to invoke change of the sort advocated by the agriculturalists is to commit a form culturcide. The basic difference between 'farmer' and 'hunter-gatherer' is therefore not simply a battle between different forms of food production, it is a brutal war of conflicting ideologies. It is a war of attrition that has been fought for millennia, and it is one that the hunter-gatherer unfortunately cannot win.

Before the advent of the 'Neolithic revolution', with its emphasis on building and domestication, the human race survived through the hunting of animals and the gathering of plant life. The hunter-gatherer societies of Europe were remarkably successful, adapting to a diverse series of landscapes, environments and climates, over several millennia. A terminal decline, however, began around 10,000-6,000 years ago. From this moment trees were cut down and vegetation erased on a scale never seen before. Enclosures and boundary ditches were created, dividing huge swathes of land. Fields were ploughed and seeds planted. Animals were corralled and controlled. New forms of permanent settlement were built. The human and animal dead were disposed of in new and novel ways. Deep cuts were made down into the earth. New forms of artefact, including pottery, sickles and querns, were used and circulated. This was the beginning of the Neolithic. The modern era had begun.

The change from hunting and gathering to reliance on agricultural production is not, however, a given, evolutionary path down which all humans are destined to travel. It is certainly not a progression towards an easier existence. To begin with, a reliance on farming and the construction of land boundaries requires a far greater input of labour than those life patterns associated with hunting and gathering. People have to cut down and remove all forms of unwanted surface vegetation. They have to break the ground, sow their crops, control their animal population and protect it from predators whilst simultaneously preventing the herd from eating or damaging crops. They must harvest the end result. They must build substantial structures, houses, shelters and food storage facilities. There is a far greater dependence on a far smaller range of resources which, if everything goes wrong, may result in nutritional deficiencies as well as increasing the risk of famine. It may also increase the chances of all-out war with the immediate neighbours, who may possess a better range of stored foodstuffs. Given these considerations, one may be excused for wondering why agriculture was adopted in the first place. It is a mystery that has bedevilled archaeologists, anthropologists, sociologists and historians for well over 100 years. It is a mystery that appears no closer to resolution.

If we wish to understand the origins of the modern world, we need to study and explain the change from the Mesolithic, or 'Middle Stone Age', to Neolithic.

We must examine both archaeological and anthropological datasets. We must attempt to understand how our ancestors lived and the ways in which they visualised the land. We must 'get into the heads' of our Mesolithic and Neolithic predecessors. We must rethink the past. To do this successfully, given that so much time has elapsed and there is no one left to interview, we need to go back to what primary evidence there is, and as the earliest information that we possess for the Neolithic, certainly in Britain, is derived from monuments, it is to these that we must turn. In short, to understand how we got to this particular point in human societal development (this 'great social quagmire' as a colleague of mine often describes it), we must go back and assess the roots of architecture.

This book is not presented as an attempt to catalogue all elements that represent the British Neolithic. It is not intended to be a comprehensive list, nor an exhaustive discussion of all the 'facts' as revealed by archaeological excavation. There are enough works like this in existence, and the better ones (in my mind anyway) are listed in the further reading section at the back of this particular work. Lists and catalogues, however worthy, can sometimes come over as deathly dull; data collection and dissemination for its own sake with little or no acknowledgement of the need to explain, interpret or understand. To this extent, the present work may appear overly selective in the data, sites, case studies and examples cited and discussed. I make no apology for this. This work is presented as an attempt to explain the Neolithic, and its impact upon the land, through the inception and establishment of the first pieces of architecture; namely the mound, the enclosure, the shaft and the uprights of timber and stone.

Many of the arguments set out here may appear somewhat one-sided; I do not challenge this. The archaeological evidence has indeed been selected in order to illustrate a particular view of the past but, rather crucially, I do not believe that my argument damages the archaeological evidence in any shape or form. It does not falsify the data; it does not fudge the issues; it does not compromise the facts. It is, however, one particular interpretation and, as Richard Reece has already noted, in his book *My Roman Britain*:

> In details most interpretations will differ. It is far more unlikely that two very different people will come to the same interpretation than different ones, yet disagreement is generally thought to be a sign of trouble, error or downright bloody mindedness. It is not, it is a sign of openness and healthy thinking.

My general take on the Neolithic is permeated by the philosophy of René Magritte (1898-1967), the foremost surrealist painter of the twentieth century. This is not an exercise in the wilfully obscure, for Magritte, throughout his life, attempted to examine the nature of reality by questioning the world around him: 'to overthrow our sense of the familiar, to sabotage our habits, to put the real world on trial'. This he attempted to achieve through the deliberate juxtaposition of materials, objects, words and landscapes, constantly confronting issues concerning the ambiguity of sight, thought and language.

In what are possibly his most famous works, *La Trahison des Images* ('The Treachery of Images'), painted in 1929, Magritte sought to examine the discrepancy between an object and the way in which that object is represented, by painting a pipe and placing above it an inscription stating 'Ceci n'est pas une pipe' (This is not a pipe). Here Magritte was demonstrating that there was no clear association between an object and the name given to categorise that object; name or category not actually representing what the object really is. Throughout his life, Magritte developed this concept further, hoping to dislocate language from precision and scientific certainty, the fundamental centre to his work being in the exploitation of all possibilities. Everyday objects were shown outsized and wildly out of context. Landscapes possessed crucial flaws in perspective. Paradoxes existed as Magritte forced the observer to question their perception of the world. An observer cannot be complacent in their outlook. They must constantly question what they perceive their reality to be.

The need to question a perceived reality is the inspiration behind this particular study of Neolithic architecture. Whilst I do not intend to subvert the complacent view of the physical world in the same way that Magritte intended, I do hope that by here questioning conservative, orthodox (some might add 'lazy') definitions and interpretations, that the ordinary and familiar may appear more extraordinary and unfamiliar. By questioning even the most apparently solid of facts, alternative inter-pretations, viewpoints and conclusions may be attained. To do this successfully, we must break down all rigid forms of classification. We must explore all possibilities. We must question what we perceive to be our own archaeological reality. This then is my own particular view of the primary archaeological resource and I actively encourage those who disagree with what is said in this book to examine the dataset for themselves, engage in debate and finally present their own take on the evidence.

This book is divided into three discrete sections. To begin with, I will examine just what we mean by monumental architecture, and what forms the earliest pieces of architecture took within the context of Neolithic Britain. Having outlined the first monuments, and attempted to explain what they may have meant to those that designed and built them, I will focus in on three specific case studies taken from the British Isles, which illustrate how such architecture first impacted upon the land. A final conclusion puts 'the Neolithic' into perspective, and suggests an explanation of why humans first made that all too significant change from a semi-nomadic, hunter-gatherer lifestyle, to a fixed society increasingly reliant upon monuments and more intensive forms of food production.

This then is a story of 'us', of how we got into this mess and why we are not all presently skinning seals off the coast of Greenland.

2 The meaning of monuments

Today we are surrounded by a host of architectural forms, be they houses, office blocks, religious buildings, ancient structures, tombs, bridges or statues (**1**, **2**, **3**, **4** and **colour plate 1**). Architecture represents the way in which humans have, and continue to alter their immediate environment by enclosing and reshaping space. Architecture changes the way we visualise, perceive or understand particular places and, whatever we think about it, it is crucial to the way in which we engage with and move through the world. Architecture generates a framework of shared experience. It imposes order.

Within the social frameworks of the modern world, daily activities are easily classified, often being set apart within discrete pieces of architecture. Modern societies, for example, often house particular religious events within clearly defined structures such as the church, synagogue, mosque or temple. Formal education usually takes place in purpose built nurseries, schools, colleges or universities, whilst offices house those engaged in a specific form of work. Places important for public services or the criminal justice system will often sit within specially designed structures such as the library, police station, fire station or court of law. Entertainment can be staged in amphitheatres, sporting arenas, race circuits, theatres or cinemas, whilst the consumption of food and drink usually occurs in restaurants, bars, pubs, cafés or burger-palaces. When we want to escape from it all we can go to the hotel or holiday camp via the railway station, bus depot, or airport. When we are unwell we go to the surgery or hospital. When we die we go to the cemetery or crematorium.

Our view of the prehistoric past is shaped by this world-view. When we examine Neolithic architecture, the first monumental structures built by prehistoric communities within the Britain, we unconsciously look for patterns and similarities, even if none exist. We interpret according to our own experience. We attempt classification. We try to explain. Such parcelling-up of the British Neolithic into a series of orderly and uncluttered categories may, however, prove somewhat misguided. Neolithic society was, in all probability, vastly different to our own. When we today use forms of architectural classification such as the 'Barrow', the 'Mine' or the 'Enclosure', we should be wary that we are interpreting these ancient monuments through the cultural frameworks of today. These terms may appear harmless enough, but they are loaded with meanings relevant to modern society. How relevant they are to the societies that originally planned and constructed the prehistoric monuments themselves is debatable.

1   *Athens: the Parthenon on the Acropolis, built between 447 and 432 BC by Callicrates and Ictinus under the direction of Phidias, is the best known of all ancient Greek structures. It glorifies the state, honours the Athenian gods and commemorates great military victories through the ordered and controlled use of geometry and mathematical precision in architecture.* Miles Russell

Let me explain

The term 'Barrow' or tumulus is perhaps the most loaded of all archaeological terms. First coined by the antiquarian investigators of the seventeenth, eighteenth and nineteenth centuries, the term is taken today to encompass all forms of earthen mound, be they circular, oval or rectangular, that cover human burials. Barrows are therefore often viewed as monuments raised to commemorate the human dead. Because so few barrow sites are known, in comparison to the numbers of people that must have lived in prehistoric times, and given the amount of time and effort required to construct such mounds, any bodies found inside a barrow mound are often taken to represent the important people in society: the powerful, successful, rich or holy. Round barrows of the British Bronze Age tend to cover single burials; hence we view this period as a time when individuals were coming to the fore of political power. Neolithic long barrows cover multiple skeletal deposits, often disarticulated or separated body parts rather than complete individuals. Hence it is common for archaeologists to view these structures as the burial mounds of more

2 Rome: the Arch of Constantine. *The grand designs and major building projects of the Roman state were made possible through use of the arch, a basic architectural form celebrated in dramatic triumphal monuments such as this. The Arch of Constantine, celebrating the triumph of the western emperor over his rival Maxentius in AD 312, synthesises the political ideology of Constantine and monumentalises the propaganda of the state. Much of the structure was assembled from pieces plundered from earlier monuments, something that would have emphasised not only the control of the past by Constantine, but also his effective rewriting of history.* Bronwen Russell

egalitarian societies, or the burial sites of the ancestral dead, the resting-place for a particular dynasty.

The 'Mine' or shaft, cut down into the natural bedrock, is almost always viewed as being purely functional. These deep cuts are usually taken to represent the earliest large-scale economic features of British prehistory; the first pieces of industrial archaeology designed to extract large amounts of subterranean flint. 'Enclosures', or causewayed camps as they are still sometimes referred to, clearly delimit an area of ground, setting it apart from its surrounding landscape. They have variously been interpreted as the earliest pieces of evidence for private ownership, structures designed to protect agriculture or enclose housing, or as a site promoting some form of ceremonial activity. The current feeling is that Neolithic enclosures represent religious centres or cult places, as the ditches related to many possess large amounts of votive or ritual deposits, including human remains.

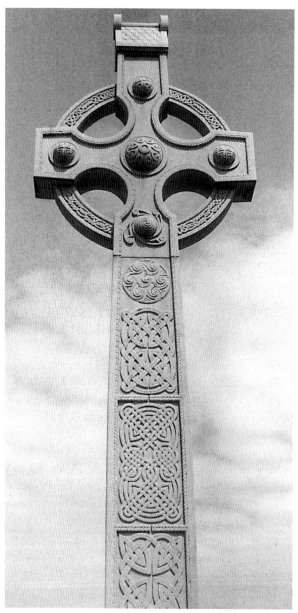

3 *Tynwald: The monumental used to commemorate those who lost their lives fighting for the state against a political ideology alien to their own.* Bronwen Russell

Unfortunately the monuments that we encounter within the British Neolithic do not fall into such neat and easily digestible packages. There are incongruities, parallels, dissimilarities and paradoxes, which are often overlooked. More importantly there are significant gaps in our knowledge, in the primary archaeological database and, more worryingly, in our own ability or willingness to understand. By constructing a series of rigid categories such as Long Barrow, Flint Mine or Causewayed Camp/Enclosure, archaeologists run the risk of imposing definitions that possess little or no validity when compared to the prehistoric reality. If we persist in seeing the Neolithic from the same

4   Rome: ruins in the forum, once the hub of the mightiest empire in the ancient world, echoing Percy Shelley's words in Ozymandias: 'Round the decay of that colossal wreck, boundless and bare, the lone and level sands stretch far away'. All works, however mighty an architectural, ideological or political statement, eventually succumb to time. Bronwen Russell

general perspective (with barrows as burial monuments, mines as industrial monuments and enclosures as ritual monuments), instead of questioning even the most fundamental of issues, then we will never come to any new conclusions about the past.

Meaning and context, as I have already noted, are not constant, either to those who originally built or developed particular monuments, or to those archaeologists, anthropologists, historians, geographers and geologists who study the sites today. In this respect there can never be definitive answers as to the nature of Neolithic architecture, but it is clear that we need to alter the questions and change our mindset, so that we can generate, develop and discuss alternatives.

To this end, this book will attempt to dispense with the usual, rigid definitions and classifications, which have achieved little but straightjacket our understanding of the Neolithic past. Of course it is never possible to do away entirely with some form of categorisation, but the terms used in this work are kept as basic as possible, defining elementary aspects of site morphology, without recourse to designations that, through constant use, have become over-familiar or imply an clear understanding of function. The terms that I would prefer to use here are therefore: shaft or vertical cut instead of mine; enclosure or horizontal cut instead of causewayed camp; and structured mound instead of long or round barrow.

The category of Neolithic shaft covers all types of deep vertical cut, set either individually or in large clusters. The majority of shafts appear to relate in some way to flint extraction, but an attempt will be made to avoid the term 'flint mine', for it is clear that a significant number of shaft sites possess attributes unrelated to general mining activity. The category of Neolithic enclosure or horizontal cut covers all areas of land fully or partially defined by a ditch and bank. As already noted, the temptation to overuse terms such as 'causewayed camp', 'cursus' or 'henge' will be avoided where possible as, although these are popular within literature, the designations themselves have lost focus due to the sheer variety of monument forms now recorded from the British Neolithic.

The category of structured mound will cover the variety of earthen and stone built features, usually accompanied by linear ditches, which have been recorded across the British Isles. Some mounds originally contained internal compartments made from stone and/or timber. The majority contained structured deposits which sometimes included human bone. The categories of structured mound examined here comprise both linear and round, the more circular forms usually representing a later development. The terms 'long', 'oval' and 'short', still used today to classify linear mounds, are not mentioned here as they are considered to be needlessly divisive. Similarly the term 'barrow' itself will be strictly avoided where possible, for it implies a burial or funerary function, something which should not be taken for granted.

Let us begin.

3 Structured mounds

The classic form of a Neolithic structured mound, a broadly rectangular earthwork flanked by two linear ditches sometimes with impressive internal stone chambers, today represents the most distinctive and easily recognisable monument type from British prehistory (**colour plates 5 and 6**). Mounds such as this, usually formed from a combination of earth and timber or earth and stone, have been identified right across the British Isles, though discrete and distinct regional clusters and forms have been noted. Recently it has become clear that the linear was not the only form of mound set up in the British Neolithic, as round forms have been identified, though overall they are much less common.

Linear structured mounds appear to have been built in Britain between 4200 and 3000 BC, the bulk being constructed between 3600-3000 BC. The earliest date for an earthen structure, 4700-3750 BC, was derived from charcoal recovered from the base of a flanking ditch at Lambourn, but this may, on present evidence, be anomalous. Radiocarbon determinations for pre-mound features, such as the 'mortuary house' (discussed below), are more limited, though dates of 4350BC-3700 BC have been produced for charcoal found within a structure at Fussell's Lodge.

In the discussion that follows, distinction will be made between two main types of structured mound, based upon their material composition: namely those mounds composed predominantly of timber and earth and those composed of, or structured with, stone. These distinctions may, as we shall see, have less to do with the geological resources to hand, and more to do with the original intent and use of the particular monument in question.

TIMBER AND EARTH

Comparing the earth and timber structured mounds of the British Neolithic is a particularly difficult task, for many have been badly hit by varying degrees of weathering, erosion, modification, antiquarian excavation and agricultural damage. The problem of comparing like with like is further compounded by the fact that comparatively few mounds have ever been fully excavated or indeed scientifically recorded.

The recorded survey and investigation of prehistoric structured mounds has been taking place for some considerable time, though there is much that remains unknown about their meaning, function, origins and chronology. The antiquarian John Aubrey was arguably the first to document linear mounds in the seventeenth century, as a form of 'sepulchre' distinct from round mounds. A series of limited examinations of long mounds were made throughout the seventeenth, eighteenth and nineteenth centuries by antiquarian explorers. Few investigations were adequately recorded, though the work of William Stukeley, Richard Colt Hoare, William Cunnington, John Thurnam, William Greenwell, John Robert Mortimer and Augustus Lane Fox Pitt-Rivers stand out as model projects of their time.

Stukeley affected the mindset of the early antiquarian excavator by interpreting long mounds as the final resting place of 'archdruids'. Druids, as any reader of the *Asterix* books is aware, were the semi-mystical, celtic priestly class in pre-Roman Gaul, referred to in obtuse terms by Julius Caesar. In Stukeley's day, without a useful dating sequence or radiocarbon chronology, any strange or non-Roman archaeological structure was automatically assigned to this vague 'Celtic' period.

The first serious pieces of investigation into Neolithic linear mounds brought disappointment; there were no well appointed graves of archdruids, only disarticulated human bone, flint and broken pottery. Cunnington dug into nearly 20 such sites across Salisbury Plain in the early nineteenth century, but the few finds did not aid interpretation. The fragmentary and disordered remains of the human dead simply did not appear compatible with the sheer size and scale of the overlying earthworks. Absence of significant burial deposits, and in some cases of burials at all, led Thurnam to note, in the latter half of the nineteenth century, that linear mounds should be regarded as distinctive monuments in their own right, rather than 'mere tombs'.

With the realisation that Bronze Age round mounds, with their often high status grave goods, were more profitable things to investigate, the examination of linear mounds effectively ceased. In 1847, John Akerman reflected the general mood when he observed that the fruits of linear mounds were not worth the effort of excavation, such work often being 'tedious, irksome and laborious'. This view was effectively countered by John Thurnam in a couple of papers published in 1868 and 1872. Thurnam, a keen student of physical anthropology, was attracted to the skeletal material contained in long mounds, and conducted a considerable programme of fieldwork upon a number of sites in Wiltshire. His work represents the first serious attempt to study the internal and external form of long mounds, date them and find a proper place for them within the social context of prehistoric Britain.

The first detailed examination of a linear mound was conducted by Augustus Lane Fox Pitt-Rivers upon Wor Barrow between 1893-4. This examination, meticulously recorded in *Excavations on Cranborne Chase volume IV*, revealed a series of timber structures, interpreted as 'a wooden version of the long chambers of stone'. Since Pitt-Rivers there have been many more investigations into Neolithic mound forms, most prominently in southern Britain, at sites such as Alfriston, Horslip and Kingston Deverill, following the threatened erasure of sites through increased agricultural and building activity.

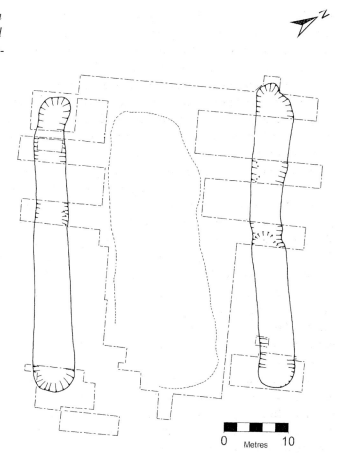

5 *South Street: plan of an 'empty' linear structured mound (centre) of rectangular type and flanking ditches as excavated.* Redrawn from Ashbee, Smith, and Evans 1979

Linear mounds

Colt Hoare and Thurnam, working at different times in the nineteenth century, observed that there were broadly two categories of linear mound structure: those resembling 'an egg or a pear cut longitudinally' and those where there was little difference in mound width at either end. These two basic forms of classification remain in use to this day, the former known as 'trapezoidal' and the latter simply as 'rectangular' (**5**). The wider end of the trapezoid is generally viewed as the business end of the mound, providing a clear visual focus to the structure. Sometimes this focus was supplemented with the building of a timber or stone forecourt or façade.

In most cases, the surviving length and width of a particular long mound represents its major defining characteristic. Measurements of mound form should in theory provide a reasonable idea of the original nature of the monument, as well as providing reasonable points of comparison with other sites. Unfortunately, any observation concerning the present condition of mounds cannot be relied upon too heavily, due to the often severe nature of plough damage sustained. A more reliable way of comparing like with like for this class of monument would perhaps derive from the measurement

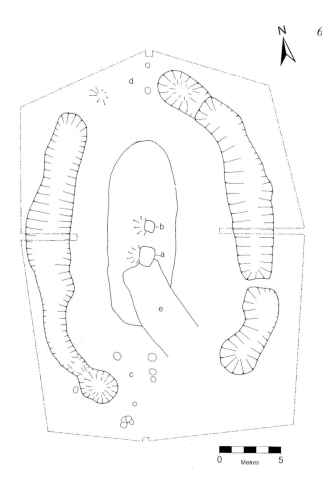

N

6 *Alfriston: plan of linear struc-tured mound as excavated. Features: a = position of intrusive human burial; b = pit of unknown date; c = postholes forming timber elab-oration at southern edge of the mound; d = postholes forming timber elaboration at northern edge of the mound; e = area of unrecorded anti-quarian disturbance.*
Redrawn from Drewett 1975

0   Metres   5

of sub-surface features, such as flanking ditches. Lack of reliable information derived from excavation or geophysical survey, however, means that major comparisons must continue to focus upon what can be seen at ground level. Despite these somewhat pessimistic observations, we can still put forward a 'best guess' for the maximum and minimum length of Neolithic long mounds in Britain, Ian Kinnes having calculated this to be in the range of 125m and 14m, the overall average being 47m.

Oval mounds

The term 'oval barrow' or 'oval mound' has crept into the archaeological literature in recent years, as an intermediary stage in evolution between the Neolithic long mound and the round mounds of the Bronze Age. The term, first proposed as a discrete class by Colt Hoare in the early nineteenth century, owes its reinstatement to the investigation of mounds at Alfriston, North Marden and Abingdon in the late 1970s and early 1980s. It is usually applied in instances where the overall length of a particular earthwork is shorter than twice its width.

At Alfriston, a linear mound, interpreted by its excavator as an oval barrow, seemed to cover the skeleton of a single adult female (**6**). This raised an interesting possibility, for it implied that the oval form was an intermediary stage between linear and circular mound. If further oval mounds could be shown to have covered single inhumations, then the class as a whole may be taken to represent the missing link between communal Neolithic burial and the more individual deposits recorded from later round mounds. The term 'oval barrow' was suddenly in vogue, and it was not long before a number of structurally and geographically diverse mounds across Britain was suddenly being reclassified.

The first signs that the sub species 'oval' was not all that it seemed came when the Alfriston skeleton was subjected to radiocarbon dating. When the dates were produced, they suggested an origin in the Late Bronze or Early Iron Age. The body was a late intrusion into the mound. Once the Alfriston inhumation was removed, significant doubts began to circulate about other oval barrow sites. At the mound of Moody's Down SE, destroyed without detailed examination during the Second World War, there was no certainty of how the single recorded skeleton had originally related to the mound. At Hambledon Hill, an oval mound had been disrupted by a bulldozer in the early 1960s, ensuring that the date and associations of the single recorded skeleton were again unknown. The more that single inhumation burials derived from oval mounds were investigated, the more they appeared to be of dubious affiliation, or worse, clear secondary insertions.

How real the class of oval barrow is in terms of identifying a discrete form of Neolithic monument is debatable and its continued application would therefore seem unnecessary. To this end, the sub-categories of linear mound that have recently sprung up, namely the 'ovate', the 'short-long', 'round-long', 'large-long' and 'long-long' (which is surely the chorus to an entry in the Eurovision Song Contest), can also be ignored. They are too divisive, too unfocussed and far too confusing. These are forms of classification which serve only to parcel up and sanitise the past. Linear mounds represent a class of structure that is distinct from the circular mounds that predominate in the Bronze Age, but to subdivide them further, into a sprawling mass of subgroups, would appear inherently futile.

Neolithic linear mounds may possess differing regional traits or they may have been built for a variety of reasons at different times by different sets of people, but the fact remains that they are, in essence, structured linear mounds of earth, timber and stone. Whether such structures were built in a predominantly rectangular, trapezoidal or oval form, does not really seem to matter. Such elements do not (and should not) serve to classify, categorise and define this particular architectural form, an issue in fact raised by Thurnam in 1868 when he observed that

> all these varieties and peculiarities of form . . . seem to be very unimportant, and to have depended on the fancy, or the greater or less care and skill, of those employed in their construction.

Round Mounds

There was a time when the circular form of structured mound was thought to have been exclusive to the Bronze Age and later periods. Since the mid-1970s, however, it has become clear that many examples containing complete or disassembled human body parts did in fact exist within the Neolithic. Unfortunately, the incredible variation of internal form makes any comparative statement problematical. Unlike linear mounds, for example, the observation of subsurface cuts such as quarry ditches cannot be used as a method of recording, for Neolithic and some Early Bronze Age round mounds never appear to have possessed such features. Furthermore, the majority of Neolithic round mounds possess little in the way of a distinctive surface form, making the potential for confusion with mounds of Bronze Age, Iron Age, Roman or Saxon date considerable.

Other problems concerning the identification and interpretation of circular mounds have been outlined by Ian Kinnes in his book *Round Barrows and Ring-ditches in the British Neolithic*. These may be summarised as: the nature of 'burial' rite (disarticulated skeletons not being exclusive to the Neolithic); the potential for Neolithic flint artefacts to be incorporated within later mounds; and issues surrounding the obliteration of surface form by ploughing. It is clear that more sites require scientific examination, but what evidence there is would suggest at least three basic mound types:

1   those composed of soil and rubble derived from the excavation of quarry ditches;
2   those comprising rubble or soil derived from other associated features (pits, shafts or turf clearance);
3   cairns or stone-structured mounds composed of material gathered from the ground surface.

Although internal composition often varies considerably from site to site, a number of Neolithic round mounds demonstrate a range of features and deposits which compare favourably with those recorded from beneath linear mounds. This is particularly true in areas of northern and north-eastern England, where earthen round mounds such as Aldro 94, Callis Wold, Copt Hill, Cowlam, Garton Slack 80, Garton Slack 81 and Seamer Moor display an internal sequence that is, as we shall see, almost identical to those recorded from linear forms.

Internal structure and composition

What evidence there is suggests that the bulk of Neolithic linear mounds were constructed from rubble derived from flanking ditches and quarries. Occasionally, however, there is the suggestion of a more complex building sequence. The core of rubble mounds excavated at Alfriston, Easton Down, Fussell's Lodge, Holdenhurst, Lambourn, Moody's Down SE and Thickthorn, for example, comprised a deposit of dark brown or black soil. At Easton Down, this was viewed as representing a dump of soil and stacked turves. If so, then turf may have represented the primary design phase, where the basic ground plan of the mound was first laid out prior to its more formal construction. Alternatively, the turf may have been deliberately hidden within the core of the rubble mound in an attempt to increase its visual appearance; to mark a dramatic contrast between the rubble of the mound and the surface vegetation that surrounded it. Burying of turves may even have been to invert the natural sequence, thus emphasising human dominance over nature; the placing of bedrock over grass.

At Nutbane, the constructional sequence would appear more complicated. Here, the covering of human skeletal remains with soil, chalk blocks, oak brushwood and a mix of soil and fine chalk may have been a way of using all the materials within the immediate landscape. Similar possibilities exist for the capping of certain mounds, such as Alfriston and Bevis' Grave, with freshly excavated nodules of flint. Julian Thomas, in his book *Understanding the Neolithic*, has suggested that the accumulation of naturally occurring materials may represent a deliberate attempt to mix bone with the samples taken directly from the land, perhaps to strengthen the ties between human society and the natural world.

The mixing of human and animal bone with the land may be evident at a number of earthen round mounds investigated within areas of Neolithic flint extraction. At Blackpatch, a series of nine round mounds was investigated between 1922 and 1932. None of the mounds possessed quarry ditches, all the material necessary for their construction having been generated from chalk and flint rubble taken from the cutting of shafts. Mounds 1, 3, 5, 6, 7 and 11 had further been covered with dense layers of freshly excavated flint, derived from basal gallery systems. Although some evidence points towards a slightly later date for a number of the mounds, stratigraphic evidence strongly implies that most, and in particularly Blackpatch 1, 3 and 12, had originally been constructed during a significant phase of Neolithic flint extraction.

Similar gathering of diverse geological material may also have occurred within the linear mound of Beckhampton Road. This earthwork was formed by the semi-alternate dumping of brickearth, chalk gravel, turf, marl and coombe rock into individually fenced rectangular chambers or bays (**7**). Such separation of building materials would, the excavator noted, have ensured that the finished structure possessed a distinct patchwork effect, from the 'yellow and brown tints' of the coombe rock, brickearth and turves, to the vividly contrasting 'white marl or gravel'. Internally fenced or bayed construction, stakes offset from a single line running the length of the mound, has been identified from other Neolithic linear mounds, most notably Giants Grave I and II, South Street, Thickthorn Down, and possibly Julliberries Grave.

The rectangular subdivision of spoil within earthen long mounds would not appear to spring from a desire to increase structural stability, but it may reflect the wish to segregate different geological materials, derived from different parts of a given landscape, during the initial construction phase. It may also reflect some form of social division during building. Ian Kinnes observed in 1992 that the division of earthen mounds into discrete segments may be similar to the segmentation evident in Neolithic ditches, a feature sometimes ascribed to the involvement of different

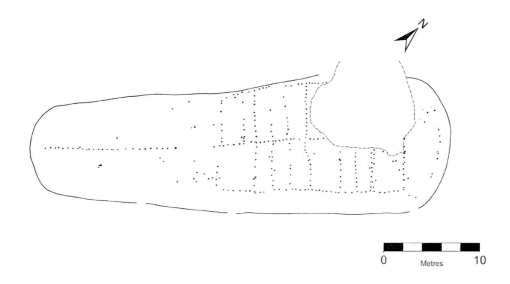

7 *Beckhampton Road: plan of linear mound as excavated showing positions of individually fenced rectangular bays, into which different geological materials had originally been segregated.* Redrawn from Ashbee, Smith and Evans 1979

social groups during construction. If differing groups were coming together to build a linear mound, each may have been allotted a separate bay to fill and complete. Such a constructional technique, different gangs working separate areas, would have emphasised the social diversity of the human group as well as the communal effort required to complete the project.

The most frequently encountered form of feature surrounding Neolithic linear mounds is the parallel set of flanking ditches running the whole length of the earthwork. Good examples of this can be seen at Bevis' Thumb, Long Burgh, Moody's Down NW and Nutbane. Other forms of ditch type are known, and these include a full circuit, with no obvious break, a full circuit interrupted at irregular intervals and the horseshoe or U-type ditch with a single break. The U-format, which usually encloses the western end of the linear mound, is evident at Thickthorn Down and Holdenhurst and would appear to be a regional variant, confined almost exclusively to the chalklands of south-west Wessex. Interrupted circuits occur at North Marden and Wor Barrow, whilst the full circuit enclosures are represented by examples at Radley, Atherfield Heath and Gib Hill. Interrupted, U-shape and continuous ditches have all been recorded from the circular forms of mound structure.

It is usual to think of ditches in purely functional terms; as features dug to provide a sufficient quantity of rubble to construct the central mound. This view has shifted somewhat, following the identification and analysis of specific artefact groups within ditch fill. Certain ditch-cuts around linear mounds, for example that at North Marden, appear furthermore to have been deliberately backfilled with earth and rubble, shortly after their initial cutting. If the ditches were designed to provide spoil for the mounds, then why (and indeed how) were some backfilled so soon after their creation? Ditch cuts may have performed a function that was originally considered to be just as important as the mound itself, a point we shall return to when we examine the artefact assemblages.

Certain Neolithic linear mounds have produced evidence for standing stones or timbers, usually at the wider of the two ends of the earthwork. These have been interpreted as façades or forestructures. A façade defines the monumental approach to an enclosure or timber building in use prior to the actual construction of the linear mound (as at Haddenham and Nutbane). Such timber structures have frequently been termed 'mortuary enclosures' or 'mortuary houses', due to the assumption that funerary activities took pre-eminence at the site prior to, during and immediately after the building of the linear mound. The term forestructure is usually applied to a set of apparently free-standing posts extending out from a potential 'mortuary enclosure' or mound structure which were presumably designed to frame the main point of access and approach. The possible significance of these chambers is discussed towards the end of this chapter.

Artefact assemblages

Artefacts other than human remains recovered from within and beneath Neolithic earth and timber mounds can vary dramatically in content, quality, quantity and state of preservation. In most cases, the disruption of the mound from ploughing and other agricultural activities means that one will never be certain what was originally present in the mound, in the ground before it was built, or inserted into the structure long after it had ceased to be of use.

The main non-human bone assemblages that occur within linear mounds are the remains of mammals, especially ox, a point first made by Thurnam in 1868. At Beckhampton Road, three ox skulls, one whole and two fragmentary, together with ox vertebrae, five sherds of Neolithic pottery, 42 worked flints (including two scrapers) and fragments of sarsen, were found at the base of the long mound, whilst at least ten antler picks, two antler rakes and multiple antler fragments were found within the core of the mound. An ox skull and foot bones were also found within the so-called mortuary house structure covered by the Fussell's Lodge mound.

Beneath the primary phase earth and timber long mound at Wayland's Smithy, pottery, struck flint, two smashed axes and a quantity of animal bone as well as a group of sarsen quernstones had been deposited. At North Marden, the area occupied by a Neolithic mound contained two scrapers, an arrowhead, firecracked flint, a large number of flakes and sherds of Neolithic pottery. At Alfriston, two antler picks and an unspecified number of sheep bones were recovered from the plough-disturbed old land surface preserved beneath the northern end of the linear mound.

Assemblages such as these may represent rubbish generated in the building or planning of a mound, or even the materials thrown out from a nearby settlement before the mound itself was ever conceived. Alternatively we may here be seeing the deliberate deposition of materials considered necessary to set down prior to the building of a particular monument. The substances may therefore express an offering to a specific deity or to the spirits of a particular place. They may represent objects made or used by the particular tribe or community engaged in the building of the mound. They may even have been objects that were in some way considered to be representative of a particular human territory or place in the landscape. They may be good luck charms. They may be 'proto-grave goods'. They may of course represent random material accidentally incorporated within or buried by a mound, but I think the structured nature of most assemblages would argue against this particular hypothesis.

The most frequently discussed find from any Neolithic mound is human bone. Dip into any text on Neolithic Britain and you will read about 'ancestor cults' and 'ancestral burial grounds', the current consensus of opinion being that mounds were a form of shrine or communal tomb. Despite the belief that linear mounds contained the selected remains of the societies that built them, finds of human bone are surprisingly scarce. A number of excavated mounds of earth and timber, such as Fussell's Lodge, do contain a relatively prolific quantity of human bone debris, but these seem to relate to structures demolished prior to the building of the mound itself.

The great majority of earth and timber long mounds across Southern Britain are curiously empty. Across the South Downs in south eastern England, for example, of all linear mounds investigated, only one, at North Marden, has produced any skeletal material and this only three small pieces. To say that this represents a limited data pool would be an understatement, especially when one compares it with the large amounts of human and animal bone recorded from the Neolithic enclosures and shafts of the same geographical area.

The two main types of human bone recorded from Neolithic mounds are articulated and disarticulated: that is to say bodies that are either complete or have in some way been disassembled. The majority of deposits, appear, like those from Fussell's Lodge as well as Wor Barrow and Nutbane, to derive from structures that pre-date the building of an earth and timber structured mound. Such buildings cannot really be used in any discussion of human burial practice within Neolithic mounds because, even though they clearly influenced the siting of the earthworks, they were built and demolished prior to the erection of the mounds. The possible significance of such structures will be discussed below, but it is worth noting here that where such early forms of building are absent, human remains from the later mound are also noticeably scarce.

The absence of human bone from earthen mound structures is only problematical if one persists in thinking of such sites as early forms of burial monument. At South Street, Horslip and Beckhampton Road, for example, the complete excavation of linear mounds failed to produce any significant human skeletal remains from primary contexts, in spite of the reasonable survival of the mounds and the potential of good bone preservation within the chalk (**8**). At Thickthorn Down, the absence of primary burial deposits was, in the words of the excavators, 'as inexplicable as it was definite'. Such a conclusion is only plausible if the mound structure in question was interpreted solely as a prehistoric burial monument.

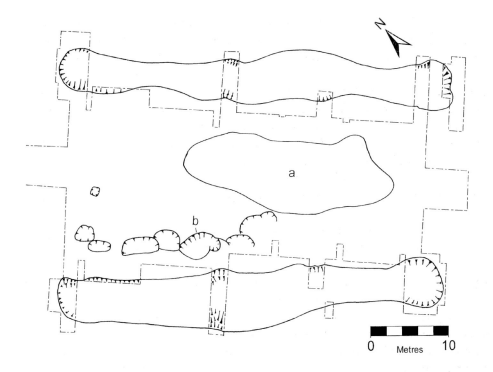

8 *Horslip: plan of an 'empty' linear mound as excavated: a = ancient land surface preserved beneath the mound structure; b = series of intersecting pits predating the more formal construction of the linear mound.* Redrawn from Ashbee, Smith and Evans 1979

Sites without obvious sign of burial can be referred to as blank mounds, cenotaphs or empty barrows, as if the dead were for some reason left out of the equation (perhaps having died or being buried elsewhere). Unfortunately, such interpretations overlook the fact that particular 'cenotaph' mound sites had often been carefully built and structured with a range of deposits (such as the ox bone material from the Beckhampton Road mound). Obsession with the supposed human funerary aspects of linear mounds can unfortunately result in the failure to see or understand significant aspects of monument construction and use.

Thurnam, writing in the latter half of the nineteenth century, observed that the scale of long mounds, when combined with the relative lack of human remains recovered, meant that they may be viewed more as monuments in their own right than as 'mere tombs'. Thurnam's words, though far-sighted, have rarely been acknowledged by later archaeologists. In 1979, the Royal Commission on the Historical Monuments of England conducted a survey of all linear mounds from Hampshire, in which they noted that 'it is questionable whether long barrows were built for the sole purpose of burying the dead'. Unfortunately, this rather significant conclusion was hidden within the introductory preface of the published survey and, like Thurnam's comments before, its potential impact was limited and was certainly not developed further.

35

If we see Neolithic linear mounds as structured heaps of soil, timber and stone containing quantities of special or ritual material, which only at times included human remains, then the clear distinction between what is and is not a 'barrow' or burial monument becomes blurred. It is worth noting that Early Neolithic shafts and enclosures have all produced human skeletal debris, sometimes more than the quantity recovered from linear mounds, yet it has never been suggested that either of these two monument types were designed for burial. Linear mounds may simply have been designed to seed the ground with representative elements of the local human community. Such material (be it bone, pottery flint or organics) could indicate a desire to establish a communal or territorial statement, or it may have been intended to tame or claim an area of wild land. If this is the case, then the evidence for the deposition of articulated, disassembled, disarticulated or cremated human bone within linear mounds may have little to do with burial in the conventional sense.

Artefacts recovered from ditch fills are usually more diverse and distinct than those retrieved from within the linear mounds. This may relate to the damage sustained by many earthworks through ploughing, which often has the effect of scattering finds over a wide area. There may, however, be a more significant aspect to the nature of deposition. Ditches tend to get overlooked within recent studies of linear mounds because it is the mound that is thought to contain human bone, therefore it is the mound that must represent the most important feature. Human and animal bone, if encountered within ditch fill, are viewed as if they were secondary burial deposits, even if, as at North Marden, there were no primary mound burials to speak of. Artefacts associated with human bone often receive even less attention, being all too easily dismissed as rubbish deposits, even if they appear to have been deliberately placed.

The finds retrieved from the ditch fill of Neolithic mounds do not often conform to the idea of randomly scattered refuse. In many cases, there appears to have been a discrete form of material separation, and in others, clear evidence of deliberate and careful selection. Julian Thomas has observed and studied the spatial patterning of Neolithic artefacts within ditch fill, noting that the patterns that emerge are ones of 'segregation within association'. In other words, specific artefact types, such as pottery and human bone, may reoccur repeatedly within the ditch, whilst never appearing in exactly the same context. Such substance segregation has been noted within the ditches of a number of linear mounds (**9**), including Alfriston (flint waste, pottery, antler and firecracked flint), Horslip (antler picks and animal bones), Kingston Deverill G1 (flint waste and antler tools), Lavant Down (antler tools, flint waste and pottery), North Marden (antler, flint waste, animal bone, pottery, firecracked flint and incised chalk), Radley (pottery, antler, flint tools and human bone) and Thickthorn Down (pottery, animal bone and flint) to name a few.

The segregation of materials within ditch fill would seem to argue against the suggestion that such assemblages represent rubbish deposits, randomly and unsystematically dumped into the nearest convenient surface hollow. These artefact groups have been deliberately structured in a way that is not always clear to a modern audience, but which may have possessed abundant meaning in the Neolithic. Thomas has viewed the main constituents recovered from such contexts as representing the

9 *Thickthorn Down: distribution of artefacts recorded from within ditch fill: a = early silts; b = later silts; c = final silts. Circles = animal bone; squares = Early Neolithic pottery; triangles = Late Neolithic pottery; open diamonds = Late Neolithic/Early Bronze Age human remains; closed diamonds = Late Neolithic/Early Bronze Age pottery. Redrawn from Barrett, Bradley and Green 1991*

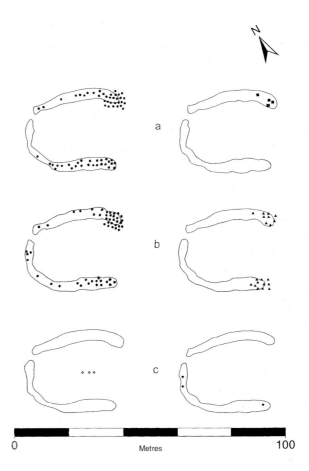

basic elements of a material code or language, similar perhaps to that observed within shafts and enclosure ditches. It is possible that certain artefact groups, which in some way were thought to be representative of a particular community, were deposited within ditch backfill as an offering to a local deity or as a way of implanting a specific social identity into the land.

STONE AND EARTH

There is a wide and diverse variety of stone-structured mounds evident in the British Neolithic. Most survive to an excellent degree, certainly when compared to their earth and timber structured relatives, and a series of discrete geographical groups and subgroups have been generated by archaeologists to classify and categorise monument type. Thus the literature is peppered with reference to 'Clyde cairns', 'Clava cairns', 'Cotswold-Severn cairns', as well as 'portal dolmens', 'stalled cairns', 'court tombs', 'passage graves', 'entrance graves' and 'rotunda graves'. Most of these terms are useful

10 Lanyon Quoit: the 'great capstone' measures just under 6m in length and is today supported by three uprights, the fourth lying to the right of the photo. The structure is today somewhat difficult to visualise in its original form, much of the cairn having been destroyed. The stone uprights themselves collapsed in 1815 and were re-erected in 1824. Miles Russell

in attempting to explain subtle variance in structural form, but they can also cause some significant degree of confusion. The terms further serve to disguise the fact that structural categories relate, in basic terms, to mounds with an internal series of stone lined chambers. A brief description of the main categories and classification factors is set out below, but it is important to reiterate here that these terms are not considered definitive and will not be used within this book to classify Neolithic structural form.

'Portal dolmen'

The so-called 'portal dolmen' represents one of the most distinctive and instantly recognisable built forms in British prehistory. Good examples have been identified in western Wales and Cornwall, at sites such as Zennor, Trethevy (**colour plates 3 and 4**), Pentre Ifan, Carnedd Hengwm, Dyffryn Ardudwy and Lanyon (**10**). The basic structure comprises an arrangement of hefty stone uprights and a large capstone, sometimes resting at a somewhat startling angle. The front of the structure is usually marked by the higher end of the capstone, supported by two or three uprights, the groups of three being set in a rough H-shaped arrangement. Debate continues as to whether these structures were ever fully covered by a mound, though some were clearly surrounded by a low cairn or platform. Most seem to have been free-standing and may therefore represent a more substantial version of the timber box chambers, or 'mortuary-houses' which predate a significant number of linear mounds in England, Scotland and Ireland (see below for discussion). Certainly there is some significant similarity concerning the basic form of the chamber with massive uprights supporting a roof, points of restricted access, provision of a façade and forecourt and the surrounding of the chamber by a fenced enclosure, low bank or cairn.

A good example of a classic 'portal dolmen' or stone box chamber, was excavated at Dyffryn Ardudwy between 1961 and 1962. Here a primary phase chamber was incorporated at the centre of a later stone-structured linear mound. The first phase chamber or dolmen had originally been surrounded by a small, oval cairn of water rounded stones, splaying out at the eastern point of entrance to create a small forecourt. No trace of any bone, animal or human, was recovered from the interior of the stone chamber, but it is possible that this area had previously been rifled by an over-enthusiastic antiquarian excavator. A pit containing Neolithic pottery was found beneath the cairn stone spread within the area of the forecourt, to the east of, and on the same central axis to, the apparently empty chamber.

'Rotunda grave'

A series of structures, restricted at least in geographical terms to the Cotswolds and Severn river valley, have been classified within archaeological literature as 'rotunda graves'. The category would appear reasonably coherent, the main defining factors being a roughly circular shaped stone cairn over an internal, roughly central, stone lined box or chamber containing human bone. One of the more commonly quoted examples of a so-called 'classic rotunda' is the structure excavated at Notgrove in 1935. This particular cairn measured around seven metres in diameter and overlay a polygonal limestone box containing the remains of a single adult male. The whole structure had later been incorporated within the body of a linear stone-structured mound of the 'Cotswold Severn' variety (**11**). The classic rotunda-style cairn recorded from Sale's Lot measured around five metres in diameter and covered a stone box which, though disturbed, was found to contain human teeth and a leaf-shaped flint arrowhead. As at Notgrove, the structure had later been incorporated within the body of a linear stone-structured mound, together with a passage grave-style cairn which lay to the immediate south east (**12**).

'Passage grave'

The term 'passage gave' is applied to a chamber accessed through a narrow passage or corridor, somewhat akin to the short galleries recorded at the base of Neolithic flint mine shafts. The passage has the effect not only of limiting access to the main chamber, but also of helping to separate the chamber from the world outside.

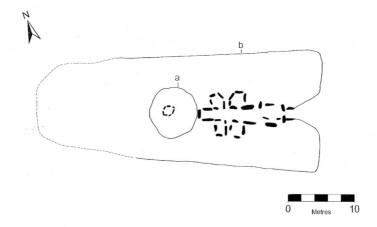

11 *Notgrove: plan of a 'rotunda grave' (a), later incorporated within the body of a linear stone-structured mound of the 'Cotswold Severn' variety (b).* Redrawn from Darvill

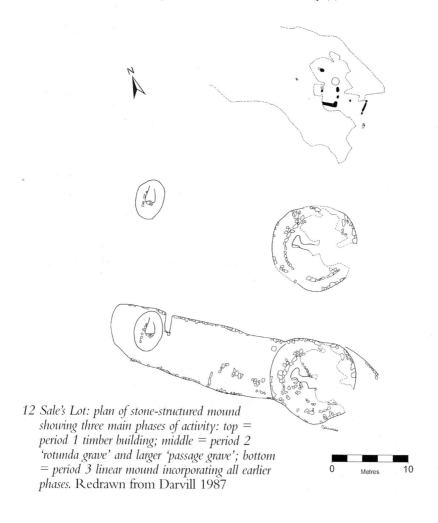

12 *Sale's Lot: plan of stone-structured mound showing three main phases of activity: top = period 1 timber building; middle = period 2 'rotunda grave' and larger 'passage grave'; bottom = period 3 linear mound incorporating all earlier phases.* Redrawn from Darvill 1987

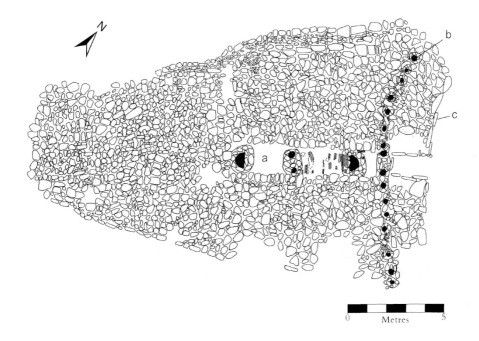

13 Lochill: plan of a stone-structured linear mound of the 'Clyde cairn' variety as excavated: a = primary phase timber chamber or 'mortuary house'; b = primary phase façade; c = final remodelling of form into 'Clyde cairn'. Redrawn from Masters 1973

Both chamber and passage are usually covered by a circular, oval or sometimes rectangular mound of earth or stone. The majority of passage grave-style cairns may be found in the areas facing the Irish Sea and up into western and northern Scotland, good examples being recorded from Balvraid, Camster Long, Ormiegill and Ty Newydd. Once again the term 'grave' is somewhat of a misnomer, for it implies that the primary use of these structures was for human burial, a theory not fully supported by the archaeological evidence.

'Clyde cairn'

The group of monuments referred to as Clyde cairns or tombs covers a large portion of the western Scottish seaboard, notably, as one would perhaps expect, around the area of the Clyde estuary. Structures are usually linear-shaped cairns with a single, rectangular stone box or chamber, almost exactly similar in form to the timber chambers or 'mortuary houses' which predate some Neolithic earth mounds such as Fussell's Lodge, Nutbane, Haddenham and Willerby Wold. At Lochill (**13**), such a timber chamber and façade had later been remodelled into a Clyde-style cairn. Internal chambers were composed of stone slabs and were

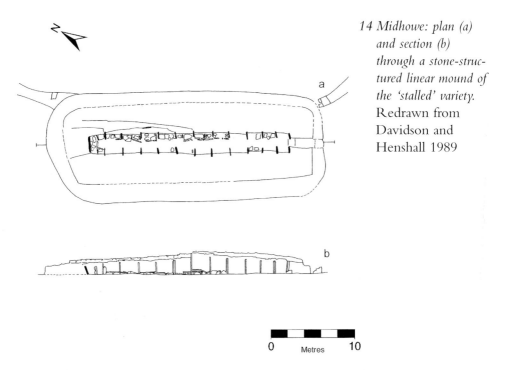

14 Midhowe: plan (a) and section (b) through a stone-structured linear mound of the 'stalled' variety. Redrawn from Davidson and Henshall 1989

0 Metres 10

anything up to a metre in height. Some Clyde cairns possessed imposing façades and concave forecourts, such as that recorded at Carn Ban.

Certain Clyde cairns underwent considerable modification during their use. The primary phase chambers of Cairnholy I and II underwent extension through the building of a second, outer chamber with concave façade. At Mid Gleniron I, two rectangular stone-lined chambers, set within two apparently independent oval cairns, both facing north east, were later divided by the construction of a third chamber, all structures then forming the core of a single linear stone mound. A concave façade, forming the business end of the new linear mound, was built directly onto the entrance of the earlier, and by then fully enclosed, eastern cairn. Extension to stone chambers has at times been thought to represent the provision of extra space for human burials, though if this was the case, the limited quantity of human bone debris is somewhat surprising.

'Stalled cairn'

A term given to a particular type of elongated stone chamber with multiple stone uprights set along the main axis, at either side of the principal through passage (**colour plate 15**). Examples of such internal compartmentalisation may be seen within the linear mounds of Midhowe (**14**) and the Point of Cott, and the more circular mound forms at Warehouse and Camster Long. Soil within the Point of Cott stalled chamber floor, excavated between 1984 and 1985, contained pottery, whale

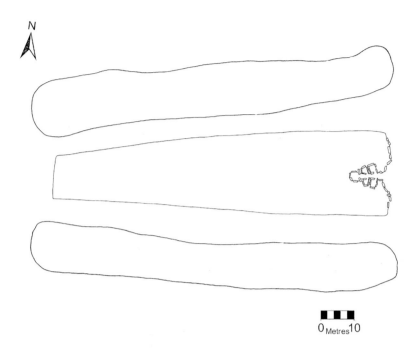

N

15 West Kennet: plan of a linear mound (centre), with flanking ditches, of the 'Cotswold Severn' variety. Internal chambers are evident at the eastern end. Redrawn from Piggott 1962

teeth, animal and bird bone. The chambered zone within the stalled cairn at Isbister, excavated in 1958 and 1976, comprised five discrete compartments and three additional 'side cells'. A series of deposits, comprising animal, human and bird (predominantly sea eagle) bone, had been placed within and beneath the main chamber and side cells.

'Cotswold–Severn tomb'

The main feature of this subgroup of Neolithic structured mound is the trapezoidal stone cairn or earth mound. The wider end of the trapezoid is usually where the main point of entrance to internal chambers can be found. Three broad categories of internal chamber may be identified within the category: single (and relatively simple) chamber or stone lined box; trancepted with pairs of chambers leading at right angles from a main passage; lateral in which passageways in the sides of the mound led to internal chambers. Chambered areas often only constitute a small fraction of the total area of a particular mound. At West Kennet, for example, the trancepted chamber extends only 12m into the eastern end of the 100m long trapezoidal structure (**15**). The Cotswold-Severn group, as the name implies, is primarily

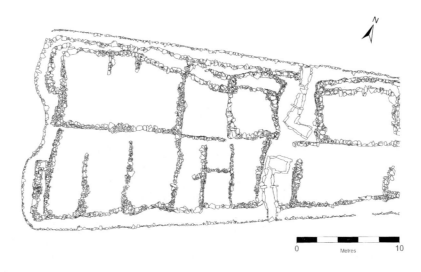

16 Hazleton North: plan of stone-structured mound as excavated showing construction as a series of roughly rectangular, stone revetted units or bays. Redrawn from Saville 1990

concentrated at either side of the Severn estuary, and between Bristol and Oxford, with some major groupings further afield in north Wales. Good examples of this class of linear mound have been excavated at Gwernvale, Hazleton North, Notgrove, Nympsfield, Parc le Bros Cwm, Stoney Littleton, Ty Isaf and Wayland's Smithy.

Structure and composition

The internal subdivision of Neolithic linear mounds into discrete, cellular units, offset from a single axial line, is not, as noted above, something that is purely restricted to earth and timber mounds. At Hazleton North, for example, a linear cairn had been built as a series of roughly rectangular, stone revetted units (**16**), whilst similar bayed construction has been recorded from stone-structured mounds at Ascott-under-Wychwood I, Belas Knap, Hetty Pegler's Tump and Randwick. So common may this building technique originally have been that Alan Saville, in his excavation report for the Hazleton North mound, wondered whether internal revetment was the norm for the Neolithic long cairns of the Cotswold-Severn region of western England and south-east Wales.

The internal components awarded most attention in the study of Neolithic structured mounds are the stone chambers. The typology of stone-chambered linear mounds, as has already been noted, varies considerably from region to region around the British Isles, but the basic format of rectangular box, walls formed by large stones (or orthostats), is universal. Sometimes the entrance to the box or chamber was via an impressive façade (**17, colour plates 7 and 9**) or forecourt. Sometimes the chamber was separated from the main entrance by a long passage (**colour plate 16**), and sometimes there are many

17 West Kennet: an impressive façade of upright sarsens, originally designed to frame the entrance into the linear structured mound, whilst simultaneously masking an earlier forecourt structure. This entrance was later blocked by the addition of a large sarsen block. The visible stones are unfortunately not all as they were in the Neolithic, having been re-erected following excavations between 1955 and 1956. Miles Russell

interlinked chambers within a single mound. Chambers can vary in size, internal dimensions, location and general orientation, but all seem to cover and contain deposits of human bone and all appear at some time to have been broadly accessible (**colour plates 13 and 14**). Generally speaking therefore, chambered mounds are perceived as structures related to the storage, movement and manipulation of human remains.

A common feature of all types of chamber or passageway is the presence of so-called constricting stones. These large slabs are clearly designed to restrict or somehow limit access to internal chambers, and may be found at the point of entrance, within the passageway, or at the very threshold of a particular chamber. Restrictions can take the form of one or two upright stones set either side of the entranceway (**18**), a slab set end on edge at the threshold, or a hole cut in a block of stone (**19**). In the southern passage of the Hazleton North mound, stone constrictions at one point reduced the available crawl space to around half a metre. A similar set of concealments and restrictions can be seen at the entrance to (and within) galleries at the base of Neolithic shafts in southern Britain and in the access points to the so-called Neolithic houses of Skara Brae in Orkney. A more severe form of restriction is the evidence for blocking of passageways and chamber entrance points in the form of stone rubble, soil, single stone uprights and drystone walling. Blocking would appear to represent the final act of sealing chambers that had gone out of use.

18 Grey Mare and her Colts: looking out through the restricting stones of the now badly denuded, stone-structured linear mound. Gareth Talbot

19 Men-an-tol: a cut stone set between two uprights. The structure, possibly representing a 'porthole' or restricting stone originally set at the entrance to a stone-structured linear mound, is almost certainly not in its original position. Miles Russell

20 West Kennet: the original forecourt structure at the business end of the linear structured mound, to the left of the photo (with a concrete skylight inserted into the roof), is still evident behind the later sarsen façade to the right. Miles Russell

The fact that access to internal chambers was not always provided at the higher, wider and visually more prominent end of certain linear mounds, such as is evident at Belas Knap and Hazleton North, has led to the suggestion that this may have been a deliberate way of creating a false entrance in order to confuse potential grave robbers. Apart from the fact that Neolithic linear mounds do not, at least by modern standards, contain anything to arouse the attention of tomb raiders (Tutankhamun's burial chamber these patently are not), anyone with determination and half an ounce of intelligence could easily determine where the main point of entrance was. These are not complicated pyramid structures with well-disguised doors and secret passageways, neither are the mounds well hidden from public view.

Linear mounds were built to a particular design; one which necessitated the presence of a 'business end' or forecourt. A forecourt need not have simply framed the main point of entrance into the mound, in fact at a number of sites it may perhaps have served as an arena for a particular set of activities (**20**). Such areas were maintained, even if the major entrances to internal chambers were elsewhere within the body of the mound. It is clear, therefore, that the shape of the structure, and its position in the landscape, are the important issues here.

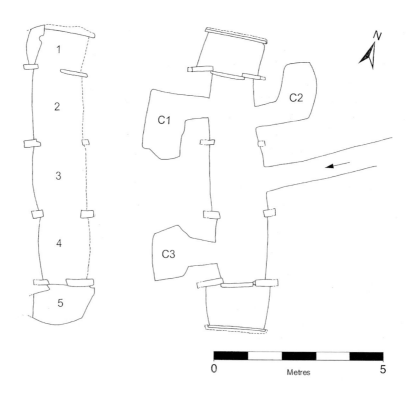

21 Isbister: outline plan of internal chambers at floor level (left) and side cells at shelf level (right). Redrawn from Hedges 1984

Artefact assemblages

At Isbister, a well-preserved, though partially investigated, long cairn of the 'stalled' or compartmentalised variety, was examined in 1958 and 1976. Human bone was found within the chambers, side cells, and cairn structure (**21**). A series of deposits, comprising animal, human and bird (predominantly sea eagle) bone, had been placed beneath the flagstone floor of compartment 5, presumably during the course of chamber construction. Unfortunately the contents of two of the main stalled compartments, namely 1 and 2, had been disrupted during the course of a previously unrecorded examination. Nevertheless, the remaining areas possessed well-preserved deposits, with disarticulated human and animal bone being found throughout the remaining area of the chamber. Human bone had been placed along the edges of the chambers, skulls in pairs in the northern two corners of compartment 2. Mixed in with the human material were shellfish, the bones of fish and sea eagle, a small amount of flint and bone points and pottery, constituting around 45 vessels, the majority of which was retrieved from compartment 3. The floor of shelved side cells C2 and C3 were covered in human skulls 'in no particular order' and the bones of sea eagle.

The minimum number of individuals represented at Isbister has been calculated as follows: seven adults, seven immatures and one infant from beneath the floor of compartment 5; 22 adults, 25 immatures and three infants from the floor of compartment 3; 51 adults, 18 immatures and five infants from the floor of compartment 4; 21 adults and six immatures from the floor of compartment 5. Remains comprising a further 18 adults, 14 immatures and four infants were recovered from side cell C3. Further human remains were retrieved from the cairn structure, chamber blocking and later modifications, bringing the minimum total number of humans represented within the cairn to 185 adults, 132 immatures (of which at least 62 were teenagers) and 24 infants. The male / female ratio (where it could be determined) was calculated at 106 males (93 adults; nine teenagers; four children) to 60 females (38 adults; 16 teenagers; four children; two infants). Of the 185 adults present, the majority were represented by skull (108), femur (191) , humerus (162) and pelvis (134). The human bone was predominantly bleached, suggesting a form of weathering or disassembly through exposure to the elements prior to inclusion within the chambers.

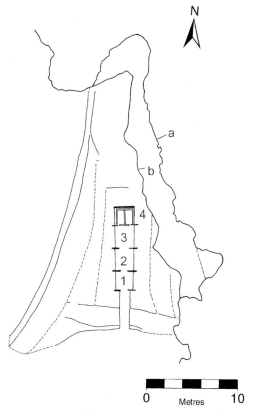

22 Point of Cott: plan of stalled linear mound showing internal chambers 1-4. Successive points of cliff erosion are shown at a (1935) and b (1983). Redrawn from Barber 1997

Of the animal bone recovered from Isbister, an assemblage that included dog, otter, pig, red deer, and seal, the majority of individuals represented were cattle (16) and sheep (16). Bird bones recovered included eagle, auk, gull, crow, owl, raven, grouse, oyster catcher, curlew, shag, goose, eider and kestrel, though as already noted, the assemblage was dominated by the white-tailed eagle (88 per cent). All bird bone appears to have been deliberately placed within the cairn.

At the Point of Cott (**22**), soil deposits across the floor of the stalled chamber contained pottery from at least five vessels, four of which derived from compartment 2, and 16 whale tooth beads, including 13 derived from compartment 3. The remaining assemblage comprised animal bone, dog and otter in compartments 1 and 3, sheep from compartments 1, 2, 3 and 4, bird bone, mostly sea eagle, from compartment 4, and human bone. The human bone assemblage comprised the

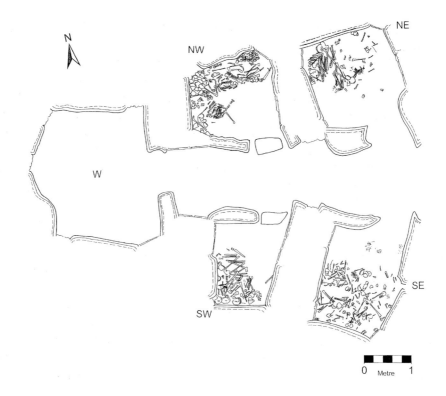

23 West Kennet: plan showing deposits of human remains as recovered by the 1955-56 excavation of the north-west, north-east, south-east and south-west chambers. The west chamber had already been emptied in 1859. Redrawn from Piggott 1962

disarticulated remains of at least five adults, two immatures and five infants. Of the assemblage, 70 per cent was derived from compartment 3, whilst 75 per cent of the infant bones came from compartments 1 and 2.

Within the trancepted chambers of the 'Cotswold-Severn' style linear mounds, great emphasis has been placed in recent years on three particular sites, namely: Hazleton North, Wayland's Smithy and West Kennet. At West Kennet, the trancepted chamber was fully excavated between 1955 and 1956. The Western terminal chamber had already been emptied, probably by Thurnam in 1859, and may have contained a series of male skeletons. The remaining four chambers did not, however, appear to have been previously disturbed. In these, the excavators found disarticulated human bone, comprising at least 46 individuals (**23**).

Scattered human bones were observed by the excavators within the north–eastern chamber. Upon clearing these, and the cremated remains of at least two adult humans, three near complete human skeletons were uncovered. The first, 'intact up to the region of the shoulders', represented the body of a young adult female. Her skull was placed against the wall of the chamber to the north. An articulated skeleton of an elderly man was tightly contracted in the north western corner of the chamber.

The excavators noted a leaf shaped arrowhead in the throat cavity, a likely indication of how the individual had died. Beneath him lay the partially disarticulated remains of an elderly female, missing the skull, mandible and certain other upper body parts. There were 50 sherds of pottery found across the floor deposits of the chamber, whilst a single deer antler lay within a recess at the western edge of the door sill.

Removal of disarticulated bone debris, including three adult mandibles, within the north-western chamber revealed a more ordered pile of human vertebrae, long bones and ribs stacked at the north-western corner, together with 'metapodials', a sacrum and a sternum. A partially disarticulated and incomplete skeleton of an elderly female lay against the northern edge of the chamber, whilst the even more fragmentary remains of an elderly male lay against the western edge. The partially articulated remains of a young adult male, missing arm bones, pelvis and legs, were found west of the chamber's central point.

Human bones within the south-eastern chamber were 'noticeably more widely scattered' than those from elsewhere in the mound, though at least two partially disassembled skeletons, male and female, were detected near the western wall. Three skulls, representing a child, a young woman and an elderly female, had been placed against the southern wall of the south west chamber. A mass of disarticulated human bone, including mandibles, ribs and long bones, had been piled up against the skulls. An incomplete and partially disarticulated skeleton of a young adult 'more or less complete from the waist downwards' had been deposited at the northern edge of this assemblage.

At Hazleton, one of the better excavated and recorded stone-chambered mounds of recent years, a complex series of deposits were encountered set within the two side chambers of the monument. The northern chamber contained the disarticulated remains of four adults, between four and six immatures and a foetus, whilst the entrance way contained pieces belonging to a further two adults and two immatures. Some cremated bone, probably representing at least one adult and one immature, together with the articulated and fully extended remains of an adult male, were also retrieved from the northern entrance. Within the area of the southern chamber the disarticulated remains of at least 14 adults, between six and eleven immatures and a foetus were found. The excavator noted that the number of long bones recovered from the southern chamber was low, and that skulls tended to have been placed along the edges of the chamber walls (**24**).

Much has been made of the complete male skeleton recovered from the entrance to the northern chamber at Hazleton (**25**), not least because it would appear to provide evidence of the deliberate interment of a fully fleshed body. Some writers have suggested this may indicate that complete bodies were usually placed close to the entrance of specific chambers until they became skeletonised, and the individual body parts could be reselected and reordered. There may well be an element of truth in this, though the discovery of similarly complete, fully articulated corpses from the final sequences of vertical shafts and enclosure ditches must provide a strong word of caution. Perhaps it is more likely that articulated skeletons from the entrances to chambers at sites like Hazleton North and Lanhill, as well as from the floor levels of

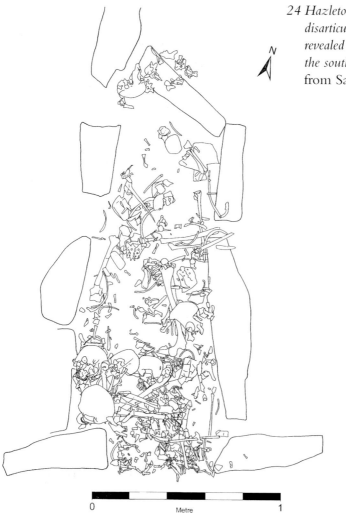

24 Hazleton North: plan showing disarticulated human remains revealed during excavations in the southern passage. Redrawn from Saville 1990

N

0   Metre   1

a number of so-called 'mortuary houses', actually indicate the final phase of deposition; a complete body intended either to hijack the significance of the structure, or emphatically to terminate it, sealing it off and ending its power forever.

Animal bones are altogether less frequent a find from stone-structured mounds than from their earthen counterparts. The fish and bird bone deposits from Isbister have already been noted, as have the whale, dog and otter bone from the Point of Cott and the cattle, pig, deer and sheep/goat remains from West Kennet. Other examples where animal bone appears to have been deliberately incorporated within the floor deposits of chambers include the sheep and cattle bones from Eyeford Hill and Luckington. At Notgrove, the near total remains of a calf were found within a chamber of the secondary phase stone-structured, linear mound. Small amounts of animal bone, including sheep/goat and dog, were found amidst the human bone debris recorded from the chambers of Hazleton North.

25 Hazleton North: plan showing disarticulated human remains, overlain by the later articulated remains of an adult male, within the northern entrance. The addition of complete individuals is common in the final stages of use for all Early Neolithic monuments. Redrawn from Saville 1990

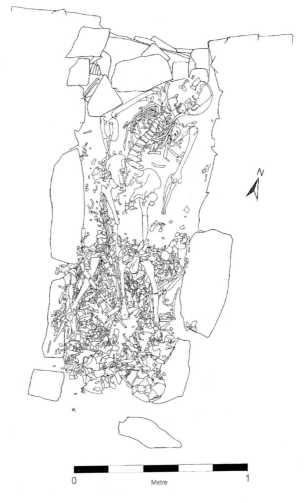

More substantial deposits of material have derived from beneath stone-structured mounds, in the old land surface or pre-mound soils. At Hazleton North, the excavation of the linear mound revealed a series of features and artefact spreads that pre-dated the structure. The artefacts comprised Neolithic flint (tools and flakes), pottery (derived from at least 25 separate vessels), animal bone (predominantly cattle, sheep and pig), pieces from a number of mauls, rubbers and saddle-querns, cereals and burnt hazelnuts. The features consisted of a small group of dubious hollows and a tighter cluster of 13 post and stakeholes associated (at least spatially) with an area of burning. This cluster was interpreted by the excavator as representing at least one side of a presumably rectangular 'indeterminate pre-cairn timber structure' of domestic character. A domestic interpretation has also been suggested for the seven postholes, two gullies and small area of burning recorded beneath the stone-structured linear mound of Sale's Lot in Gloucestershire.

PRE-MOUND STRUCTURES

The structured mound, although undeniably striking, usually represents the final element in the overall stages of monument use. The excavation of both earthen and stone-structured Neolithic mounds has at times revealed a complex of archaeological features sealed beneath the main earthwork. These features have included single pits, pit lines, postholes, post slots, substantial palisades, stone chambers, stakeholes and occasionally ard or plough marks.

Pre-mound timber structures have proved particularly difficult to interpret with any certainty, and there has been a tendency to view such remains as evidence of an earlier phase of burial monument. Unfortunately, quite apart from the fact that linear mounds may well not have been intended as monuments to the dead, there is no certainty that any pre-mound feature relates in any way to later activities enacted on the same site. Structural remains could, for example, represent part of an earlier house, destroyed or demolished to make way for the mound. They may well represent a structure long abandoned (and forgotten) by the time the first stages of mound construction got underway. John Barrett, in his book *Fragments from Antiquity*, has suggested that traces of pre-mound activity may represent all that is left from the gathering and interaction of people at or in places considered important by the local community. This could in turn imply that the siting of certain mounds was dependent upon what had previously happened at that site, perhaps within the living memory of those who constructed the later earthwork.

Alternatively, any pits, postholes or other features preserved beneath a linear mound could represent the traces of activities enacted only just before the construction of the mound commenced. In such a scenario, the linear mound represents the final event, the monumental end statement, effectively sealing all trace of what had only just occurred. This would provide a more significant meaning to the various scattered pits and postholes found beneath some mounds which are often dealt with so cursorily by archaeologists. It could also provide a context for evidence for the intense breaking up of the soil noted beneath certain mounds. At South Street, for example, a series of linear cuts, criss-crossing through the pre-mound soil (**26**), have been interpreted as evidence of ploughing or root clearance. Alternatively, it is possible that the breaking up of the ground was a deliberate action designed to prepare the soil for the planting of the human dead or of other important artefacts (such as pottery, animal bone or flint).

Evidence for substantial forms of pre-mound building have been found beneath comparatively few Neolithic linear earthworks, but these buildings demonstrate a compelling similarity in structural form. The pre-mound timber buildings that have taken pre-eminent place in the archaeological literature are, perhaps unsurprisingly, those from the Wessex heartland such as Wayland's Smithy, Fussell's Lodge, Wor Barrow and Nutbane, but other sites certainly exist, such as Dalladies, Cross Thorns, Haddenham, Kemp Howe, Kilham, Lochill, Market Weighton, Raiset Pike, Raisthorpe, Rudston, Street House, Westow and Willerby Wold.

At Nutbane, the examination of the eastern terminal end of an earthen mound in 1957 revealed a complex set of timber structural remains (**27**). The earliest phase

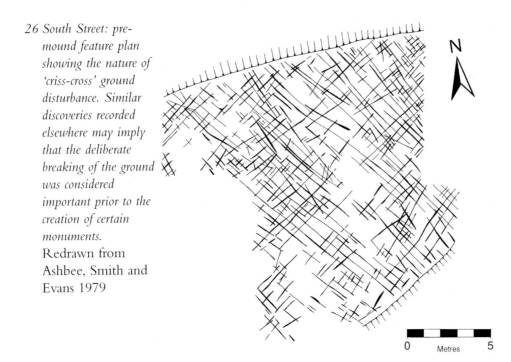

26 South Street: pre-
mound feature plan
showing the nature of
'criss-cross' ground
disturbance. Similar
discoveries recorded
elsewhere may imply
that the deliberate
breaking of the ground
was considered
important prior to the
creation of certain
monuments.
Redrawn from
Ashbee, Smith and
Evans 1979

0   Metres   5

of activity on the site consisted of four postholes, each containing between three and four individual posts, demarcating an area that was roughly square. To the immediate west of these, two irregular ditches were cut, defining a rough east – west aligned oval. Spoil from the excavation of the ditches seems to have been thrown outwards to form a low bank, whilst two sets of two posts were embedded within the eastern and western terminals. A further two posts were set within the area defined by the two ditches, along the axis of the structure. At some stage in the lifespan of this structure, and presumably in the final moments of use, three human corpses were added: two crouched and partially disturbed (or decayed) adult males, lying on their left with heads to the east, and a crouched skeleton of a child, lying on its right with head to the south.

A second major phase of building resulted in the destruction of the first post structure, with some posts removed from their sockets, and the remainder being snapped off. The area of the primary building was then enlarged with an additional three postholes placed inside, along the central north – south axis. The ditches were backfilled with chalk, and the western internal post was removed. A palisade or fence, marking at least three sides of a rectangle, was constructed around the outer edge of the infilled ditch cuts. A fourth male skeleton, crouched on its right with the head to the south, was set down within this fenced enclosure, directly over the infilled void left by the removal of the internal post.

Following this, two north – south aligned trench slots were cut at the eastern end of the fenced enclosure, apparently blocking the earlier entrance. The slots held vertical posts which supported a series of horizontally set boards. Rubble generated from the

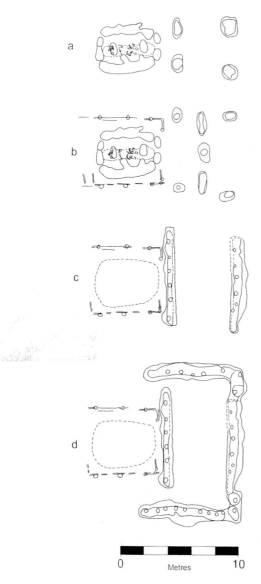

excavation of the slots was used to form a chalk cairn within the area enclosed by the rectangular fence to the west. The eastern slot was then enlarged at its northern and southern edges by the addition of two east – west aligned arms, to create a façade. In the final stages, two parallel ditches, orientated east – west, were cut to the north and south of the earlier features. Spoil generated from the excavation of these ditches was used to form a linear mound which covered everything up to the post slots to the east. The posts were then burnt right down into their sockets, and chalk rubble, containing the bones of ox and red deer, was thrown over the remains, thus completing the formation of the mound structure.

At Fussell's Lodge (also excavated in 1957), the exact sequence remains unclear, though the primary phase structure was represented by a roughly rectangular ditched enclosure, slightly wider at its eastern end. The cut originally held a series of closely packed upright timbers and was continuous except for a break at the eastern end. A setting of four postholes framed this point of entry into the enclosure (**28**). The entrance gap was later blocked by a large post, one of three that ran back along the central axis of the enclosure. Removal of the middle post allowed for the deposition of human remains, which clustered into at least five groups of disarticulated bone. These comprised a minimum of ten men, nine women, 12 children and an additional 13 adults of unknown sex. The long bones had been carefully stacked along the main axis of the structure, whilst the skulls were placed to the sides. A flint cairn was finally thrown over the remains, the whole later being covered by a linear mound, formed from rubble generated by the cutting of two flanking ditches.

At Wayland's Smithy, excavations conducted between 1962 and 1963 revealed a complex set of monumental construction and phasing. The primary building was represented by a paved zone of sarsen slabs, set between two massive timber posts and flanked by two linear sarsen cairns. The remains of at least 14 humans had been placed over this

27 Nutbane: suggested phasing of pre-mound features recorded from excavation: a = period 1 postholes and ditches with final phase human deposits; b = period 2 postholes and fence; c = period 3 palisade trenches and chalk cairn; d = period 4 enlarged palisade (façade). Redrawn from Cunliffe 1993

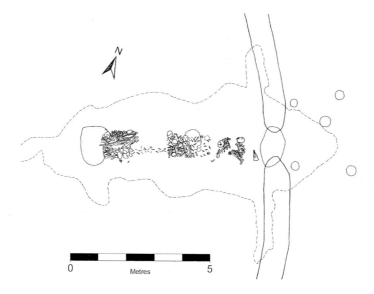

28 Fussell's Lodge: plan showing final phase of pre-mound features. Here the entrance gap for the primary phase rectangular ditched enclosure, originally framed by a series of postholes, has been blocked by one of three larger posts, forming the timber chamber or 'mortuary house'. Removal of the centre post has facilitated the deposition of carefully stacked human remains. Note the position of a single ox skull at the extreme east of the bone deposits. Redrawn from Ashbee 1966

pavement, in articulated and disassembled form. To the immediate south east of this area, a five post rectangular setting was recorded. The whole had eventually been covered by an elongated chalk cairn, derived from material generated from the cutting of two flanking ditches. A third major phase of rebuilding replaced the earthen linear mound (Wayland's Smithy I) with a larger stone-chambered example (Wayland's Smithy II).

The features revealed beneath the Haddenham mound were waterlogged and therefore relatively well preserved (**29**). Excavation at the wider, north-eastern end of the mound exposed a rectangular box-like feature, which the excavators noted appeared to be 'closely related in size, shape and construction techniques to the megalithic chambered tombs'. The sides of the chamber comprised oak planks which possibly rose to a height of 1.3m. The whole was supported by an exterior bank of clay silt, and three vertical posts placed one at either end of the chamber and one just off-centre. The effect was to subdivide the timber structure into what has been described as a short vestibule and a 'longer inner chamber'. A north-west – south-east aligned linear slot, with two shorter extending arms forming an overall C-shape, flanked the north-eastern edge of the chamber. A palisade or fence ran from the terminals of this linear slot to form a rectangular enclosure. The slot had originally held a series of timber uprights, which presumably formed a façade similar to the final pre-mound structure at Nutbane.

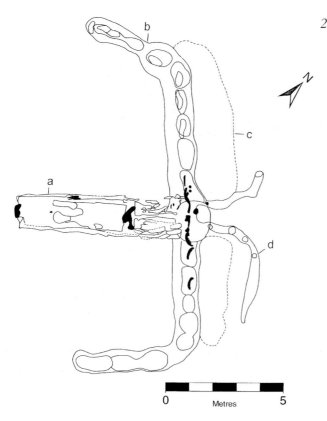

29 Haddenham: plan of pre-mound features revealed during excavation: a = timber chamber; b = timber façade; c = gravel bank; d = timber forecourt or passage. Redrawn from Hodder and Shand 1988

Soil derived from the cutting of the Haddenham façade had been dumped outside to the north east, whilst a series of timber posts supporting a fence structure created a funnel-like forecourt or entrance to the chamber. Gravel appeared to have been spread in front of this entrance, perhaps in order to provide a more durable surface for those attempting access. The partially articulated remains of at least five humans were recovered from the inner segment of the timber chamber, whilst a series of 'special deposits, including whole pots' was recorded from the area of the forecourt. The dismantling and partial burning of the phase one building was followed by the construction of a two-phase linear mound.

The primary phase timber structure recorded beneath the Willerby Wold linear mound, excavated between 1958 and 1960, also comprised a rectangular area or shallow chamber attached to the centre of a linear palisade trench or façade. The structure, which did not survive as well as that from Haddenham, was represented by a shallow deposit of burnt soil and fused chalk, overlying an oval pit. The deposit was interpreted as a crematorium, though it is just as likely to represent the remains of a timber chamber destroyed by fire, especially as the façade seems to have been burnt prior to the construction of the linear mound. A deposit of disarticulated human bone was found at the western end of the 'crematorium', and comprised three skulls and a number of long bones. Human bone had also been retrieved from this area during the course of excavations conducted prior to 1870. Pottery, flintwork and ox bone were retrieved from the eastern segment of the later-dating covering mound.

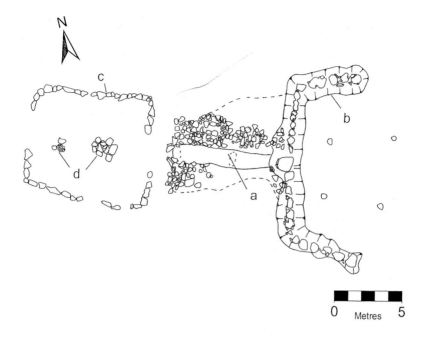

30 Streethouse: plan of pre-mound features revealed during excavation: a = chamber or 'mortuary house'; b = façade trench; c = stone fronted enclosure; d = paving. Redrawn from Vyner 1984

The primary phase structure preserved beneath a small stone-structured linear mound at Streethouse demonstrated a similar range of features, namely a C-shaped palisade trench or façade, fronting a narrow passage or chamber supported on three large posts (**30 & 31**). A stone-fronted rectangular enclosure was recorded to the immediate west of the chamber, whilst a series of postholes, presumably representing part of an avenue or forestructure, was found to the east of the façade. Soil derived from the excavation of the linear trench had formed a bank of clay and stone surrounding the chamber. Façade and chamber had both been set alight during their final period of use. Burnt human bone comprising 'a number of individuals of all ages represented by all parts of the skeleton' were found on the base of the chamber and within the burnt sandstone rubble above. The majority of bone appears to have been in a disarticulated state at deposition.

The buildings recorded from beneath the Raisthorpe, Kemp Howe and Lochill linear mounds also consisted of gently concave post slots or facades, fronting pits and rectangular areas. The Raisthorpe example comprised burnt chalk rubble, which presumably marked the remains of a chamber destroyed by fire at the same time as the façade. At Lochill the primary chamber consisted of a shallow, plank-lined, rectangular cut. Three large postholes divided the chamber, the end cuts each containing a large post, the middle supporting two. Both façade and chamber were burnt prior to restructuring in stone. The structure at Kemp Howe consisted of two

N

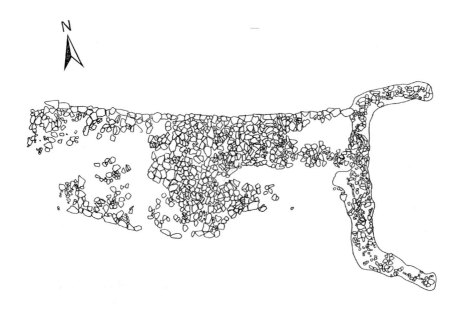

31 Streethouse: plan of the final phase linear stone-structured mound.
Redrawn from Vyner 1984

0   Metres   5

roughly parallel shallow slots with an area of burning nearby. The disarticulated remains of at least three adult humans, as well as some pottery and animal bone, were recorded from this area. Two settings of postholes extending out from the façade trench formed a funnel-like passageway presumably directing access towards the chamber. As at Raisthorpe and Lochill, the façade had been burnt prior to the construction of a linear mound.

As has already been noted, primary phase structures, such as those noted from Haddenham, Willerby Wold, Fussell's Lodge *et al.*, were not always covered by linear mounds. In certain instances the position of timber chambers appears to have been permanently marked within the landscape by the construction of a round mound or circular cairn. At Callis Wold, for example, a round mound (barrow 275) excavated in 1892 and re-examined in 1974, was found to overlay a roughly rectangular platform of stones, bordered at each end by large, D-shaped postholes (**32**). At the south-eastern end of the platform was a linear post slot, or façade trench, whilst a similar, if curving, façade was examined to the north west.

In the final stages of platform use, at least ten contracted adult bodies had been placed, together with three leaf-shaped arrowheads, apparently 'in contact with' the human remains. Finds from the two large postholes comprised disarticulated human bone (including long bones and the skull of an infant), a human cremation, pottery and animal bone. Once final deposition was complete, a low circular mound was set up over the structure, later replaced by a two-phase round mound, the latter stage consisting of material taken from a surrounding quarry ditch. Similar rectangular

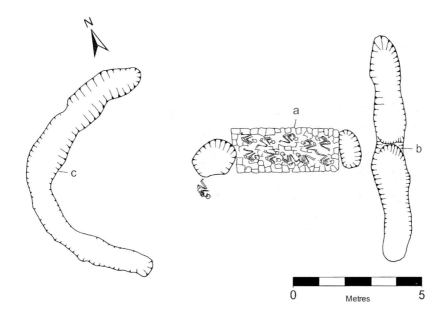

32 Callis Wold: plan of features recorded beneath circular mound 275: a = stone platform/chamber, showing approximate positions of human bodies placed during the final phase of use; b = linear post slot (façade); c = curved post slot (façade?). Redrawn from Coombs 1976

structures, filled in their final stage of use with human bodies and body parts, have also been found beneath the round mounds of Aldro 88, Aldro 94, Cowlam 277, Garton Slack 80, Garton Slack 81, Copt Hill and Whiteleaf.

The structures revealed beneath these later circular and linear mounds are all regularly referred to in the archaeological literature as 'mortuary houses'. This is an unfortunate term, for it presupposes function, implying that the buildings were in some way related to the storage and disassembly of the human dead. Unfortunately, there is nothing contained within the archaeological record that can conclusively confirm such an interpretation. In fact, when one re-examines the original database, the main argument for interpreting the structures as a form of 'mortuary house' or 'mortuary chamber' is due primarily to two main factors:

First, the buildings in question were found beneath long barrows and long barrows are equated in the modern mind with burial. But, as we have already noted, and will discuss again later, there is no compelling evidence to suggest that such linear mounds were primarily (or even exclusively) associated with the human dead.

Second, the human skeletal evidence recovered from within the recorded buildings is used as evidence of the structure's use and function. Here we have a real problem, for the bone material recorded clearly relates to the very final phase of structural use. In other words, corpses have been added to the timber buildings at the very end of the building's life. In such a scenario, the human remains may perhaps more realistically be interpreted as a form of special deposit, similar in character to the bodies added to Neolithic shafts or to the backfilling ditches of Neolithic enclosures.

If we mean to retain the term 'mortuary house' to describe the timber buildings beneath Nutbane *et al.*, then we will have to rename flint mines with skeletal material as 'mortuary shafts' and the cuts fronting Neolithic enclosures as 'mortuary ditches', something which would, in all honesty, be somewhat ridiculous.

If the major timber structures found beneath certain Neolithic structured mounds were not obviously associated with the storage, disassembly, protection or display of the human dead, then what were they intended for? They were clearly significant buildings, judging not only by the amount of time put into their construction, but also because of the nature of deposits added to them at their closure, as well as the size extent of the linear mounds eventually thrown over them to seal and mark their place in the landscape forever. Perhaps the answer lies in how we view and interpret Neolithic linear mounds in totality. If these are not mere tombs, graves or ancestral burial grounds, then what are they? What reasons can we put forward for their construction and for the amazing similarity of form evident in sites across, not only Britain, but the whole of Western Europe? These are questions to which I will repeatedly return in the next section.

The meaning of mounds

So, where did the concept of mound as monumental building originate? There are, as Ian Hodder noted in 1990, 1994 and 1998, clear points of comparison between long mounds and the post-built long house structures of the European Neolithic. Both types of structure were broadly rectangular in shape. Both possessed a wider, 'business end' within which the main entrance was usually set. Points of entrance were generally orientated south-east and were sometimes provided with porches or elaborate forms of timber or stone-structured façade. Both types of building were often flanked by ditches: in the case of the mound to provide soil to shape the earthwork and in the case of the house to provide material to form the walls. Both structures also seemed to possess a clear, threefold internal division and similar forms of internal decoration. In short, Hodder has argued, the similarities between the two types of building would appear so clear, that it seems perverse to argue that they were not in some way related.

This is all well and good, but unfortunately leaves us with the problem of which came first; long house or long mound? Unlike the chicken and egg scenario, however, even if we can establish which came first, we still cannot exactly be sure of why. Why did Neolithic society build structured mounds in the first place? Furthermore, what possible significance could such structures have had?

We can argue that the large, European free-standing post structures were a type of house (though even this point is debatable) and that linear mounds were a symbolic form of house or home for the recently deceased. Perhaps the house, as centre of domestic life, served as the blueprint for the communal tomb; a sort of Neolithic family vault. The long mound could therefore have come to represent, not just a particular social group (tribe, clan or household), but also all aspects of daily life that were centred on or in the house. The long mound as 'house tomb' would, in this model, have expressed all the social, economic, religious and political interrelationships of a particular community. Over time, such family tombs would have become important marker points in the landscape. They would point to the final resting place of those who had first domesticated the land. They would also serve as a useful reminder of who continued to claim the land by right of descent. An ancestral land claim made eternally clear through monumental architecture: a sort of 'we were here first' sign.

As already observed, the datasets recovered from the structured earthen mounds have confirmed that the disposal of human remains did not play a prominent role within the majority of such structures. Certain linear mounds, such as Alfriston, Beckhampton Road, Holdenhurst, Horslip, Kingston Deverill G1, North Marden, South Street, Thickthorn Down and Woodford G2, though comparatively well preserved, have yet produced little or no convincing evidence of human burial from the primary levels. Those earthen mounds that do cover human remains are often little more than marker mounds for timber structures (or 'mortuary houses') that have been filled with bone (animal and human) and other artefacts, before being demolished or burnt. The mound itself is not, therefore, in these cases a tomb, merely a marker for an earlier range of material, deliberately set into the ground. Sometimes it would appear that the importance of the mound lay more within its construction and composition, as is clear at Beckhampton Road, rather than with any artefactual associations.

Elsewhere, the stone-chambered or stone-structured long mounds of Western Britain have produced sometimes considerable quantities of articulated, disarticulated, disassembled and cremated human bone. It is these assemblages that, as noted, demand centre stage within discussions surrounding Neolithic burial activities. Certainly the samples contained within stone-chambered mounds are substantial when compared to their non-chambered earthen cousins, but it is worth noting a few points here.

First, the spatial patterning of human remains within the chambered mounds is confined to a very small part of the mound, usually the wider, 'business' end. In fact the dimensions of these structured mounds often present a great contrast to the numbers and distribution of human body parts. In all, the zone of depositional activity within stone-structured mounds often represents less than five per cent of the total area covered by the structure. Furthermore, if one is treating the mounds purely as places of human burial, then one should acknowledge that these are not sites in which every member of society could participate. Richard Atkinson, in an article published in 1968, observed that the total amount of human bone recovered from mounds across southern and eastern England would suggest that the Neolithic population never exceeded between 40 and 75 individuals at any one time. To say that such a society was not viable, in simple economic and biological terms, would be an understatement.

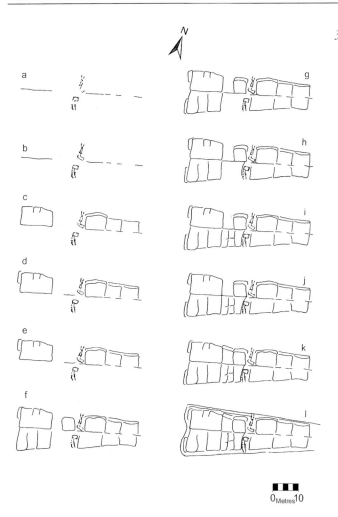

33 Hazleton North: proposed building sequence for the stone-structured mound from the establishment of stone-lined chambers and passageways (a) to final form (l). Redrawn from Saville 1990

Sometimes the chambers themselves may actually represent an earlier element of structure, established prior to mound building, such as at Hazleton North (**33**). Perhaps stone chambers, for all their apparent monumentality, were simply a stone form of the timber 'mortuary structures' recovered beneath certain earth and timber mounds. The only difference here would seem to be that the stone chambers remained accessible, whilst those of timber were sealed by, or destroyed prior to, the building of the linear mound. At other sites, the human remains recovered from chambers appear to have been intermingled with animal bone and pottery. Other sites show that the incorporation of human remains represented the final act of deposition, prior to the physical sealing of chamber entrances. Thus the extended, articulated male skeleton found in the entrance to Hazleton North may be paralleled by the articulated skeletons recovered from the final fills of Neolithic enclosure ditches, pits and shaft fill, or the fully articulated female skeleton sealing the entrance to a gallery in Shaft 27 at Cissbury. All these factors appear to suggest that the *disposal* of human remains did not provide the primary motivating force behind the building of monumental linear mounds.

So if the evidence from long mounds, especially the non-chambered, earthen examples from the southern English chalk, suggests that these sites were not 'tombs', where does this leave our understanding of their context within an articulated Neolithic social system? They were certainly the first major pieces of structural engineering, whose creation involved a considerable input of labour from the local population. Bill Startin has attempted to calculate just how long a structured mound of the Neolithic would take to complete, estimating that the average would have been between 7,000 and 16,000 person-hours. All is of course dependant upon the monument in question, its location from the nearest settlement, condition of ground surface and vegetation cover prior to construction, hardness of bedrock and availability of good building materials other than that generated from the cutting of ditches. With these considerations in mind, Tim Darvill has suggested that the average block of work necessary would be the equivalent of ten people working an eight hour day, seven days a week for between three and seven months.

Earth and timber long mounds were not, it seems clear, intended to act as tombs. These structures were, it is my contention, intended to act as a form of cultural or social archive. Hence the 'symbolic house' that was the long mound would contain the markers or identifiers specific to the social group that constructed it. These community markers may have been represented by the accumulation and separation of different soils or geological materials common to a particular territory, as has been suggested for the earth and timber mounds of Beckhampton Road and Nutbane. Social identifiers may also have been generated through the deposition of artefacts made by, or common to, a particular group; such as worked flint or pottery. Alternatively the remains of domesticated or wild animals that had lived or had been killed within a particular territory may have been deposited within the mounds.

Occasionally human bone, a representative sample of the community, could be incorporated within the structure of the earth and timber mound or within the ditch segments. Other materials of an organic nature (textiles, artefacts of leather and timber, food and drink), could also have played their part. More often than not, the final version of the archive appears to have been stored within a timber box or chamber, accessed via a façade or timber forecourt, as at Nutbane at Haddenham, and the earth mound merely acted as a marker, covering and sealing the material remains for eternity.

Stone-structured or chambered mounds may, cautiously, justify the term 'tomb', but not with any real sense of conviction, for the actual burial components of such monuments often only comprise a very small percentage of the total structure. Perhaps the only real point of divergence between the earthen long mounds and those possessing stone chambers is that the latter category gave members of society the opportunity, if desired, continually to access, catalogue, examine and reorder the community database: human and animal bones could be taken out and replaced; meanings could be altered through the addition of new pottery styles or flint artefacts. The earthen long mounds, in contrast to those of stone, represented the final narrative statement, which served to both seal the archive and mark its presence within the landscape.

It is this aspect of access and prevention of access to the community archive that perhaps best links the linear mounds of the British Neolithic to other structures of this period, most notably the shafts, flint mines and monumental 'houses' such as Skara Brae. In the galleries of a vertical shaft, the chambers of a mound, and the tunnels linking space at Skara Brae, an attempt was made to remove the human presence (both dead and living) from the real world outside. For those crawling along the restricted subterranean galleries of the flint mine, the feelings of being somewhere alien and strange are tangible: there is very little natural light; there are none of the comforting sights and sounds of the natural world; there are no significant variations in temperature; there is no sense of reality.

There is, however, every sense of having been dislocated from society and being alone in the dark, deep within the earth (**colour plates 11, 12, 13 & 14**). Such a sense of separation may also be attained within the stone-lined chambers of the linear and circular structured mound for, once in the chamber or crawling through the access passage, one has the sense of having left the real behind. It is dark, it is cold and one is quite clearly alone. It is perhaps possible, therefore, that the stone- and timber-lined chambers, be they within a mound or free-standing, were designed not only to store and retain the community archive, but to ensure that those accessing the database were clear that they were entering a different and somewhat unsettling supernatural world.

Timothy Taylor and Julian Cope have recently put forward interesting ideas to explain the form taken by the forecourt or monumental entrance structure, leading to the internal chambers of stone-structured mounds. In his book *The Prehistory of Sex*, Taylor views the basic structure of a Neolithic linear mound, with an entrance and internal chambers, as monumental representation of female genitalia: a sort of 'womb tomb'. The entrance, Taylor notes

> is often described as an opening between two 'arms' – an unfortunate coyness that obscures the obvious fact that arms do not converge on an opening, legs do.

The modelling of linear mound as part phallic mound, part womb, may therefore be a necessary prerequisite for the storing of the dead. Unfortunately, such a theory is somewhat hindered by the lack of any meaningful quantity of human bone recovered from a number of structured mounds, though it is just as applicable to the variety of material remains recorded. Disassembled human bodies, animal body parts, pottery, flintwork, et cetera could in this respect have been placed or planted 'like seeds' within a mound. If the ground had further been ploughed or broken up prior to mound construction, as at South Street, then the symbolic nature of land re-fertilisation through social markers may have been significantly increased.

A further interesting point, touched upon by Taylor, Cope and others, is the nature of constricting stones or portholes found at the threshold of many stone-structured mounds. As has already been noted, such concealments have the effect of limiting access to internal chambers, sometimes drastically. At Hazleton North, for

34 West Kennet/Silbury: approaching the linear or circular structured mound in the Neolithic would undoubtedly have meant a separation from the familiar world of home; a dislocation from society. Today these feelings are all but lost to us, the modern worlds of business and tourism imposing their own, intrusive order to the land. Miles Russell

example, constricting stones decrease the crawl space to less than half a metre. If structured mounds were designed as a permanent form of implanted community archive, then the narrowness of entranceways may reflect who could and could not regularly access the database. Access to, and modification of, social identifiers stored within timber- or stone-lined chambers may therefore have possessed an element of initiation, an activity geared specifically to the immatures, or those of slighter build, within society.

Entrance to certain mounds, with their associated feelings of isolation, separation and dislocation from the living human community (**34**), may thus have been linked to concepts surrounding the 'coming of age'. An immature, could, in such a scenario, gain entry to the internal chambers and access the database, containing information on the nature and identity of the land and the human and animal population that inhabited it. Final emergence from the mound, through a porthole placed at the opening, between two symbolic 'legs', would have made a suitable and dramatic rebirth, as a fully fledged adult, for the individual concerned (**colour plate 10**).

In this model of mound as communal archive, the presence of human bone does not of course represent the major defining factor. Presence or absence of human body parts may well have been dependent upon their availability or importance at the time of chamber design or mound construction. Alternative artefact assemblages, such as

67

flint waste, pottery, carved chalk or animal bone may have at times been viewed as more representative of the social group or of the land that they laid claim to; hence such items may sometimes have gained prominence over human bone. It is possible that, having been established as community identifiers, some mounds would over time have been further modified and adapted. In some regions of Britain, the long mound may have become gradually more synonymous with the deposition of human body parts, though whether such sites could be justified as tombs remains questionable.

Archive mounds were presumably created within specific parts of the landscape for a host of different reasons, though the main impetus may well have been land claim. Such claims need not have been political, however; there may have been as much reason to dedicate important items to a particular deity in order to ensure the long term good will of supernatural forces. The deposition of cultural or social markers could also have been designed as a way of taming a new or wild space by seeding it with the identity of the local community. Such a concept could, as already noted, explain the ard or plough marks preserved beneath mounds like South Street, or the pits under mounds like Moody's Down SE and Alfriston, which may originally have held some form of archaeologically undetectable libation or offering.

The desire for increased fertility of the soil or the tribe, the need for ample food, the availability of game and the provision of flint may also have been important to the group, and this could explain the range of artefacts deposited within and around shafts and enclosure ditches. The need to establish a clear identity within certain tracts of land may also have been important to newcomers, seeking a form of moral or ideological dominance over indigenous communities, by those who felt threatened by newcomers, or those who feared a shortage of resources due to the steady increase in the local population.

If linear mounds did represent a form of cultural archive or community statement imposed upon the landscape, then any discussion of burial rites, mortuary rituals, or ancestral worship in the British Neolithic is unnecessary. Bone deposits were not part of some burial rite applied only to the great and the good. The human bone placed within Neolithic mounds could instead be seen as representing the disassembly of one or more persons considered to be representative of the community.

How such body parts were acquired would also be a moot point, for there is no certainty that bone had come from those who had died from natural causes. It is possible that certain individuals, be they male or female, adult or immature, who were selected for disassembly and inclusion in the archive may not have gone willingly. Particular cases in point here may be the skeletons recorded from West Kennet and Ascott-under-Wychwood. At West Kennet, an elderly adult male had been killed by an arrow fired to the throat; a woman in the Ascott-under-Wychwood by an arrow to the spine. Other examples of leaf-shaped projectile points as probable causes of death, rather than as grave goods, within structured mounds may also be cited from Adam's Grave, Blackpatch 12, Notgrove, Rodmarton, Sale's Lot, Ty Isaf and West Tump. The people represented within or beneath linear mounds may not therefore have been the powerful, the successful, the wealthy, the religious or spiritual leaders. The average person selected or sacrificed for disposal and storage in the structured

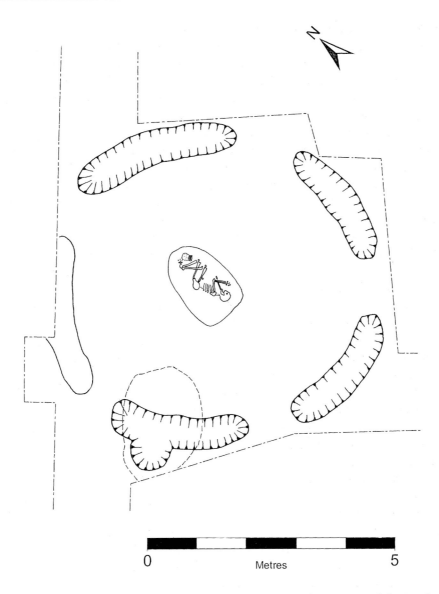

35 Stockbridge: plan of features recorded during the excavation of a Later Neolithic/Early Bronze Age round mound. The segmented ditch represents the primary phase monument; at the centre (hearth-point) was placed the body of an adult female. A flint cairn was later set over the structure, sealing all deposits. Redrawn from Stone and Gray Hill 1940

mound could just as easily have been poor or dispossessed, a captive or a slave.

The development of round mounds, and the transformation from linear to circular forms throughout the Neolithic and into the Early Bronze Age, is usually interpreted by archaeologists as evidence of 'the rise of the individual'. That is to say that political or religious power was moving from the communal, as represented by the linear mound, towards a social system with chiefs, kings, queens and priests. How then does the suggestion that the disposal of human remains did not consti- tute the primary motive for the building of linear mounds affect such a theory? Surprisingly well as it happens, especially if the perceived importance of a linear mound lay more in its construction, composition and location, rather than with any specific association with the human dead.

It is possible, for example, that the move from linear to circular mounds may represent the abandonment of the community archive or community marker, in which the material essence of a particular social group is stored in order to claim an area of land. The fact that circular forms of mound appear at a time when circular domestic structures were becoming more common may alternatively suggest that the concept of mound as symbolic home containing a series of representative community identifiers continued beyond the Early Neolithic. The development of round mounds, with bodies placed at the centre (**35**), in the area of a house normally occupied by the hearth, may add further weight to this idea.

In this model, the appearance of a single articulated body may indicate that the nature of society in specific areas had altered to the point that individuals could now act for the wider community. Individual burials, sometimes with singular dress items, including daggers, hair braids and archery equipment, would then have become the main way of imprinting social identity into the land. A single, well-appointed skeleton would not therefore indicate that the person in question had been powerful, wealthy or in any way successful when alive; merely that they were powerful in death, as a representative of a new social group or the descendants of the earlier group that still sought to claim the land.

The need to establish clear identity and ownership of specific parts of the landscape may have gained in importance throughout the Late Neolithic and Early Bronze Age as social pressures on the land from new or competing human groups increased. Perhaps communities felt the need to hijack the monuments of earlier periods, such as the enclosures, linear mounds and shafts, in order to strengthen or legitimise their claim. Such capture of sites could have occurred through the addition of later pottery types (Grooved Ware or Beaker), flintwork or a contemporary and complete member of society, deep into a backfilling ditch or shaft or weathering mound. Such inserted bodies again need not be those of the religious leaders, the politically powerful or the financially successful, for these individuals may have been chosen due to the fact that they were perceived as being representative, not unique.

4 Enclosures

The first identification of a distinctive type of Neolithic enclosure in Britain came in the 1920s. Prior to this, many earthworks now known to be Neolithic had been attributed to the Romans or the (somewhat unspecified) 'ancient British'. The early examination of Neolithic enclosures was small scale, limited excavations occurring at Maiden Bower at the end of the nineteenth century and at Knap Hill (**colour plate 19**) between 1908-9. In 1922 the Rev H.G.O. Kendall commenced an excavation at Windmill Hill (**36**) and effectively kick-started research into this class of Neolithic site in a very big way.

Kendall brought the Windmill Hill site to the attention of O.G.S. Crawford, archaeological officer for the Ordnance Survey, who, when it appeared likely that the hill was to be permanently scarred by the construction of a radio mast, contacted millionaire Alexander Keiller. Keiller purchased the site and, from 1924, commenced a detailed programme of survey and excavation. The nature of discoveries at Windmill Hill led to the publication in 1930 of an article on *Neolithic Camps* by Elliot Curwen, which brought together for the first time 16 sites possessing a similar range of characteristics.

It was the distinctively interrupted, or broken, circuit of ditch (**37**) which first provided a name for this class of Early Neolithic monument, namely 'Causewayed Camp'. The causewayed element was clear enough, the word camp was applied because the ramparts appeared so lacking in definition that they were thought to have been occupied on a temporary basis. Discussion of Neolithic enclosures has, for most of the twentieth century, continued to focus upon the breaks in the ditch circuit and the possible reasons for these as means of defence, attack or simple entrance and exit.

Ditches have also provided rich grounds for interpretation and discussion. Crawford interpreted individual ditch segments as separate sunken feature buildings, a sort of Neolithic ribbon housing development, based on ethnographic examples of nomadic campsites in Africa. Interpretation of the ditch as a 'pit-dwelling' was fairly common throughout the 1930s; Curwen, when reviewing the ditches at Whitehawk in 1937, saw the finds contained within them as domestic refuse, something which suggested that the original occupants had lived amidst a mass of 'filthy litter'.

Since the 1970s it has become apparent that ditch cuts do not represent the sole defining feature of Neolithic enclosures, a number of embanked and, at times, only partially ditched sites being recorded from the uplands of Cornwall, Devon, Derbyshire, Cumbria and Northumberland. The most famous of these is Carn Brae, where excavations between 1970-3 revealed a series of irregular stone ramparts, broken at intervals. The majority of such sites are, somewhat bizarrely, often

36 Windmill Hill: an aerial view of the Neolithic enclosure. The three circuits of bank and ditch are visible at the centre of the photo, overlain by modern field boundaries, three circular structured mounds and a small plantation. Sussex Archaeological Society: Holleyman Collection

37 Whitehawk: the distinctively 'causewayed', or interrupted, ditch is visible in this photograph of the third circuit under excavation in 1932. The two excavators (and dog) are standing in the western segment of ditch, the eastern (in the foreground) is partially overlain by a modern pipeline. Between the two ditch segments lies 'Causeway I,' a break in the circuit further defined by two postholes (just visible in the photo), possibly the remains of a gate structure or timber façade. Sussex Archaeological Society: Curwen Collection

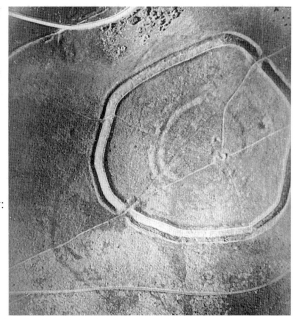

38 The Trundle: the distinctive imprint of the interrupted Neolithic enclosure is evident within the area enclosed by the well-defined ramparts of the Iron Age hillfort in this aerial photograph. Traces of the outer Neolithic rampart are clear to the north of (i.e. outside) the Iron Age ramparts at the top of the photograph, and also as dark lines visible to the south west. The extent of enclosed space recorded here would suggest that the Trundle was one of the largest enclosures of its period in the British Isles. Sussex Archaeological Society: Curwen Collection

excluded from discussion on Neolithic enclosure on the grounds that they do not possess obvious ditches. Because of this, the Cornish sites are often ascribed a category all of their own as 'Tor enclosures'. When Tor enclosures have been examined, however, they demonstrate that they were contemporary with the 'causewayed' sites noted from softer rock geologies. At the very least the Tor sites clearly 'enclose' and, as such, should not be excluded from the discussion purely because they superficially look different.

Just over 70 Neolithic enclosures have today been identified in the British Isles. The majority of sites cluster within the lowlands of southern, south-eastern and south-western England, with outliers recorded from southern Scotland, northern England, north Wales and the Isle of Man. The construction of enclosures within Early Neolithic Britain appears to have been between 4200 and 3000 BC, though the main periods of building and redefinition seem to have occurred between 3700 and 3300 BC. The earliest dated enclosure circuit for the British Isles is Billown, charcoal from the primary phases of ditch fill suggesting a date of between 4780-4530 BC for the initial phases. Other enclosures in Britain possess slightly later radiocarbon determinations for primary ditch circuit definition, notably 4200-4010 BC for Court Hill I, and 4320-3900 BC for the Trundle (**38**).

Ditch structure

The possible significance of multiple breaks in the ditch circuit of Neolithic enclosures has been discussed at length. Interpretations have ranged from a possible way of improving the defensive capabilities of the enclosure, to the result of small teams of people excavating

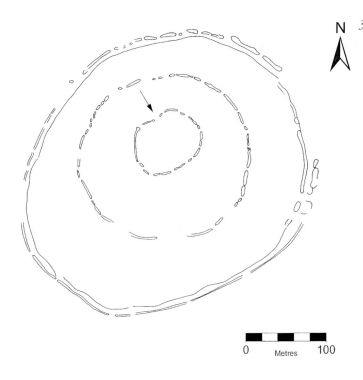

N

*39 Windmill Hill: plan
of the enclosure
showing possible
approach and entrance
point (arrowed) for the
inner, primary phase
ditch circuit.*
Redrawn from
Whittle, Pollard and
Grigson 1999

0   Metres   100

spoil in relative isolation from one another (**colour plate 20**). Whatever the origins for this early ditch excavation technique, it would appear that the primary concern was to provide sufficient spoil for the construction of an internal rampart.

Unfortunately, the internal banks of Neolithic enclosures do not always survive, either because at some stage during their use they were deliberately levelled, or because post-Neolithic activities, such as ploughing, have erased all traces of them. If breaks in the ditch and bank did perhaps indicate numerous points of entrance and exit, then these could reflect the desire to provide an easily accessible circuit, or one where access was granted only to a limited number of people from specific social backgrounds. Alternatively multiple entrances could indicate a need to provide obvious points of access to different sectors of the surrounding landscape. Enclosures without continuous ditch sequences, such as the upland sites of Carn Brae and Helmon Tor, appear to possess ramparts that are interrupted less frequently and by somewhat narrow breaks.

Within some enclosures there may have been any number of ditch or bank circuit interruptions, but perhaps only one or two major points of approach and entrance. Christopher Evans has noted that the inner ditches of certain multi-circuit enclosures often possess a flattened side, or area where the clear inward curve of ditch segments may relate to a façade or 'hornwork'. Such inturning of the ditch is, for example, clearly visible within the north-western sector of the inner circuit at Windmill Hill (**39**) and the eastern sector of the inner circuit at Briar Hill. If interpreted correctly, such hornworks, perhaps similar to the façades noted from certain structured mounds, may have been intended to emphasise the correct direction of approach, one which was designed to take visitors through a monumental form of ditch and rampart interruption.

40 *Whitehawk: suggested three*
  phase plan of the enclosure
  showing (clockwise from top
  left): phase 1 inner circuit
  with possible entrance points
  and directions of approach
  arrowed; phase 2 outer
  circuits showing possible
  entrance gaps and directions
  of approach arrowed; phase 3
  outermost circuit with possible
  direction of approach and
  entrance gaps arrowed. The
  later phase entrance points
  are defined by possible gate
  structures recorded during
  archaeological excavation.
  Redrawn from Russell
  and Rudling 1996

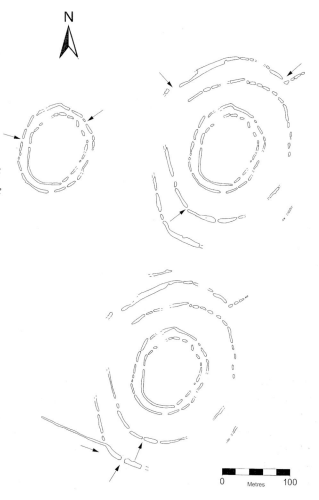

At Whitehawk, once the secondary phase of construction (as defined by the outer two circuits) has been removed, it is possible to suggest the presence of at least two points of entrance within the primary phase double circuit; at the western and the extreme north-eastern sectors (**40**). These represent the only two points within the inner enclosure circuit where interruptions in the double ditch correspond and where the ditch segments curve appreciably inwards. Of the two possible entrances, that set within the western sector would perhaps appear the most credible as it is positioned at the approximate centre of the longest, flattened side of the circuit. It must be noted, however, that the second gap was aligned towards a north-eastern tangential ditch, which could have acted as a device intended to direct the movement of people or animals towards the intended entrance.

Similar inturning of the primary ditch circuit is detectable at the eastern margins of the Trundle, the northern margins of Offham, the southern circuit of Halnaker Hill and south-western side of Barkhale. The plan of the Trundle indicates that two segments of the inner ditch circuit curve appreciably inwards along the eastern side

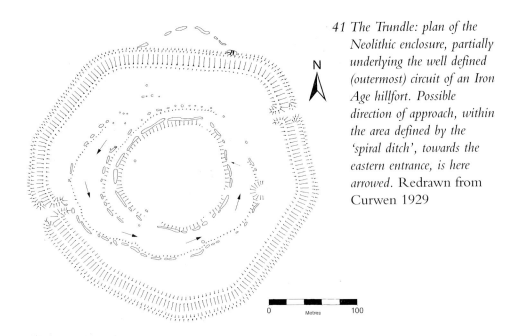

41 The Trundle: plan of the Neolithic enclosure, partially underlying the well defined (outermost) circuit of an Iron Age hillfort. Possible direction of approach, within the area defined by the 'spiral ditch', towards the eastern entrance, is here arrowed. Redrawn from Curwen 1929

N

0   Metres   100

of the monument, where a gap in the ditch is mirrored by an interruption in the bank. It is interesting that the so-called spiral ditch, which traverses the western and southern margins of the hill, first diverges from the inner circuit at a point just to the north of this possible entrance. This could suggest that the spiral represents a feature designed to channel movement around the summit of the hill to the main access point at the east (**41**). A similar explanation, albeit with regard to a later phase construct, may explain the tangential ditch systems recorded from the north-eastern and south-western margins of outermost circuit at Whitehawk.

If such façades did originally indicate the main point of access to enclosures such as Whitehawk, Windmill Hill, Briar Hill and the Trundle, then it is interesting to note that secondary remodelling of the circuits did not usually follow or even respect it. At Briar Hill, Christopher Evans has observed that the secondary enclosure phase appeared to reverse the primary orientation to the east. At Whitehawk, the outer circuits also inverted the major point of access, continuous sections of bank and ditch being placed in front of the two earlier possible entrances (at the north-eastern and eastern sides) and at least two entrances set out at the south-west.

Within circuit 3 at Whitehawk the line of the ditch was originally continuous until a substantial period of recutting apparently altered the basic design, interrupting it and creating two discrete segments of ditch cut (**42**). The new gap, which measured around two metres, was accompanied by two postholes, possibly part of a gate, along its inner lip. A second gap in the south-western ditch, to the north-west of the first, may also have represented a new entrance through the third circuit. The importance of these new entrance gaps at Whitehawk may be reflected in the artefacts recovered from the accompanying ditch terminals. Deposits here comprised of charcoal rich soil containing worked flint, pottery and the contracted skeletons of two young women,

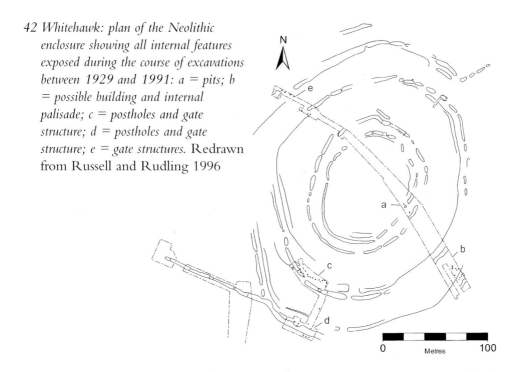

42 *Whitehawk: plan of the Neolithic enclosure showing all internal features exposed during the course of excavations between 1929 and 1991: a = pits; b = possible building and internal palisade; c = postholes and gate structure; d = postholes and gate structure; e = gate structures.* Redrawn from Russell and Rudling 1996

one having possibly died in childbirth. A gap in the outer circuit at Whitehawk also appears to have comprised an earlier segment of continuous ditch replaced by a defined break or causeway. Within the area of the earlier ditch, left untouched by the secondary break, the skeleton of a partially dismembered roe deer had been placed.

Despite extensive investigation into Neolithic enclosures, little research had, until the late 1980s, been conducted into their spatial organisation. Evans was one of the first to consider the configuration of multi-ditch sites and relate their patterning to aspects of phasing, orientation and function. Evans suggested that, despite the inadequacies of the radiocarbon chronology, the phasing of multi-circuit enclosures could potentially be determined through the coherence and integrity of ditch construction. At Briar Hill, for example, the innermost enclosure ditch possessed 'an independent integrity apart from the two outermost rings'. This could imply that the two outer ditches were 'out of phase' with the inner. A number of additional enclosure sites were, Evans suggested, of similar sequence, representing not a single period of monumental construction, but a number of distinct phases. The final form of these circuits of ditch and bank would not therefore represent the ultimate design, but the product of gradual accumulation and experimentation.

At Whitehawk, the innermost double ditch circuit is aligned independently from the outer two, which together possessed a mutual cohesion, possibly suggesting a two phase sequence of development. An additional phase of circuit definition may be suggested by the presence of a tangential ditch at the south-western margins of the enclosure. This ditch appears to have been directly joined to the outer ditch circuit at its south-western margins.

43 Whitehawk: a pair of large postholes placed along the inner lip of a secondary break in the Neolithic ditch circuit as photographed (at night) in 1933. It is likely that this represents part of a timber gate structure designed to frame the main direction of approach. Sussex Archaeological Society: Curwen Collection

It is also possible to infer a sequential development for the Early Neolithic enclosures at Offham Hill and the Trundle. At Offham, environmental data recovered from the ditches suggested a significant time had elapsed between the cutting of the inner and outer circuits, whilst the plan clearly shows that the two surviving areas of enclosure circuit follow noticeably divergent paths. The plan of the Trundle indicates that the inner circuits possess a cohesion distinct from that of the 'spiral' and fourth circuits. The spiral ditch may represent a later act of enclosure, partially extending from the primary phase second ditch, or, as already noted, a form of tangential ditch similar to the examples recorded from Whitehawk.

Gate and rampart structures

Despite the suggestion of major points of entrance, evidence for gateways within Neolithic enclosures is comparatively rare. Examination at Carn Brae revealed good evidence of at least one reasonably well-defined gate structure, the placing of which was largely reliant upon the nature of the granite bedrock, a clear break in the geology

44 Whitehawk: a line of four postholes, three of which are visible in this photograph, running back from a break in the fourth ditch circuit, as revealed in 1935. This postline, Curwen speculated, may have formed one side of a timber-lined entrance passage through the rampart of the fourth circuit. Sussex Archaeological Society: Curwen Collection

being emphasised by paving and the setting up of stone uprights or orthostats. Establishment of these uprights created a restricted gap, just over one metre wide, something which would seem to imply that only foot traffic could gain entry.

Two possible gate structures have been recorded from the Whitehawk enclosure during excavations conducted in 1932-3 and 1935 (**43**). A break in the line of ditch circuit 3 possessed, along its inner lip, two small postholes set around two metres apart. Elliot Curwen suggested that both had originally linked to a pair of similar postholes to the north forming a potential timber-lined entrance passage. Evidence of a second possible passage through the rampart was found within a break in the outer ditch, where a line of four postholes was recorded running along an east–west line from the southern edge of the causeway (**44**).

If these areas at Whitehawk and Carn Brae were Neolithic gate structures, then the evidence does not unfortunately provide a clear idea of what form they originally took. From a modern perspective, they do not make particularly convincing defensible structures, though given the levels of disturbance to the enclosure sites in the last 200 years this may not seem surprising. It is also fair to say that we do not know what form of warfare was fought within Neolithic society. The impressive series of ramparts and walls that surround Iron Age and Medieval defences can affect our view of how early prehistoric societies attempted to prevent their neighbours from killing them. The earthworks and post structures of Whitehawk may, against the less organised and less heavily armoured armies of the Neolithic, have therefore represented a defence system that was, for its time, state of the art.

The placing of timber posts at a break in the ditch and rampart circuit at Whitehawk may alternatively have been purely to dramatise a point of entrance and frame it more

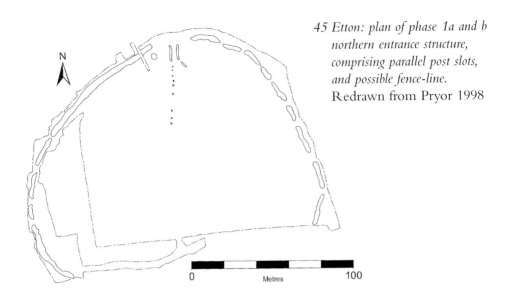

45 Etton: plan of phase 1a and b northern entrance structure, comprising parallel post slots, and possible fence-line.
Redrawn from Pryor 1998

N

0   Metres   100

clearly within the landscape. Rodney Castleden, in his book, *The Wilmington Giant: the Quest for a Lost Myth*, has suggested that the paired postholes at Whitehawk were designed to hold immense, free standing timbers, forming a type of dipylon gate or ceremonial entranceway. Such a suggestion may not be too far off the mark; after all, when similar sized postholes are encountered at one end of a Neolithic linear mound, they are generally interpreted as a form of façade or visual focus and not a form of defence.

More convincing evidence for timber-lined entrance passages has been found at the enclosures of Crickley Hill and Etton. At Etton, the passageway running back into the enclosure from a break in the northern ditch circuit, and defined by two parallel post slots rather than individual postholes, measured three metres in width and was around eight metres long (**45**). The southern end of the passageway appeared to be linked to a low fenceline and a shallow, curved gulley, interpreted as a form of screen. At Crickley Hill a long series of twinned postholes extended back from at least four of the possible entrance breaks, creating passageways of between 15 and 35m in overall length.

A complex series of postholes, pits and shallow gulleys was noted within the causeway through the outer ditches and palisade slot at Orsett (**46**). Three postholes, located at the central point of the trench slot causeway, may have been part of a double gate structure, whilst further postholes to the south-west could represent a later blocking. The evidence may, however, suggest a more complicated sequence. There is a certain linearity of features through the southern ditch gap which is mirrored in the orientation of the eastern half of the palisade slot. The excavators, Hedges and Buckley, interpreted this as a secondary stage of entrance definition, but it may alternatively indicate a structure designed to move people through the ditch and post trench circuits and into the central area of the enclosure in a certain way, along a fixed route: a form of Neolithic crash barrier.

Evidence for the timberisation of Neolithic ramparts is rare in Britain, possibly because few circuits have been fully examined, or because so many sites have been

46 Orsett: feature plan showing possible gate structure through the outer ditch, inner ditch and internal palisade trench with possible direction of entrance and approach arrowed. Redrawn from Hedges and Buckley 1978

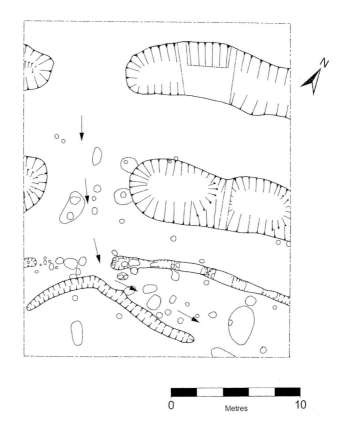

0   Metres   10

badly hit by development or modern agricultural practice. At Orsett, a thin linear cut was found behind the second ditch circuit and interpreted as the remains of a palisade trench or post slot. Evidence from the fill suggested the former presence of timber posts measuring around 0.2m in diameter. The occasional charcoal-rich deposit showed that at least some of the posts had been burnt *in situ*. An original entrance point for the enclosure may be indicated within the north-western quadrant, where a break in both slot and main ditch coincided.

A similar, gently curving cut, has been found behind the main ditch of the Haddenham enclosure (**47**). The faint trace of decayed posts evident within the gravel fill of the slot implied that the average timber measured around 0.3m in diameter, and had been spaced at a distance of roughly 0.4m. Certain sections of the palisade were associated with evidence of burning, possibly indicating a period of destruction. The post slot appeared to have been dug in separate, straight lengths, each individual section measuring around three to four metres, each section separated by a clear break, measuring less than a metre. Evidence to suggest timber structure to Neolithic ramparts has also been recorded from Whitehawk. Here, three circular postholes were found to the north-east of the inner edge of ditch 3, whilst postholes have also been found within the rubble bank accompanying it. All have been interpreted as part of a continuous timber palisade. Postholes surrounding ditch segments at the Trundle (**48**) may have been designed to add an extra visual dimension to the rapidly backfilling hollows.

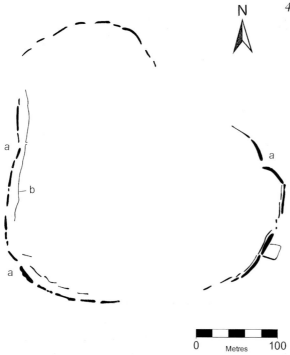

N

47 Haddenham: feature plan for the enclosure as detected through excavation and survey: a = three possible points of entrance and approach; b = internal palisade trench

a

a

b

a

0   Metres   100

48 The Trundle: a segment of the second ditch as excavated in 1930, showing postholes cut along the very edges of the feature. Possibly these were intended as a way of adding further emphasis to the backfilling or overgrown ditch cut. Sussex Archaeological Society: Curwen Collection

49 Etton: plan of phase 1c palisade trench, replacing part of the north-western ditch circuit and reinforcing the east/west divide down the centre of the earlier enclosure. Redrawn from Pryor 1998

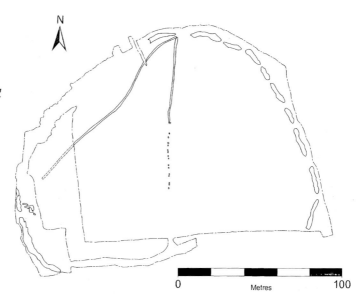

0   Metres   100

Other fence or palisade trenches accompanying ditch circuits may be in evidence in southern England at the Neolithic enclosures of Crickley Hill, Etton and the Stepleton enclosure at Hambledon Hill. The Crickley Hill feature comprised a linear, segmented cut set back from, and parallel to, the 'phase 1d' ditch circuit (**49**). At Etton, the palisade slot recorded appears to have been built as a replacement for the primary phase, waterlogged ditch, whilst the Stepleton enclosure possessed a series of postholes in two parallel rows set beneath, and presumably within, the internal earth rampart (**50**).

Internal features

An impressive range of internal features has been recorded from the upland enclosure sites situated on hard rock geology where later agricultural activity has been relatively limited in effect. The complex series of internal features recorded from Crickley Hill has unfortunately yet to be published in detail, though preliminary data suggest a number of important elements, including possible house structures, pathways and storage pits.

At Carn Brae, excavations conducted between 1970 and 1973 have revealed so much structural data that Roger Mercer has referred to the site as an 'enclosed village'. Behind a section of the south-western enclosure wall in trench A1, a shallow and irregular sided pit or working hollow was examined. The hollow contained evidence of burning and appeared to have been placed directly across a line of stake-holes and small pits (**51**). Mercer felt that, in combination, these features represented multiple phases of structure, though the basic design of a roughly rectangular building would appear clear enough. Whether this represented a timber backing to the stone

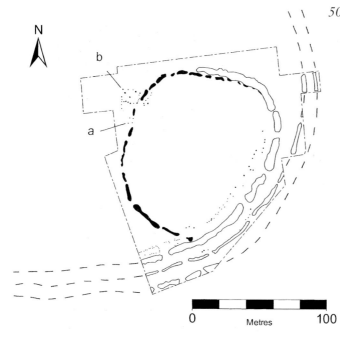

50 Hambledon Hill: feature plan of the Stepleton enclosure as derived from excavation and survey: a = possible entrance structure; b = linear set of postholes interpreted by the excavator as 'the barbican', and all postholes comprising potential timber structured rampart.
Redrawn from Oswald, Dyer and Barber 2001

N

b

a

0   Metres   100

rampart, or part of an independent structure, is unfortunately unclear, given the relatively small area examined. Given the sometimes substantial nature of postholes and the evidence for *in situ* burning, there would appear little doubt that the features revealed originally formed part of a prominent building, possibly a house.

Stakeholes were also noted in trench A2 and K at Carn Brae, though the layout suggested to the excavator 'no coherent pattern'. Better structural information, in the form of postholes, was revealed at the site within trench D, together with a dark deposit of burnt material interpreted as an occupation surface. Unlike the features from A1 however, the trench D features are more difficult to assign a form, though they clearly relate to an independent building. Mercer suggested that the traces of at least one external wall could be made out at the southern edge of the dark deposit, though no stakeholes were discovered.

Compared to upland sites, the presence of internal features from within the Neolithic enclosure circuits of south-eastern Britain would appear sparse. This may be a sampling problem, or it could be that thousands of years of weathering has erased all but the most significant of features. Plough damage may be responsible for the relative absence of features within excavated enclosures, though it is possible, given the relative fluidity of Neolithic society, that sites did not possess a significant amount of building anyway. Perhaps the error lies in the assumption that the enclosures of the British Neolithic should contain large, permanent-style longhouses, of a kind identified on the Continent, whereas the majority of Early Neolithic built forms may well have been more archaeologically ephemeral.

At Whitehawk, a large cluster of features was located midway between the third and fourth ditch at the south-eastern edge of the 1935 excavation trench. The group

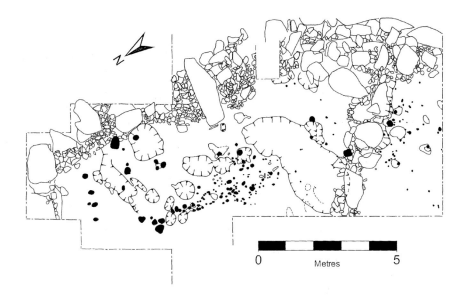

51 Carn Brae: plan of features revealed in trench A1 showing enclosure wall, hollows and post/stakeholes comprising the roughly rectangular building. Redrawn from Mercer 1981

comprised eight irregular cuts, six of which were interpreted as pits and the remaining two as postholes. Curwen was uncertain how to interpret these features, noting that they were apparently 'arranged without any obvious plan'. It is likely that certain aspects have been lost through ploughing or chemical erosion, however. Given the location, form and finds content of the features, it is perhaps more likely than not that they originally constituted timber structures or buildings.

The scattered pits and postholes recorded within the interior of enclosure sites such as Abingdon, Staines and Windmill Hill could well relate to the corralling of livestock or perhaps more seasonal forms of settlement activity. Unfortunately we do not possess a good enough dataset from 'normal' areas of contemporary Neolithic settlement in Britain to be able to make any definitive form of statement or comparison. As with the ditches of structured mounds and the fill of shafts, there would appear to be a significant quantity of placed deposits or structured debris recorded from the internal pits of Neolithic enclosure sites. Such material could of course be taken as suggesting that the primary function of pits was as receptacle for the residue of ritual activity. Alternatively the deliberate selection of material from domestic refuse and its placing in such features may have been necessary as a form of community identifier, designed to claim the land, or as an offering to certain subterranean or supernatural forces.

Artefact assemblages

Artefacts derived from the ditches of Neolithic enclosures vary considerably in quality and quantity, but the basic range of finds, namely pottery, worked flint, animal bone (predominantly ox, pig and sheep/goat) and human bone (complete skeletons and body parts) would however seem relatively stable. Much of this material, especially the articulated human and animal carcasses, would furthermore appear to have been deliberately placed within the ditches of enclosures, sometimes with a tangible sense of order and uniformity.

Quite why large concentrations of flint waste, bone and pottery were permitted to accumulate within Neolithic ditches and why these features were not cleaned out on a regular basis, is a question that has perplexed archaeologists for some time. It is a particular problem if one considers Neolithic enclosures as a form of defensive structure, for surely the deliberate infilling of ditches with rubbish and soil would negate their usefulness. Also, would not the stench of decomposing matter be a problem for those living close to the rampart circuits as well as providing an attraction for rodents and other animals?

Perhaps, but these are really only issues of concern if one visualises Neolithic enclosures from the same perspective say as an Iron Age hillfort or a Medieval castle. In these instances defence was paramount and the removal of waste and repair of ramparts may have been more efficiently organised. Neolithic enclosures, on the other hand, represent the first significant pieces of land division and demarcation and may, therefore, have possessed vastly different constraints and organising concepts.

Etton represents a site where not only the quality of preserved deposits demands attention, but also the exceptional differences of artefact deposition within ditch fills is of particular interest. Excavated by Francis Pryor between 1982 and 1987, the enclosure seemed to have originally been divided into two distinct halves, as indicated by the eastern and western ditch arcs. Material from the western ditches, which may well have been waterlogged throughout their existence, comprised predominantly *in situ* waste derived from the working of antler, wood and bark. The cultural assemblage recovered from the eastern half comprised antler, animal bone (mostly cattle, sheep and pig), human bone and complete pottery vessels. Disarticulated cattle bone was 'often found arranged in linear spreads', whilst the skeletal remains of sheep and pig were more commonly in a state of partial articulation. Human bone was always disarticulated, consisted mostly of skull fragments, and showed evidence of dog gnawing prior to inclusion within ditch fill. This indicated to Pryor that human corpses had been defleshed, presumably through exposure or excarnation, whilst animal carcasses had been butchered.

There have been many attempts to use artefacts recorded from Neolithic ditches as a way of attaching meaning to the enclosures themselves. The basic problem is that the quantity of material retrieved may relate either to domestic refuse, making the enclosures places of long-term settlement, or the deliberate placement of items, in which case the enclosures may have been ceremonial centres. Roger Mercer used the quantity of human remains recovered from Hambledon Hill, for example, to interpret the enclosure as a 'vast reeking cemetery, its silence broken only by the din of crows and ravens'. O.G.S. Crawford and Elliot Curwen, on the other hand, saw the artefact clusters and the structural nature of the ditch cuts as incontrovertible evidence of permanent settlement. Some have seen the artefactual evidence as an indication that enclosures were a type of central place where various goods were bought, sold or redistributed. Others have seen the density of animal bone as proof that the sites were areas of mass consumption, not redistribution.

It may be more complicated than this.

The longevity of monument use and the possible multiplicity of interpretation through time may have ensured that there was never a single meaning attached to Neolithic enclosures, or that any perceived meaning was constantly undergoing revision. Analysis of the artefactual evidence retrieved from a number of multi-ditch enclosures in Britain, notably Abingdon, Briar Hill, Hambledon Hill, Orsett, Whitehawk and Windmill Hill, seems furthermore to indicate that there are discrete differences in the artefacts and artefactual assemblages recovered from the various circuits. In cases such as these, any alteration in the quantity, quality and range of artefact data, especially with regard to human remains, may be taken to imply functional differences between the inner and outer ramparts and the activities enacted by human groups within the areas enclosed by them. Alternatively, and perhaps more plausibly, it is possible that any difference in artefacts from inner to outer circuits is chronological and relates to discrete phases of rebuilding and modification.

One particular area where the range of artefacts recorded from Neolithic enclosure ditches has been used to interpret enclosure function is the chalklands of South Eastern England. Here, in 1988, Peter Drewett suggested that there were two basic types of Neolithic enclosure: fortified settlements and unfortified ceremonial sites. On the South Downs, these two categories were represented by Whitehawk and the Trundle (fortified settlement enclosures), and Barkhale, Combe Hill, Bury Hill and Offham (unfortified ceremonial enclosures). The major factor in determining the argument that the latter four were of ritual or ceremonial importance was that their ditches possessed only a limited number of artefacts, whilst the ditches of the Trundle and Whitehawk contained a wider range of material which implied some form of domestic settlement and manufacturing activity combined with agriculture.

Unfortunately for this particular theory, the evidence of craft activities (namely weaving, wood and bone working and the manufacturing of pottery and flint tools) recovered from the Trundle and Whitehawk is not exclusive to these sites, having also been discovered at Barkhale (knapping scatters, borers, pottery), Bury Hill (knapping scatters, hammerstones, awls and pottery), Combe Hill and Offham (knapping scatters and pottery). Evidence of agriculture and 'seasonal food collection' in the form of animal bone, flint axes, sickles and scrapers has also been found elsewhere, particularly at Barkhale, Bury Hill, Combe Hill and Offham. The more the enclosure sites are examined, the more the 'limited artefactual assemblages' appear at odds with the archaeological evidence. At Bury Hill a mass of Early Neolithic pottery, struck flint and animal and human bone have been recorded, whilst at Barkhale large quantities of struck flint and pottery were also recovered. Significant quantities of worked flint, pottery and animal and human bone have also been retrieved from Combe Hill and Offham.

Attempts to play down the possible significance of the human and animal bone component recovered from Whitehawk and the Trundle unfortunately do little to support the argument for a clear divide between settlement and ceremonial enclosures. In fact the quantity of faunal 'rarities' recorded from the four potential ceremonial enclosures comprises entirely of two beaver teeth from Offham; hardly as significant, from the perspective of placed deposits, as the partially dismembered roe deer found in pit 5 at Whitehawk (or indeed the articulated dog, pig and sheep skeletons from Windmill Hill). Artefacts of 'non-domestic' nature recovered from the Trundle and Whitehawk, such as the carved chalk, are downplayed in Drewett's argument, whilst any significance surrounding artefacts related to food preparation recovered from Barkhale and Bury Hill is largely ignored, apparently in order to sustain the divide. As a result of these and other points, the suggestion that the archaeological data imply the presence of two discrete classes of Neolithic enclosure is here thoroughly rejected.

The artefact type most often debated within discussion of Neolithic enclosure is the human body part. Disarticulated human bone and fully articulated skeletons have long been recognised from the backfill of Neolithic enclosure ditches and, when recovered, such material is often interpreted as the residue of excarnation or of the defleshing of cadavers. Few attempts have, however, been made to relate human skeletal material to distinct phases of constructional activity, the assumption being that as most enclosures comprised a single phase of monumental building, all bodies recovered must relate to this primary phase. Recent work on the recorded enclosures of Britain has, as noted, emphasised longevity of use and sequence. If human skeletal material was deposited throughout all periods of enclosure use, then our understanding of what these bodies and body parts actually mean within the context of enclosure must undergo careful consideration.

The Neolithic enclosure where human remains are most often discussed is that of Hambledon Hill. Here, the quantity of skeletal remains prompted the excavator to suggest that the site may have been a gigantic necropolis for the exposure of corpses prior to more definite disposal elsewhere. Certainly the quantity of body parts recovered is large, but the range and nature of the material itself does not appear unusual within the context of Neolithic enclosure ditch backfill. Human body parts were recorded from the primary silting of the main enclosure circuit, a deposit which also contained animal bone, pottery and flint working debris. Roger Mercer has suggested that the nature and context of this artefactual assemblage indicated deliberate and careful deposition, rather than simple tipping or the accidental inclusion of surface debris.

Of particular note within the primary silt of the main enclosure was the occurrence of a number of human skulls. Absence of mandibles and associated vertebrae seemed to indicate that the skulls had arrived into the ditch cut in an advanced state of decay, rather than having been deliberately severed from the body. Also of significance was the articulated lower trunk of a young adult male, noted from the primary fill of the south eastern area of the main enclosure ditch. This body part did not display evidence of deliberate dismemberment, though animal gnawing was evident across the femora. One must presume, therefore, that these partial remains were introduced into the ditch at an advanced stage of decomposition, but before the muscle tissue of the lower body had completely broken down.

The accumulation of human body parts seems to have continued throughout the gradual backfill of the main enclosure ditch at Hambledon, until it had almost completely filled with spoil. At this time a series of steep-sided cuts was excavated along the line of the ditch, presumably in an attempt to redefine the feature. Disarticulated human skeletal material, especially fragments of skull and mandible, were frequently located within these secondary cuttings.

Of the ditch systems recorded beyond the main Neolithic enclosure at Hambledon, the inner outwork to the east contained one still partially articulated adult human forearm. The infrequently causewayed Stepleton enclosure, to the south-east of the main site, has also produced a range of human body parts from the primary and secondary fills, including a mandible, a femur and at least four skulls, two of which were represented as crania. Associated with these was a quantity of flint knapping debris and animal bone. Human bone, including at least one skull, was recovered from the primary fill of the inner earthwork to the south of the Stepleton enclosure.

At Whitehawk, disarticulated human skeletal material was retrieved throughout the ditch fill of the inner three circuits. The pieces recovered from inner ditches 1 and 2 consisted of lower body parts (humeri, ulna, femora, vertebrae and a pelvis) and, whilst two humeri were also retrieved from ditch 3, upper body parts (skull and jaw fragments) appeared to be restricted solely to the secondary fills of the third enclosure circuit. Much of this material was found in association with animal bone (sheep/goat, ox, pig, red and roe deer). No human material was recovered from the substantially remodified outer circuit, though the skeleton of a partially dismembered roe-deer was retrieved from a feature at the northern margins of the secondary recut.

At Abingdon, the remains of two or more young people were represented by cranial fragments recovered from within the fill of the innermost enclosure ditch. Fragments of human pelvis were further noted from the outer circuit. At Windmill Hill, human remains noted within the primary rubble of the outer ditch comprised a complete and two fragmentary humeri, a vertebra and pieces from two skulls. The primary rubble of the middle ditch produced parts of two femora, a fragment of maxilla and parts of two skulls, one from a child and one an adolescent. Part of a maxilla was also retrieved from the upper levels of the middle ditch circuit. Basal deposits from the inner ditch produced part of a child's skull, a left ulna, a temporal bone and part of a humerus. Two human mandibles, a fibula and a femur were recorded from the outer ditch at Offham, whilst a phalanx and a fragment of rib were retrieved from the inner.

At Staines, two human skulls, part of a mandible and a right radius and ulna were recovered from an organic rich layer at the bottom of the outer ditch cut. One of the skulls appears to have been originally removed from the body by force, a series of wounds to the head perhaps further indicating that the individual concerned had met a violent death. Further damage to the bones appears to have occurred after death, but before deposition into ditch fill. As at Whitehawk, the organic layer within which

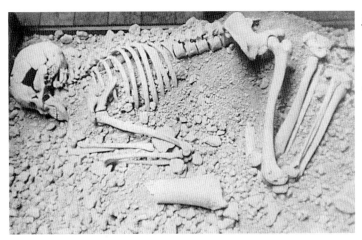

52 Whitehawk: skeleton II, of an adult female, recovered from the secondary fill of the third ditch circuit, re-laid for display in Brighton Museum. Note the crouched position, hands to the face and the ox radius placed just below the left elbow. Sussex Archaeological Society: Curwen Collection

all human bone was recorded also contained large amounts of animal bone (cattle, sheep/goat and pig), Early Neolithic pottery and worked flint material. Additional human body parts recovered from the outer ditch included a single mandible, associated with animal bone (cattle, sheep/goat and pig), a complete ulna and a group of disarticulated carpals and metacarpals (representing the greater part of a hand).

Within the inner ditch of the Staines enclosure, the upper part of a right forearm (which the excavator notes may have been part of the same individual represented by pieces retrieved from the outer circuit) and part of an infant fibula (possibly just post-natal) were recovered from areas of primary ditch silt. The close association, at Staines, of disassembled body parts with what has been interpreted as occupation debris (large quantities of pottery, flint tools, and animal bone), has been taken to indicate that bodies had been decomposing around the site before certain pieces were eventually incorporated into ditch fill.

In addition to such examples of disassembled human body parts, fully articulated human remains are also occasionally found, though such deposits tend to be less frequent and relate more to secondary phases of enclosure use. At Whitehawk, for example, three articulated skeletons, two adults and an infant, were recorded from a dark band of secondary fill within the third ditch. Curwen described this dark layer as an occupation deposit containing not only corpses, but also flintwork, faunal remains, charcoal and pottery. Skeletons I and II, within this deposit, comprised crouched adult females (**52**). Slight displacement of the bones of skeleton II may have been due to animal or root disturbance, or to partial dismemberment prior to deposition. The remains of an infant, apparently only a few weeks old, lay within a space between the left elbow and knees of the adult.

A fourth articulated skeleton (numbered III), the contracted body of an adult male, was found within the area enclosed by ditch circuit 2 at Whitehawk. The skeleton did not appear to be within a defined cut and is described as simply lying on the undisturbed chalk surface which may indicate deposition within the earth bank, all traces of which had been removed by the mechanical stripping of topsoil prior to archaeological investigation. A fifth articulated individual, Skeleton IV, a child aged around seven, was recovered half way down a cylindrical cut located to the north-west (outside of) the third ditch circuit. At the Trundle, the crouched skeleton of an adult female was recovered from the secondary fills of the outer ditch (**53**), the remains of a crouched adult male were recorded from a pit cut into the fill of the outer ditch at Offham, whilst at Staines a crouched adult female was recovered from an oval pit just within the area enclosed by the innermost ditch.

At Hambledon, the main enclosure ditch produced the articulated remains of two infants, both bodies having been placed within defined niches or pits, cut into the floor. Within the ditch of the Stepleton enclosure at Hambledon, above the burnt remains of a timber palisade, a more dramatic discovery was made. This comprised the extended skeleton of a young man in his late teens lying face down, over the skeleton of a post-natal infant. A single leaf-shaped arrowhead was recovered from within the throat of the adult, which may suggest the individual had died violently. His body had been covered with chalk rubble derived from the collapsing bank, almost immediately after its deposition.

53 The Trundle: the crouched remains of an adult female, from the secondary fill of the outer ditch, under excavation in 1928. Sussex Archaeological Society: Curwen Collection

The crouched remains of a two- to three-year-old child was found at the base of the outer ditch of Windmill Hill (**54**), the skeleton of an immature pig being recovered from the same level. A second articulated infant, this time aged around seven months, and the body of an immature goat were found in the secondary fill of the outer ditch, whilst the skeleton of a dog was observed from the primary silt of the middle ditch. The crouched skeleton of an adult human male aged between 35 and 40 years was found in an oval pit sealed by the bank of the outer enclosure circuit, together with a quantity of pig bones.

The apparent frequency with which human remains have been found within Neolithic enclosure ditches is usually taken by archaeologists to represent their greatest defining factor. Therefore enclosures are regularly considered as necropoli, cult centres or areas solely associated with the dead: liminal places at the very edges of human existence. The discovery of a similar range, if not quantity, of bone material from within the backfill of other Neolithic monuments, most notably certain shafts (see below), may alternatively suggest that such a definition is wholly unwarrantable. Human remains,

*54 Windmill Hill: the crouched remains
of a child are visible in the foreground, to the bottom right of the
modern ladder, in this photograph of
the outer ditch taken in 1929.*
Sussex Archaeological Society:
Curwen Collection

especially upper body parts like the skull, occur in ditch fill with significant quantities of other Neolithic cultural debris, such as pottery, flintwork and faunal remains. As has been argued for structured mounds, this could indicate the collation of a representative sample of social markers placed into the land by a specific group, in order to stamp it indelibly with their own cultural identity.

If human bone debris was incorporated within ditches of Neolithic enclosures (as well as within shafts and structured mounds) in an attempt to imprint the monument with a specific social label or identity, then discussion concerning burial in the conventional sense becomes invalid. The accumulation of human body parts within cuts, such as the ditch, would be likelier to represent part of a more general process of structured deposition than be the defining element of that process. The fact that within the disarticulated bone assemblages from enclosure ditch-fill skulls would appear to predominate may reflect the desire to incorporate the more identifiable elements of particular individuals into the fill of a feature thought to lie at the ideological or political centre of one or more prehistoric territories. Discovery of similar deposits within certain shafts, such as those from Cissbury, may also have emphasised their importance within the monument frameworks of Neolithic Britain.

The deposition of complete human bodies within enclosure ditch fill does not cause a problem with such a model, merely a development of it. Fully articulated remains, as noted above, appear to be associated with secondary-phase activity, usually in the outermost ditch cuts of multi-circuit sites (as at Whitehawk). The incorporation of complete individuals into ditch fill, rather than selected body parts, may reflect the changing ideology as indicated within structured round mounds, in that individuals could later embody or 'stand for' the values, belief systems and outlook of an entire community. Part of this social embodiment may be seen in the differential treatment of females and immatures as opposed to adult males. Whilst the disarticulated remains can, where identified, display a reasonable equality in age and sex, the later articulated remains seem to be biased towards adult females and immatures

The fact that some skeletons, both in an articulated and disassembled state, show signs of violence immediately prior to death, as is evident at sites like Staines and Hambledon Hill, may suggest that certain people did not go to their final resting place peacefully. This could indicate that the bodies in question were not those of the powerful or successful, who had died of natural causes, but individuals chosen to represent examples of the 'typical' or social norm, in much the same way as the articulated deer from Whitehawk and the pig, sheep and dog from Windmill Hill.

The meaning of enclosures

The interpretation of Neolithic enclosures in Britain and north-western Europe has always been difficult and resulted in much agonised discussion within archaeological literature. Part of the problem is that, when one looks at other monument types of this period, most notably the linear mounds or the vertical shaft, one can usually impose a functional interpretation (burial mound or flint mine) and go home happy. Enclosures, however, appear to fall into an interpretational void. This is partly due to the observation that they seem to represent a combination of the monumental, domestic, functional, ceremonial and ritual. Most attempts to establish a single interpretation based on all the available evidence, as noted, will fail, the majority of writers suggesting that some sites were for settlement whilst others were designed for an ill-defined ritual purpose.

Perhaps the only thing we can be sure of with regards to Neolithic enclosures is that our understanding of this type of monument has been significantly hindered by some of the more rigid forms of classification that have been imposed. A particular problem is the clear divide, certainly within modern western society, between secular and religious. Trying to fit a particular type of Neolithic structure into one of these two categories, based solely on the archaeological material retrieved from ditch fill, is ultimately doomed to failure, though this has not stopped people trying.

Although it may be almost impossible to answer the question 'where did the idea for the Neolithic enclosures in Britain come from?', some useful observations may be derived from analysis of the nearest comparable examples in central and north-western Europe. Here it may be interesting to note an apparent relationship between enclosure and settlement within sites of the primary Neolithic or Linienbandkeramik (LBK), of western Europe constructed from the mid- to late sixth millennium BC. The evidence, such as it is, may suggest that certain enclosure sites materialised prior to a total reordering of basic settlement form.

At Langweiler 8, in Western Germany, an enclosure was built at the margins of a Neolithic settlement, within the final phases of longhouse development. At Langweiler 9, the monument was apparently established in order to enclose a largely blank area between two former longhouse clusters. Enclosures such as these may have been designed to increase the definition of a communal zone, between what by then had become defunct areas of settlement. This may have been in order to personify or commemorate the deserted community, or to emphasise the status of a small part or element of that former community, clan or household.

Richard Bradley noted in 1998 that, following the main phase of the LBK, continental enclosure building appeared to become increasingly important whilst the enclosures themselves began to take on strong ritual connotations. The ritual interpretation, of course, is one that has dominated the archaeological discussion of Neolithic enclosures. The consensus of opinion tends to be that because there is, as is often, little sign of occupation and no evidence of houses, enclosures must have possessed some other purpose. This has had the unfortunate side effect of ensuring that when occupation evidence is recovered, such material is usually explained as being of purely ceremonial importance. Thus areas of ditch fill where significant quantities of animal bone has been found become evidence of ritualised meat feasting, demonstrating the deliberate wasting of food.

One particular attempt to resolve this apparent schism (between the domestic/secular and the ceremonial/religious) has been by reviewing the defensive capabilities of Neolithic enclosure sites. The sites of Offham, Bury Hill, Barkhale and Combe Hill, for example, have all been interpreted by Peter Drewett as ceremonial, partly because all possessed a placement that seemed to indicate that defence was not the main consideration. These sites, however, represent the earliest form of enclosure built within the British Isles and we should not impose our own concept of what is or is not a strategic or defensible location.

Similarly the modern view concerning the nature of war should not necessarily be imposed upon the Neolithic past. Whilst we can assume that disputes between discrete Neolithic human groups may well at times have become violent, as the Stepleton Enclosure skeletons from Hambledon Hill and the mass of arrowheads from Hambledon, Crickley Hill, Billown and Carn Brae suggest, we cannot be sure that any conflict was conducted along the same lines as modern warfare. Intertribal disputes may have been resolved by small-scale or highly ritualised conflict with specific rules of engagement. Under such circumstances a psychological or social barrier could be as effective as a physical one.

In other words, we cannot determine the defensive capability of Neolithic enclosures without being able to reconstruct fully the outlook, ideology and belief systems of the societies that constructed them. The main issue here must be that, irrespective of current views on the importance of strategic defence, the circuits of bank and ditch at enclosures such as Barkhale, Offham, Windmill Hill and Hambledon Hill represent the first significant acts of enclosure in Britain. As such, these sites must have presented a very formidable barrier, even without 360 degree visibility, strong gates, high ramparts and towers.

It is the contention here that Neolithic enclosures were designed as areas of clearly demarcated settlement, but settlement only in the context of what was happening in Early Neolithic Britain relative to the rest of Europe. Alasdair Whittle has argued persuasively against the assumption that the arrival of the Neolithic should be equated with sedentary agriculture. The spectrum of Neolithic settlement mobility proposed by Whittle contains an aspect of attachment or 'anchoring to place' through the use of specific places and monumental architecture. Enclosures fit into this structured framework as they represent bounded or inscribed places where people could return at semi-regular intervals in order to interact with others, engage in trade, corral livestock, reaffirm allegiances, and, perhaps more importantly, re-establish patterns of temporary, seasonal settlement. All this could occur within the confines of the enclosure, which would therefore act as a theoretically safe haven. At such times, distinct social groups may have reaffirmed or imprinted their own cultural identity through the cleaning out and remodelling of rampart circuits, or the deposition of discrete community markers within pits, slumped ramparts or rapidly backfilling segments of ditch.

Many people have drawn attention to the concept of ancestral veneration that may be reflected in the density of human body parts within enclosure ditch fill and all other forms of Neolithic monumental architecture. Whilst agreeing that the presence of human remains within the makeup of Neolithic mounds, enclosure banks, ditches, pits and shafts implies some form of desire to incorporate elements of 'the dead' into the monumental architecture of 'the living', I would argue that the human remains them-selves did not originally imply a wish to affirm an ancestral presence over a section of the land. Instead it was part of a process designed to imprint a particular place with the identity of a particular social group. Such an imprint would probably have taken the form of the deliberate incorporation of deposits that best identified or defined the social group in question. In such instances the 'the typical' or social norm was likely to have been the pottery, flintwork and other artefacts made by the group, examples of the geology that defined their area, the animals that they reared or hunted, food that they grew and sometimes even the body parts of deceased members of the community itself, all in varying degrees of quality and quantity.

Whether this material should be considered as refuse or midden material generated by the social group (and left lying around), or as artefacts that were specially separated from the discard process and selected for deliberate deposition, unfortunately cannot be determined with any certainty. The issue may however be largely irrelevant, for the fact remains that the material under consideration was incorporated, sometimes in great numbers, into the backfill of ditches and pits with no apparent concern that it was in any sense contributing to the decay or social pollution of the structure in question. Unlike today, there was perhaps no concern that relinquished materials eroded or detracted from a sense of place. In fact it might be that discarded material was deliberately allowed, or positively encouraged, to accumulate as it was considered to represent a vital component in the reaffirmation of land claim by specific human groups and the subsequent taming of wild, strange or alien places. The significance of the deposits is therefore not diminished by the different hypotheses concerning their ultimate origin.

The main assertion here is that the material assemblage recovered from the ditches of Neolithic enclosure circuits does not necessarily represent evidence of ceremonial activity such as feasting, exposure burial or some form of 'ritualistic flint knapping' (and I defy anyone to explain what this is supposed to mean). The artefacts recovered, which include varying degrees of charcoal, quern stones, animal bone, human bone, flint waste, marine shell, and pottery, could alternatively be viewed as representing evidence of hunting, butchery, eating and the selected discard of domestic waste. Given the paucity of similar material from elsewhere, and the absence of any substantial body of data relating to 'normal settlements' of the period, it would perhaps be obtuse to argue for the exclusion of enclosures from models of Neolithic settlement activity.

Yes, there is clear evidence for the deposition of the special or unusual in Neolithic enclosure ditches, but this should not detract from the observation that the main component of the ditch-fill assemblage was primarily derived from settlement debris, however selective or structured these deposits were subsequently made. The argument that such material cannot represent occupation debris because no trace of any type of house or permanent structure has been recorded from within the enclosures is, given the relative absence of such structures from anywhere else in Britain, somewhat of a self-fulfilling, and wholly damning, prophesy.

Interrogation of the artefactual and ecofactual data has implied that the majority of Early Neolithic enclosures, in southern England at least, were constructed away from agricultural land, at the periphery of the major concentrations of worked flint. Thus the argument has developed that such sites are not central to territories, but placed at the edges of settlement, possibly within the marginal landscapes of the dead. This may be true, though it is equally plausible, assuming the enclosures performed as some sort of gathering-site for settlement (however temporary) and other communal activities, that the sites themselves were placed not within the centre of any one particular social group, but where a number of conjoining territories met.

It has already been suggested that enclosures with multiple circuits of bank and ditch represent the product of lengthy periods of exploitation within which they were likely to have performed a variety of functions and possessed a wealth of changing meanings and associations to different human groups. Some of the enclosures recorded from Britain appear to have been built, used, and allowed to decay without any apparently significant modification to the original design. Nevertheless the sites themselves remained as prominent earthwork features and would presumably have retained influence in the way the immediate landscape was conceptualised and structured. At sites like Windmill Hill, Briar Hill, Whitehawk, and the Trundle, however, we see evidence of substantial remodelling over a considerable period of time. The phases of reordering and restructuring at these sites may have been such that, as Richard Bradley observed in 1998 'the idea of 'completion' may be inappropriate'. These sites were 'projects', rather than defined monuments with a set design, sequence and plan.

As certain enclosures evolved, with the subsequent elaboration of entrances, there was intensification of earthwork circuits, the filling-in or recutting of earlier ditches, so the next stage of human social development may be reflected in the density, range and distribution of artefacts within ditch fill. The progressive expansion of enclosed space may have been conducted to increase the social standing of particular sites as they began to dominate the land with ever more daring circuits of bank and ditch, or through the provision of timber posts in the form of ramparts or monumental gateways. Some enclosures, such as Whitehawk, Hambledon Hill and Orsett, may have evolved into more substantial and permanent forms of settlement with heavily structured ramparts and entrances. Some, such as Carn Brae, Billown and Crickley Hill may even have been attacked and partially destroyed, possibly by those who did not feel part of the new social structure or settlement system, or who felt in some way threatened by it.

1 *The sculpture 'Worker and Woman Collective Farmer' at VDNKh, Moscow, originally constructed as a monument to the Soviet state, in reality commemorates a much earlier revolution than that of 1917; intensive farming, industrial production and the building of monuments were all fundamental aspects of the Neolithic.* Miles Russell

2 *A prehistoric round house at Michelham Priory. The form of the 'house' is crucial to the design of certain Neolithic and Bronze Age*

3 Trethvery Quoit: a 'portal dolmen' with a sloping capstone from the side. Miles Russell

4 Trethvery Quoit: a 'portal dolmen' with a sloping capstone from the front. Miles Russell

5 *Adam's Grave: a linear structured mound dominating the landscape around Walker's Hill in Wiltshire.* Miles Russell

6 *Bevis' Thumb: a linear, earthen structured mound, the flanking ditches of which have been badly disturbed by ploughing.* Miles Russell

7   *Wayland's Smithy: a linear stone-structured mound with a more than partially restored stone façade.* Jane Russell

8   *Wideford: the outer face and inner revetment walls to a stone-structured mound.* Jane Russell

9 *Wayland's Smithy: the restored stone façade and point of entrance to the inner chamber.*
Jane Russell

10 *King Orry's Grave 1: the stone façade and restricting stones, complete with immature.*
Miles Russell

11 West Kennet: looking in to the chambers of the stone-structured mound. Miles Russell

12 West Kennet: looking out from the chambers of the stone-structured mound. Miles Russell

13 West Kennet: looking in to north-east chamber of the stone-structured mound. Miles
Russell

*14 Hetty Pegler's Tump: accessing what is left of the communal archive within the stone-
structured mound.* Miles Russell

15 Blackhammer: the interior of a (newly re-covered) stall-chambered linear mound. Jane Russell

*16 Maes Howe: looking out from the chamber along the main passage of the circular struc-
tured mound. Jane Russell*

17 Nether Largie: looking in to the main chamber of the stone-structured mound. Gareth Talbot

18 Skara Brae: the interior and side cells of 'hut' 8. Gareth Talbot

19 Knap Hill: the primary phase Neolithic enclosure crowning the upper slopes of the hill.
Miles Russell

20 Whitehawk: the outer ditch of the Neolithic enclosure being hastily examined in 1991 prior to its destruction. Miles Russell

21 Maumbury Rings: looking through the (now heavily modified) northern entrance of the 'henge' to the interior. Miles Russell

22 Avebury: the internal ditch/external bank comprising the 'henge' and the restored stone uprights. Miles Russell

23 King Stone: a stone upright imprisoned behind an iron fence so that its original context is now almost impossible to gauge. Miles Russell

24 Billown: an earth-fast jar, possibly the main way of imprinting the ground with a specific social identity, under excavation in 1996. Miles Russell

25 Stonehenge: an impressive series of stone uprights joined with lintels. Phil Rowley

26 Stonehenge: the final word in the brutal domestication of nature during the Neolithic?
Phil Rowley

5 Shafts

Throughout the eighteenth and nineteenth centuries, the distinctive, crater-like hollows of Neolithic shafts at Cissbury and Harrow Hill (**55**) in West Sussex, and Grimes Graves in Norfolk, were interpreted as primitive huts or a form of pond or crude reservoir. In 1739, the Rev. Francis Blomefield suggested that the dished hollows at Grimes Graves represented part of a curious Danish encampment; a sort of sunken Viking holiday camp. In 1849, the Rev. Edward Turner interpreted a similar range of features at Cissbury as a place where the druids of ancient Britain had undertaken some of their more unspeakable rites (what they were, he unfortunately did not elaborate). George Irving, following excavations conducted in 1857, preferred to see the hollows as types of animal pen. In 1852, the Rev. C.R. Maning interpreted Grimes Graves as a fortified settlement belonging to the Iron Age Iceni tribe, whilst in 1866, the Rev. S.T. Pettigrew suggested that the craters had been formed in the course of a war between Saxons and Vikings (presumably with the Dark Age equivalent of hand grenades).

To be fair, most of these interpretations appeared eminently plausible at the time they were first suggested. Few of the hollows had been archaeologically investigated, and none had been comprehensively emptied of fill. Attempting to fit these bizarre features into the established historical framework of Britain was difficult, and few people possessed any real idea as to the full age and antiquity of human endeavour.

Colonel Augustus Lane Fox was the first to surmise correctly the purpose of the Cissbury shafts, noting in 1868 that they had been cut for the purpose of extracting good quality flint. The full extent of the Grimes Graves shafts was revealed between 1868-70 by Canon Greenwell, who cleared a shaft to its full depth of over 12m. Three horizontal seams of flint, termed by Greenwell as 'topstone', 'wallstone' and 'floorstone', had been cut by this shaft, clearly demonstrating the Neolithic extraction procedure.

Since Greenwell, there have been numerous investigations of Neolithic shafts, including those at Blackpatch, Church Hill, Cissbury, Durrington, Easton Down, Grimes Graves, Harrow Hill, Long Down and Martin's Clump. Single shafts have also been noted at Cranborne Chase in Dorset, Salisbury Plain in Wiltshire and Beachy Head in Sussex. Up until the 1990s, the vast majority of archaeological investigation had been undertaken upon shafts recorded in the chalkland of southern England. Since then, however, evidence for Neolithic pits and shafts has been found further afield, such as at the Den of Boddam and Skelmuir Hill in Grampian and Billown on the Isle of Man.

The current radiocarbon chronology for the Early Neolithic shafts of Britain suggests that the initial phases of excavation began on the southern chalk, at sites such

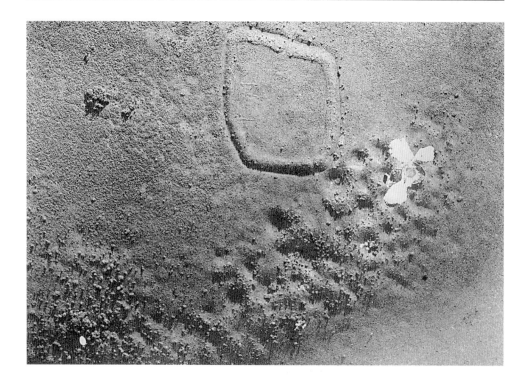

55 Harrow Hill: The distinctive impression of Neolithic shafts, appearing as surface hollows or pock-marks, are visible running diagonally across this 1925 aerial photograph, to the north-east (bottom right) of a Later Bronze Age enclosure. The three areas of 'whiteout' in the middle right represent areas of chalk rubble spoil, generated during the excavation of Shaft 21. Sussex Archaeological Society: Curwen Collection

as Blackpatch, Church Hill, Harrow Hill and Martin's Clump, at some stage between 4350-3500 BC, 4500-3750 BC, 4250-3500 BC, and 4230-3780 BC respectively. Shafts appear at Billown by 4900-4500 BC, whilst the spectacular shaft at Fir Tree Field has produced dates of 4340-3990 BC, though the exact nature of this particular feature is in debate and it may represent a natural solution hollow. The cutting of shafts at Grimes Graves appears to have commenced before 3000 BC, ending at some stage after 2200 BC. Shaft cutting along the southern chalk may well have continued to a similar date.

Internal structure and composition

Flint mine sites often cover large tracts of land, though comparatively few sites have been excavated or recorded in any significant detail. One of the largest areas of shaft cutting would appear to be that recorded at the Den of Boddam, a recent survey indicating that the original area of activity extended over 12 hectares, comprising at least

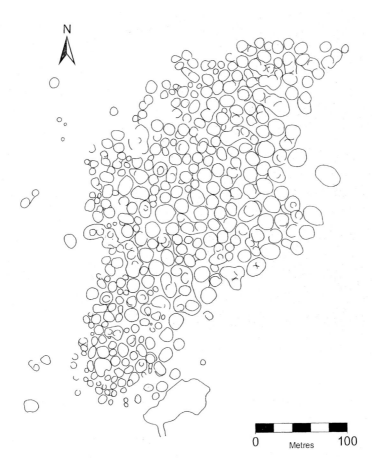

N

0   Metres   100

56 Grimes Graves: plan of surface features constituting the main area of shafts. Redrawn
   from Barber, Field and Topping 1999

1000 separate cuts. The nearby site of Skelmuir Hill may originally have been
comparable in scale, though only 25 separate shafts appear to have escaped the effects
of ploughing. At Martin's Clump, the cutting of shafts originally covered an area of
at least eight hectares, possibly with as many as 1000 separate shafts.

Grimes Graves represents the single largest concentration of deep shafts so far
recorded in Britain, with at least 433 covering an area of around 7.6 hectares (**56**).
Cissbury possesses at least 270 shafts, though a significant number probably await
discovery beneath the ramparts of an Iron Age hillfort which partially obscures the
site. Around 160 shafts have been recorded from Harrow Hill, whilst at Blackpatch
something like 100 shafts are known to have existed over an area of 1.5 hectares. At
Easton Down, 90 shafts are known from a 16 hectare block of land, although more
shafts almost certainly existed here. The remaining areas of Neolithic shafts which
survive to a reasonable degree comprise Stoke Down with at least 70 shafts, Long

57 Harrow Hill: looking down from ground level into Shaft I during the course of excavation in 1936. Note the main basal gallery has here been exposed and cleared. Sussex Archaeological Society: Holleyman Collection

Down with around 50, Church Hill with 26, and Nore Down with 9. Single shafts, possible representing only part of a larger complex, have also been observed, most notably from Slonk Hill and Monkton Up Wimborne.

As one would perhaps expect, the nature and form of Neolithic shafts varies significantly from site to site. Much of this variation relates to geology and topography, especially as the majority of shafts appear to have been cut to extract subterranean flint. The smallest recorded shafts, or pit-shafts, are the two cuts examined at Durrington, which bottomed at depths of just over two metres. Other vertical cuts have been recorded from Durrington, but few of these descend below half a metre and are really little more than shallow surface workings. The pit-shafts recorded from Tolmere are broadly similar in scale, descending to depths of no more than two metres. The shafts at the Den of Boddam and Skelmuir Hill are only slightly deeper, descending to depths of between 2 and 4m. Most appear to have been roughly bell-shaped, in that they were wider at the base than at the surface, and seem to have been cut in order to extract rounded flint cobbles from the local gravels.

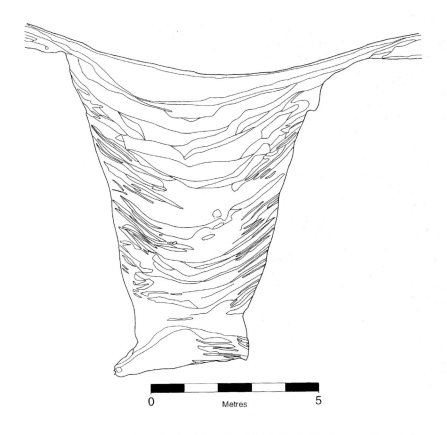

58 Grimes Graves: section through the fill of the 1971 Shaft. Redrawn from Mercer 1981

Deeper shafts are known from the more extensive flint extraction sites of Grimes Graves, Cissbury, Harrow Hill (**57**), Easton Down, Church Hill and Blackpatch. At Grimes Graves, arguably the most famous flint mine site in Britain, the scale, form and general dimensions of shafts varied considerably. 108 years of excavation at the site (1868–1976) have cleared at least 35 shafts to basal levels, revealing a diverse range of digging techniques. Roger Mercer's shaft, excavated in 1971, descended to just over 12m (**58**), like Greenwell's before him, whilst other shafts examined at the site bottom at depths between 3 and 9m. The 20 or so shafts archaeologically examined at Cissbury between 1873 and 1956 demonstrate an equal amount of variation, ending at depths of between 2 and at least 13m, whilst those at Blackpatch and Church Hill average between 1 and 6m.

The single shaft examined by Martin Green and Mike Allen at Fir Tree Field is spectacularly deep by any standards, excavation to date suggesting an overall depth in excess of 25m. Bone from the upper fill has produced a date of between 4340 and 3990 BC, though, as the excavators have noted, cultural debris is largely restricted to the upper three metres of weathering cone. Below this, the nature of fill and its apparently rapid accumulation may indicate that the feature is of natural origin,

59 Harrow Hill: looking into the entrance of a subterranean gallery excavated at the base of Shaft II in 1936. Sussex Archaeological Society: Holleyman Collection

perhaps created from water dissolving through the chalk bedrock, such features being relatively common in some areas of Dorset and Wiltshire. Whatever the origin of this 'shaft', it was a feature that was clearly visible in the Later Mesolithic, and its presence may have prompted the deposition of pottery, bone and flintwork within.

Extensive tunnels or galleries extended from the base of most Neolithic shafts (**59**). At Cissbury, for example, the number of recorded galleries varied from two to eight. Many were further accompanied by additional workings and areas of limited undercutting of the shaft wall. Certain galleries, such as those in No.1 Escarp Shaft, widened at the work face, whilst others, most notably in the Cave Pit, terminated in a more domed chamber. A number of galleries, especially those examined within Shaft 27, were linked to other tunnels by small windows, perhaps to aid in the circulation of air. A similar picture is in evidence at Grimes Graves, for example at the base of Shaft 15 where nine galleries radiate out connecting the shaft to a further six shafts in the immediate vicinity. A few shafts, most notably Harrow Hill 13, were surrounded by smaller satellites, whilst others, for example Harrow Hill 4 and 5, were originally paired.

Many of the shaft gallery systems connect, sometimes producing a complicated plan of interlinked tunnels (**60**). Joining may have been accidental, or it could represent a deliberate and highly organised technique whereby desired seams of flint were systematically removed through the cutting of interconnected galleries.

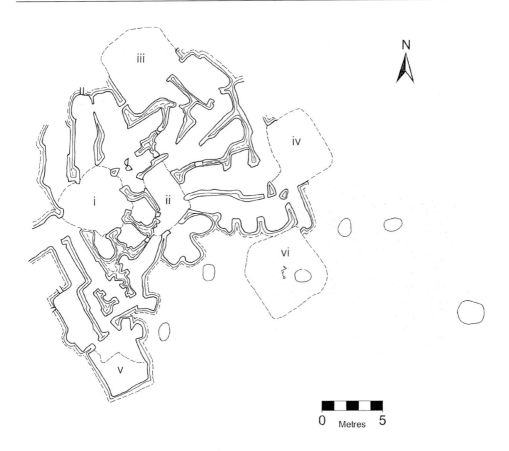

60 Cissbury: basal plan of Shafts iii, iv, v and vi showing the nature of inter-linking galleries and passages. The approximate location of the articulated body of a human male is shown within the fill of Shaft vi. Redrawn from Harrison 1878

Conjoined shafts could therefore have provided multiple points of entrance and exit. Loose rubble generated from gallery cutting appears to have been cleared from the work face and dumped elsewhere in the shaft. No firm evidence to suggest the use of pit props has yet been located within gallery systems, though voids recorded in the fill at Grimes Graves may suggest the former presence of roof supports. Props may well have been unnecessary, workers in the shafts throughout the 1970s commenting favourably on the structural integrity of all gallery systems.

Whether those originally working within subterranean gallery systems would have required a source of artificial light is debatable. Areas of smoke discoloration have been noted from the roof of gallery systems at Blackpatch 2 and Harrow Hill 21, but these could relate more to the nocturnal activities of illicit visitors during the 1920s' and '30s' excavations. Certainly no new areas of soot have been revealed in the later flint mine excavations and it would appear that the majority of subterranean working areas possessed an ample supply of natural light if worked during daylight hours.

Not all shafts possessed complicated subterranean networks of tunnels. The shaft cleared at Cissbury by Plumpton Tindall in 1874, for example, did not possess any form of gallery system. Neither did a similar shaft opened at Long Down possess galleries or any evidence of the undercutting of the shaft wall. The Billown shafts and four of the five shafts cleared at Easton Down (B1a, B19, B45 and B67) do not appear to have been dug explicitly for the extraction of flint. Flint seams were encountered within the Monkton Up Wimborne shaft, and, though removed, there did not appear to have been any attempt to exploit the material systematically.

The main forms of internal structure recorded from Neolithic shafts would seem to relate more to entrance and exit and the removal of excavated chalk and flint rubble. Cut footholds do not seem to have been prominent, though examples may have been recorded at Grimes Graves in Shafts III, IV, V, VI and 13. The apparent steps cut into the edge of Grimes Graves V and the Cissbury Cave Pit may originally have descended to a short ledge left in the shaft wall. The Monkton Up Wimborne shaft appears to have been from the south-eastern margin of a ten metre wide circular cut. This may possibly have acted as a form of platform, designed to aid access to and from the shaft, although there is no certainty of this. Whatever the explanation, the Monkton shaft is somewhat unusual, having been surrounded in its final phases by a ring of oval pits.

Rubble derived from the lower levels of shafts could originally have been removed using baskets or bags hauled to the surface with rope. The walls of Cissbury 27 and Blackpatch 5, for example, had been rubbed smooth by such haulage activity. More drastic wear patterns, in the form of wide rope-gauged grooves, have also been seen above the entrance to galleries in Grimes Graves 1, 2 and D, perhaps indicating the removal of material from these horizontal workplaces. Two slanting holes found at the base of Church Hill 7 may represent the base of a ladder or slide along which bags of rubble could originally have been pulled. A vertical break detected within the central fill of Cissbury 27 may be all that is left of a small tree trunk or ladder used as the main way of entrance and exit by workers in the shaft.

Slightly more convincing internal structural evidence from a Neolithic shaft came from a series of small circular holes found in the walls of the 1971 shaft at Grimes Graves. These may represent a form of internal timber structure, such as a platform or secure landing for a ladder, to aid in the extraction process. Alternatively the holes may have been formed by a type of timber screen designed to protect workers in the bottom of the shaft from the ever present danger of falling rubble. Assuming that ladders or climbing poles were used by the original excavation team, then we may suppose that the rubble was carried in containers lashed to a form of back or head frame; ascending a ladder with only one hand, the other grasping a basket of mining debris, would be tantamount to suicide.

Incisions, apparently unrelated to the integrity of shafts, have been noted from the walls of a number of Neolithic cuts, most notably in Norfolk and Sussex. The first to be identified were a series of vertical and horizontal lines cut opposite a gallery entrance in Willett's Shaft 2. A second engraving, which had the appearance of the number '16', was later noted above the entrance to a second gallery in the shaft.

*61 Harrow Hill: a series of linear incisions 'forming an irregular chess-board design',
recovered from the 'west jamb' of gallery vi in Shaft 21.* The Sussex Archaeological
Society: Curwen Collection

Additional linear incisions were later observed at Cissbury in No. 2 Escarp Shaft, Shaft
VI and the Cave Pit, whilst a series of dots, lines and cup-shaped marks were noticed
in Shaft III. A group of linear vertical and diagonal marks were also noted from
Grimes Graves 2 and from the entrance to galleries in Harrow Hill 21 (**61**). In Church
Hill 4, a series of circular cuts was recorded above three of the five gallery entrances,
whilst more realistic depictions of a short-horned bull, two red deer, and a possible
fish head were discovered within galleries explored at the base of Cissbury 27.

Harrison originally suggested that the linear incisions were a form of writing, a
sign of ownership or a tally mark. At Grimes Graves, Clarke suggested that the cuts
may have served as a primitive form of sundial. At Harrow Hill, the excavators
wondered whether the irregular chessboard design from Shaft 21 was a simple form
of doodle such as 'a schoolboy would draw on his blotting paper'. It may, in fact, be
tempting to view all these pieces as a tool intended to aid the extraction process: a
map or mark made to indicate the quantity of flint removed. The discovery of similar
pieces of engraved stone from the ditches of certain enclosure sites, such as
Whitehawk and the Trundle, or from the entrances to passageways at Skara Brae, may

however contradict such a theory, for none of these are extraction sites. The carvings may perhaps indicate a form of social, tribal or community identifier.

Just how many people were originally engaged in the digging of shafts is unknown, a problem compounded by the fact that we have no idea just how long each shaft was originally worked. Gale Sieveking and P.J. Felder have calculated that, for the Grimes Graves mines, assuming that an individual required a minimum of one square metre of working space, the initial phases of shaft cutting could have been conducted by at least 20 people. As the shaft descended, more people would have been required to remove rubble to the surface. With regard to the cutting of galleries, given their dimensions and way in which each had been cut it was unlikely that more than one person was ever active at the workface. If each person had at least one assistant removing spoil (or alternating digging duties), and if the average number of galleries per shaft was four, then the maximum number of people working in the shaft at any one time was unlikely to exceed eight.

As galleries extended away from the shaft, the number of individuals helping to remove rubble would of course have increased. To extend this argument of 'ifs' and 'buts' further, if a single miner could, with backup, extract flint from a one metre area of gallery in a single day, then the time taken to exploit all the flint from the base of an average shaft would have been around 15 days. If correct (and of course there is no guarantee of this), the calculation would imply that a vertical shaft could orig-inally have been completed within a minimum of 93 days.

During the examination of Greenwell's shaft at Grimes Graves, Felder calculated that, of the 75,735kg of flint potentially available within the shaft and its attendant galleries, at least 63,639kg (or 84 per cent of the total), was exploited. This would suggest that for every square metre worked, around 330kg of flint could have been successfully won. A similar calculation conducted for Shaft 15D at Grimes Graves suggested that the figure here was closer to 312.69kg per square metre. Using Felder's observations, Ian Longworth and Gillian Varndell have attempted to calculate the total quantity of flint extracted from the Grimes Graves site. Given a potentially considerable margin of error, it may be further possible to suggest the possible removal of 17,955.63 metric tonnes of flint. It is worth noting, however, that not all flint taken from the shafts was used in the manufacture of tools. Considerable amounts of the stone remain at the site, either in the form of knapping waste, or as untouched nodules piled back into abandoned shafts, or left on the surface.

Artefact assemblages

Evidence for the range of tools originally used in the shafts, which can include picks, rakes, punches and mallets made from deer antler, bone shovels and stone axes, has been recorded from within a number of sites. Such finds are often found in signifi-cant quantities and usually appear as if freshly discarded. The abandonment of perfectly useable digging equipment may seem curious from a modern perspective, though it could of course relate to the sudden abandonment of the workface due to rock instability. Alternatively, it may relate to the deliberate placing of objects as an offering to a specific deity or spirit residing within a particular area of ground. Or, as has been suggested for the material recovered from the structured mounds, it could have been a way of imprinting the ground with the identity of a specific social group.

Red deer antler appears to have been the main resource for tools used during the cutting of shafts and the subsequent extraction of flint. Antler, with its sharply pointed brow tine, represented an ideal digging tool used to pick away at the natural fissures in the bedrock. As well as picks, a variety of other tools was used by those cutting into the natural rock. Antler punches were used with some success within Blackpatch 1 and 7 and Harrow Hill 21, as can be seen by the impression left in gallery walls. Some form of wooden bar or lever seems to have been used to break up the rock face in Church Hill 4 and 7. Stone axes were also, on occasion, used by the original excavators, as can be seen from the walls of Greenwell's Pit and Shafts 1 and 2 at Grimes Graves. The ox shoulder blade or scapula is a fairly common find from the Sussex mines, though it is found less frequently in Norfolk. It does not appear to have been used in the same way as a modern shovel would, but rather to have been employed as a scrape or paddle to clear difficult material from the path of those moving through the cramped galleries.

A significant number of Neolithic shafts appear, on completion, to have been backfilled with rubble. This may have been a necessity, as empty shafts pose a potential hazard, or it may have been to clear the surface of unwanted mining debris. It may of course have been an activity of more special significance, perhaps intended to heal partially the wound caused by the sinking of the shaft in the first place. The large heaps of mining debris still evident at mining sites would, however, suggest that total backfilling was never a reality for the majority of vertical cuts. Whether complete or only partial, one thing about the backfilling of shafts is clear: the soil used often contained a significant quantity of cultural material.

At Cissbury, in Tindall's shaft, two ox skulls, a human skull, the skull of a wild boar and a quantity of bones, included including otter and roe deer and possibly badger, goat and dog, were found in the fill at a depth of below eight metres. Animal bone, including goat, pig, roe deer, red deer, horse and ox, was found in the Large Pit at Cissbury from a depth of two metres. In the Skeleton Shaft at Cissbury, Lane Fox found the remains of an adult human female lying upside down within the fill with the bones of pig, ox, goat, roe deer and fox. In Cissbury VI, Harrison recovered scorched antler picks, large numbers of flints, an ox bone and a human skeleton, this time male, buried in a contracted position, at a depth of around six metres. Cissbury 24 produced a large quantity of pig bones at a depth of two metres, whilst the fill of Cissbury 27 produced tabular flint, the scorched and partially butchered skeleton of an ox and the articulated skeleton of an adult human female (**62**).

Mixed in with flint knapping debris in the upper fill of Blackpatch 1 was a set of sheep mandibles, whilst two thirds of the way down the fill of Blackpatch 7, a large quantity of animal bones, mostly ox, was observed. In Grimes Graves 2, a set of disarticulated human bone, comprising lower limbs and parts of the lower jaw, vertebrae and ribs, was recovered with flint knapping debris and the bones of ox, sheep, red

62 Cissbury: John Pull (with pipe) standing at the entrance to gallery 1 in 1953. The pelvis and slightly flexed right leg of the female skeleton may be seen to the left of the shot. The body appears to have lain directly across the gallery entrance, the skull facing inwards towards the main area of extraction. © Worthing Museum and Art Gallery

deer, roe deer, fox, dog and vole. Some of the ox bone appeared blackened by fire. A piece of human skull was recovered from Grimes Graves 1, together with flint implements, knapping debris and the bones of roe deer, red deer, pig and ox. A single human fibula came from the fill of Church Hill 6.

One of the more spectacular deposits associated with a Neolithic shaft has recently been examined by Martin Green at Monkton Up Wimborne. Here, at the northern edge of a roughly circular cut containing, at its south-eastern edge, a seven metres deep shaft, a separate pit was found to contain the crouched remains of four humans: one adult female and three immatures. DNA analysis suggests that the adult female was the biological mother of at least one of the immatures, a female aged around five years. The others comprised a girl of around ten and a boy aged nine. The shaft fill contained, amongst other things, a cattle skull and a pick of deer antler.

As faunal remains appear to occur in significant numbers in shaft fill when human remains are present, it is possible that there was originally a link between the two types of deposit. Similar associations have also been made concerning the fill of Neolithic enclosure ditches. Enclosures, however, are often viewed as places where human bodies were deliberately disassembled. The discovery of a similar range of material from Neolithic shafts may of course suggest that this interpretation is invalid. Human and animal remains, especially upper body parts like the skull, occur in ditch and mine shaft fill with significant quantities of Neolithic cultural debris, such as pottery, flintwork and other refuse. This could indicate cannibalism, with human body parts being discarded with elements of more general food residue. Alternatively the combination of human and animal bone with pottery and flint waste could reflect an urge to gather a representative sample of social markers, which could then be placed into redundant features in order to stamp the land with an indelible, distinctive form of cultural identity.

If human bone had originally been incorporated within shafts in an attempt to imprint the monument with a specific social label, then discussion concerning human burial, as noted for the enclosures and mounds, becomes defunct. The accumulation of human body parts within shafts could instead be seen as part of a more general process of structured deposition and not the final, defining element of that process.

The meaning of shafts

Neolithic shafts are generally classified as forms of economic or industrial monument: the earliest pieces of evidence relating to 'heavy industry' within the British Isles. Recent analysis and examination of both stone tools and the places from which the stone was originally extracted suggests, however, that such a categorisation may be too simplistic. Richard Bradley and Mark Edmonds, in their study of stone production sites in northern England, Martyn Barber, Dave Field and Peter Topping in their analysis of English flint mines and the present author in his study of Neolithic shafts in Britain, have all come to fairly similar conclusions: that though the desire to generate good quality stone certainly provided one of reasons for cutting shafts, the range of non-functional finds and features suggests that ceremonial activity was just as important.

As previously noted, we cannot judge Neolithic people and the monuments they created by the standards or mind set of today's highly urbanised society. Vertical shafts cannot be treated as simple industrial features in the same way that one may today view a modern coal, tin or gold mine. Neolithic shafts were planned, excavated and operated within a landscape dominated by the non-functional and, to our minds at least, non-rational. A careful consideration of the less obvious elements of Neolithic shafts, such as their siting, the experience of mining, the symbolic nature of extraction, the significance of carvings, the density of placed objects (including human remains), points towards an alternative way of visualising, conceptualising and understanding these prehistoric land cuts. In other words, to comprehend Neolithic shafts, we need to distance ourselves from the modern world view and cut our way free of present considerations.

The siting of shafts was not based solely upon economic principles. Specific places were chosen for a specific variety of reasons. Such areas may have been important in spiritual, tribal or 'ancestral' ways, for the extraction of flint was certainly not conducted on a systematic basis (even though good sources of flint may be found across much of southern England). The southern English shafts appear to have been placed in particular places in order to dominate a number of key, if restricted, views.

63 Blackpatch: the galleries extending out from the base of Shaft 1 can be dark and cramped, emphasising isolation and separation from the real and familiar world above. The Sussex Archaeological Society: Curwen Collection

The Sussex shafts, for example, are usually sited to face a significant portion of the coastal plain where the main areas of Neolithic settlement may have concentrated, whilst at the same time remaining invisible to other major monument types. Obscuring or partially concealing sites from other monuments, such as the enclosure or structured mound, may have enhanced the mystery or special significance of the shaft. Tools made from the stone derived from deep within such hills could also have possessed significant or magical properties. Similar observations have been made by Mark Edmonds and Richard Bradley for the Neolithic upland stone quarries, perched high in the rugged landscapes of Cumbria.

The majority of Neolithic shafts seem to have been set some way from contemporary enclosures, and were perhaps peripheral to the main focus of settlement. If so, then the process of digging shafts would, for those involved in their working, perhaps have meant a significant dislocation from their respective communities. Such dislocation would have been increased for those actually entering into the shafts and working within deep, subterranean galleries. Even today, once in the deep galleries of Neolithic shafts, the sense of isolation and separation from the 'real world' is immense (**63**). Galleries are dark, damp and cold. Anyone today who manages to crawl to the end of a gallery at Grimes Graves will appreciate just how alien their environment suddenly becomes. It is the Neolithic equivalent of a sensory deprivation tank (a similar sense having already been noted for the stone chambers of structured mounds). There are no familiar noises, what sounds there are being muffled

64 Harrow Hill: the restricted nature of space available for most of the subterranean galleries is demonstrated in this photo taken at the base of Shaft II in 1936. Sussex Archaeological Society: Holleyman Collection

and distorted. One cannot feel the sun, wind or rain on one's face. There are no bright colours. There is often no real sense of day or night.

Galleries are difficult to negotiate, working areas are often cramped. Points of entrance and exit, like the passageways to chambers within structured mounds, are often restricted (**64**), making access to the workface difficult to all but the slight of build. Given these considerations, it is possible that the act of descending into shafts and the extraction of flint in the Neolithic formed a rite of passage. Constrictions controlled who could and who could not access the riches of the earth: who could gain entrance to the community archive and add elements of their own identity to the database. It could be that the rites of passage related specifically to the immature within Neolithic society; those about to enter into adulthood.

Working within shafts could further have been part of a wider social event with people from disparate groups coming together to co-operate in the excavation and extraction and thus affirm their individual community identities and interclan loyalty. Such inter communal activity could explain the absence of large enclosures and structured mounds within the central block of the South Downs, for here shafts themselves acted as centres of social activity. This could in turn explain the nature of artefacts recovered from backfilled mine shafts and why such assemblages appear to mirror the range, if not the quantity, of material retrieved from the backfill of enclosure circuits and linear mounds. These were all types of community or tribal marker with which individual groups hoped to imprint their identity into the land.

So, were those who dug and worked in the deep shafts specialists? Almost certainly, but only perhaps in the sense that those who farmed the land required specialist knowledge of what crops to grow, where and how to look after them. We should not view shafts in the same sense of a modern mine whereby those who work within them gain their livelihood from doing so. In fact the relatively small number of known shafts, when compared with the extensive range of dates provided for the period of their cutting, would appear to argue that mining was not the sole activity of a specialist group of mining folk. The act of shaft cutting and flint extraction in the Neolithic may even have been undertaken on a seasonal basis, perhaps at a time when the generation of food was not paramount.

Thus far there has been an unconscious tendency for archaeologists to visualise those working within Neolithic shafts as being exclusively adult male. This is perhaps due to the male-orientated interpretation of the past as depicted in reconstruction drawings. In such recreations past activities have been categorized according to sex, so prehistoric males are often shown returning from the hunt, laden down with dead animals, whilst prehistoric females sit at home preparing dinner or weaving. Children are invariably absent. There is, however, no archaeological evidence that can be used to support these hypothetical divisions of labour and there is certainly no evidence to support the predominance of adult males within the mines and shafts.

In fact if we are to examine the, admittedly limited, archaeological evidence from the shafts, it is worth noting a few points. At Cissbury, of the three articulated bodies recovered from shaft fill, only a single adult male appears to have been deposited with any formal solemnity. The Shaft 27 skeleton was, due to its anomalous position, thought to have died accidentally, the victim of an early mining tragedy. This particular interpretation, though popular at the time of discovery, was dropped once the skeleton was found to be female. This is unfortunate for there is no reason to suggest that working in the shafts was exclusive to the adult male.

Indeed, to extend this argument, it is unlikely that many of the muscle-bound males depicted in modern reconstructions of flint mining would ever have been able to fit within the recorded basal galleries and side chambers. It is certainly clear that many of the modern adult excavators of the Worthing mine sites had severe problems negotiating the narrow spaces within cleared galleries and the possibility that individuals of slighter build, perhaps even immatures (of either sex) worked within such areas is one that should not be overlooked. Perhaps the work was originally more evenly balanced between the sexes or perhaps only the female members of the community could enter and work in the shafts. Alternatively, as already noted, it may be that only the infants or immatures of a given community could access the shafts as a rite of passage towards adult life.

6 Secondary developments

From the mid- to late fourth millennium BC, the earliest architectural forms to impact upon the landscapes of Britain were in a state of flux. Certain enclosures were being modified and added to, whilst others were clearly going out of use, some by around 3300 BC. Evidence from Hambledon Hill, Crickley Hill, Billown and Carn Brae suggests that termination of use was not always gradual nor peaceful; dense quantities of flint projectile points and evidence of burning and demolition suggesting a somewhat sudden and violent end. Late Neolithic activity at most enclosure sites comprises of limited artefact deposition, usually of distinctive forms of pottery. There is no evidence, to date, of continued use or significant reoccupation of the first enclosures into the third millennium BC.

What, if anything, replaced this system of enclosure across Britain is not known. There are a small number of circular, Later Neolithic interrupted ditch enclosures known from southern Britain, of which Flagstones and Stonehenge 1 are certainly members, whilst Melbourne and perhaps Briar Hill 1 are possible examples. The Flagstones enclosure, at present dated to around 3370-2190 BC and the enclosure forming the first phase at Stonehenge, dated to between 3340-3220 BC, are certainly striking in layout and apparently similar in chronology, but they do not alone indicate a major shift in patterns of land demarcation into the third millennium BC.

Shaft cutting remained a practice, certainly in Norfolk and possibly also across the chalk of southern and south-western Britain, until the mid-third millennium BC, though, as previously noted, shaft form appears to have changed somewhat from earlier examples. The majority of shafts, especially those from Grimes Graves and Blackpatch, appear to have been cut for the extraction of flint, though other, non-flint related shafts have been recorded from Cranborne Chase, the South Dorset Ridgeway and the South Downs. Linear structured mounds became common across larger swathes of Britain from around 3500 BC, but appear to have reached a climax by at least 2800 BC, being gradually replaced by more circular forms of structure. The third millennium BC, more crucially, was a time when new elements in the architectural repertoire of prehistoric communities began to appear. These secondary monumental components are usually categorised in the archaeological literature as the 'cursus', the 'bank barrow', the 'henge' and the circles of timber and stone.

Before we continue, I must first apologise for the repeated use of apostrophes in the text that follows (particularly as a previous reviewer of my work noted that they look 'as if a drunken, ink-splattered spider has crawled across the printed page'). I do, however, feel that it is necessary to note my severe objection to the terms 'cursus',

65 Dorchester-on-Thames: the mid section of the cursus, looking south-east, is visible as two darker lines running across the approximate centre of the aerial photo, to the immediate right of the main road. To the top right of the cursus are the distinctively curved, darker lines of the double ditches comprising the Big Rings 'Henge'. Sussex Archaeological Society: Holleyman Collection

'bank barrow' and 'henge'. These are antiquarian terms of categorisation, hijacked by modern archaeologists, and successively reinterpreted and reclassified, so that their original meaning has been totally lost.

I do not like these terms: they are too vague, too unfocussed and far too woolly. They are also often used to cover a multitude of archaeological sins. Thus if a site is found not quite to fit within the current definition of, say, a classic 'henge', it may, in the archaeological literature, be legitimately referred to as being 'henge-like', 'henge-esque' or (particularly offensive in my view) 'hengi-form'. Similar written atrocities have occurred for other site types, hence the appearance of 'mini-bank barrow', 'bank barrow-form', 'cursus-like' and 'cursus-esque'. Problems with the term 'cursus' are further acerbated by the fact that there appears to be no consensus of opinion as to what the plural is; 'cursus', 'cursuss', 'cursi', cursuses' and even cursu-podi' all having been used at some stage. Personally, if I am made to use the term at all, I would prefer to avoid the issue entirely and say 'cursus monument'.

Unfortunately, even though 'cursus', 'bank barrow' and 'henge' have become largely meaningless forms of categorisation, they remain in the archaeological literature as a useful (or perhaps lazy) form of shorthand. As no one has yet found a suitable replacement for them, other than perhaps 'elongated secondary enclosure' for 'cursus', 'elongated secondary structured mound' for 'bank barrow' and 'secondary circular enclosure' for 'henge', archaeologists will remain lumbered with the literary baggage of the recent past. 'Cursus', 'bank barrow' and 'henge' will therefore stay for the moment; but so will the apostrophes.

Secondary linear

The first great linear ditched Neolithic enclosure to be archaeologically observed and recorded was at Amesbury. In 1740, William Stukeley published *Stonehenge: A Temple Restor'd to the British Druids*, within which he noted the elongated site, suggesting that it 'resembled a course suitable for the racing of chariots by the ancient Britons'. The Latin term 'cursus' was applied by Stukeley to the distinctive monument, where, unfortunately, it has stuck. Even if modern archaeologists do not see the 'cursus' as the charioteering version of Brands Hatch, the earthwork class as a whole is still affected by Stukeley's perspective; they are viewed as some form of monumental path or 'processional way'. Along such processional ways, it has been argued, a large contingent of the prehistoric population would travel, possibly to ancestral burial grounds, in a highly structured and ordered way.

'Cursus' monuments, though small in number when compared to earlier Neolithic architectural forms such as the structured mound, have been found throughout the British Isles, at least 107 now having been tentatively identified from Wales (8), lowland Scotland (43) and England (56). Most of these have been recognised through aerial photography (**65**). Few 'cursus' sites have been adequately examined, their sheer size and scale often precluding this, though there have recently been gallant attempts to archaeologically sample a number; notable excavations taking place at Dorchester-on-Thames, Cranborne Chase (popularly referred to as 'the Dorset cursus'), Drayton, Sarn-y-bryn-caled, Springfield and Stonehenge (lesser and greater sites).

The form taken by 'cursus' monuments would appear clear enough: two ditches with accompanying banks (generally placed inside the ditches) forming an elongated rectangle, usually closed at both of the smaller ends (**66**). Breaks in ditch circuit are rare, though entrance points, where detected, would seem to be more common set within the longer sides, close to the terminal end. Scale can vary immensely. The Dorset 'cursus', for example, comprises two conjoined structures (sometimes referred to as the Pentridge and Gussage sites), which together covers a distance of 9.8km (**67**). The Springfield 'cursus' is far more modest in scale, measuring only 700m in length.

'Cursus' monuments often cut a swathe across a variety of landscape types, will take in valleys and hill slopes, and will sometimes possess an association with water, either cutting across streams or terminating close to a major river. Construction of

66 Drayton: the southern butt-end of the Drayton South 'Cursus' is visible to the top right of this aerial photograph, together with a number of later circular ditched features. Sussex Archaeological Society: Holleyman Collection

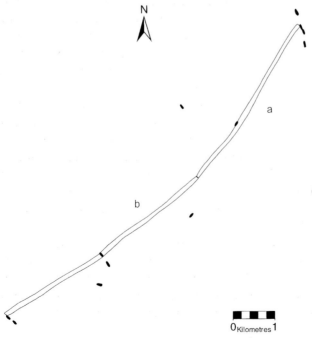

N

67 The Dorset 'cursus': plan of the cursus showing its relationship to linear struc-tured mounds of the earlier Neolithic (solid rectangles): a = Pentridge 'cursus'; b = Gussage 'cursus'. Redrawn from Barclay and Harding 1999

a

b

0 Kilometres 1

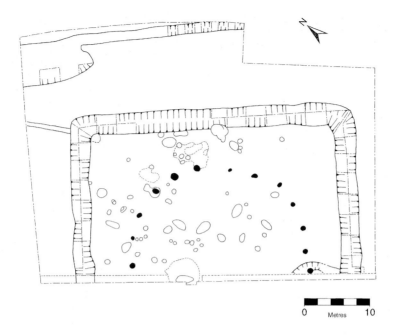

68 Springfield: feature plan as revealed by excavations within the eastern 'cursus' terminal. Line of the post circle shown in solid. Redrawn from Hedges and Buckley 1981

most would appear episodic, with additions, extensions and occasional periods of ditch realignment and recutting. Alignment towards basic astronomical events (solar or lunar) is clear at a number of 'cursus' sites, most notably at the Dorset 'cursus' where the midwinter sun sets behind a linear structured mound enclosed between the two internal banks of the new monument. Other sites may have possessed more specific alignment upon prominent landscape features or towards structures dating from an earlier period of Neolithic building activity.

Unlike the ditches that accompanied structured mounds and enclosures and the backfill of shafts, deposition of cultural material within 'cursus' ditches was negligible. There are no significant assemblages of flint or pottery, no meaningful quantities of faunal remains and no human bone. This may of course reflect the limited percentage of 'cursus' ditches so far investigated, though it must be admitted that activity of any kind from 'cursus' sites is rare. Investigation of monument interiors has also been fairly small scale to date, though structural evidence has been observed from at least three sites; namely Holywood North, Holywood South and Springfield. At Springfield, excavations within the eastern terminal revealed half of what appeared to be a circle of postholes and a small number of pits containing charcoal rich soil and burnt flint (**68**). At Holywood North, postholes lined the inner edge of the northern terminal, whilst a series of postholes, possibly forming part of an independent structure, was revealed during excavations within the northern terminal of Holywood South.

N

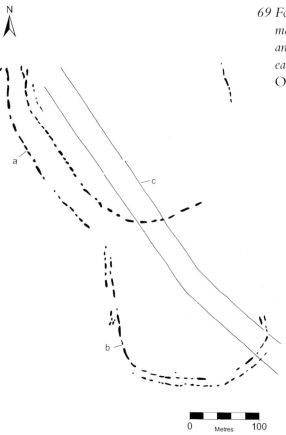

a

c

b

0   Metres   100

'Bank barrows' have received less attention within the archaeological literature than the 'cursus', though it is clear that they represent a similar development of linear monumental form. One of the best known 'bank barrow' structures is the example overlying the Early Neolithic enclosure of Maiden Castle, now fully enveloped by the multiple earthworks of the Late Iron Age hillfort made famous by the excavations of Mortimer Wheeler in the late 1930s. The Maiden Castle structure comprises an earthen mound, measuring over 540m in length, flanked by two roughly parallel ditches set, on average, 20m apart. The monument may have started as a discrete linear mound, positioned just to the west of the Neolithic enclosure, before being extended over the rampart sequence and further to the west, along the ridge of the hill. Excavations by Wheeler, through the ditch and at the eastern end, provided material for radiocarbon dating (see below) but little conclusive evidence for use and function. 'Bank barrows' tend to cluster within southern England, most prominently at Crickley Hill and along the South Dorset Ridgeway, though sites have been recorded from northern England (such as at Scorton) and Scotland (Cleaven Dyke).

The radiocarbon chronology for secondary linears is extremely patchy, with only 22 determinations available for the 'cursus' and 25 available for the 'bank barrow' in the most recent overview of the monument class conducted by Alistair Barclay and

70 Billown: plan derived from geophysical survey, aerial photography and excavation: a = main Neolithic enclosure; b = lesser enclosure; c = line of parallel ditches forming probable bank barrow overlying the main enclosure. Redrawn from Darvill 2000

Jan Harding in 1999. Most dates do not, unfortunately, derive from primary contexts. What dates there are suggest that the linear ditched 'cursus' was being constructed from around the middle of the fourth millennium; single determinations of 3960-3630 BC, 3790-3340 BC, 3650-2900 BC, 3500-2900 BC, 3360-3030 BC and 2900-2470 BC being produced respectively for Sarn-y-bryn-caled, Drayton, Stonehenge lesser, Dorchester-on-Thames, Dorset and Stonehenge greater. The more limited dating conducted upon linear embanked 'barrows' suggests a broadly similar constructional date range; single determinations of 3650-3100 BC, 3620-3570 or 3540-3350 BC and 3350-2920 for Maiden Castle, North Stoke and Fordington respectively.

The limited date ranges suggest a significant overlap between the construction of secondary linear monuments and the later phases of the enclosure and linear structured mound. Stratigraphic relationships, however, seem to indicate that the 'cursus' and the 'bank barrow', where they coincide with the structured mound and enclosure, were always an addition to, or elaboration of, earlier monumental forms. Their relationship to early Neolithic enclosures, for example, appears clear enough. At Fornham All Saints, a 'cursus' ploughed straight through the centre of the main enclosure and secondary elaboration (**69**), effectively ending any usefulness the original site may have served. At Etton, the so-called 'Etton cursus' hacked its way across the south-eastern portion of the enclosure, terminating within the area previously enclosed. At Maiden Castle, Crickley Hill and Billown (**70**), a series of 'bank barrows' cut through and sealed early features and rampart sequences. As well as enclosures, many structured mounds also appear to have been hijacked in the course of building secondary linear monuments; such features being incorporated, for example, within the alignment of the Dorset, Eynesbury and Stonehenge greater 'cursus' sites.

The meaning of secondary linears

Although few archaeologists would seriously argue today that 'cursus' monuments were originally designed to facilitate Neolithic chariot racing, the idea that they formed some type of processional way, perhaps associated with the movement or treatment of the dead, is one that has firmly embedded itself in the archaeological subconscious. Much has been said about the nature, form, survival, associations and geographical extent of 'cursus' sites in Britain within recent years, most notably by Roy Loveday, Alastair Barclay and Jan Harding, but we still appear no closer to discovering what these mysterious, elongated structures were actually designed for and how they were initially used. Secondary linear monuments, especially when they ride over enclosures or incorporate earlier mounds, give the impression that they have been created in order to erase former significance and rewrite the meaning of landscape. Some clearly incorporate astronomical alignments. Others incorporate watercourses.

It is this final aspect, that of tying the placement of monuments with a specific water course, such as a river or stream, that has perhaps most affected the interpretation of sites in recent years. There has even been discussion surrounding a possible 'cult of wet or watery places', perhaps with the flow of water directing the flow of people along the monument itself. This, together with the association of 'cursus' sites with earlier structured mounds, would seem to be missing the point somewhat. 'Cursus' monuments were designed to incorporate wide swathes of land, sometimes to take in as many varied aspects of the topography or local ground conditions as possible. Therefore we see 'cursus' sites that cut across hillslopes, dry valleys, gravel spreads, spring lines and rivers. We see 'cursus' sites riding over enclosures and incorporating linear structured mounds.

'Cursus' sites could be seen as an extension of earlier concepts regarding the claiming, use and control of land. These discrete sites could therefore have been designed to enclose monumentally a representative swathe of land used by, or claimed by, a discrete social group: the hills that they hunted across; the valleys they ploughed; the land they inhabited; the rivers they fished in. The placing of timber structures at the terminal end of some 'cursus' sites could, in this light, be seen as the symbolic representation of the house or human settlement; the centre of community life. There was no longer a need to claim land by seeding freshly cut ditches or pits with distinctive cultural material (such as human or animal bone, pottery, flint, or organics). The domination of land and marking of territory through identity imprinture had already been achieved by enclosure and the structured mound. 'Cursus' style enclosures mark the first attempt to dominate the land further, by emphatically taking a distinctive slice through the landscape; a ceremonial form of 'land-grab'. There was no need to place cultural markers in the ditches of the 'cursus', for the 'cursus' itself was controlling the land and who moved through it. This was the first way of marking territory through selective enclosure.

New forms of linear structure such as the 'bank barrow' also appear to have been increasing land domination through monumental architecture. Whether the mound would have acted as a raised form of processional way, as has been hinted at Crickley Hill, is debatable. It would seem reasonable however to view the 'bank barrow' as a structure designed to dominate in much the same way as the 'cursus'. The 'bank barrow' may not have enclosed land, nor cut across such varied forms of landscape as the 'cursus', but its position within the land ensured that it was certainly more visually striking. Perhaps the grouping of large numbers of 'bank barrows' within discrete geographical zones, such as is evident along the South Dorset Ridgeway, was the embanked version of the 'cursus', with many elongated mounds having the same desired effect that a smaller cluster of 'cursus' structures would have had. Perhaps the 'bank barrow' is no more than a more monumental version of the archive mound: a more emphatic equivalent of the 'keep out' sign.

Incorporating earlier pieces of architecture, such as the structured mound within the 'cursus' or 'bank barrow', was not a way of associating the new linear monument with the ancestral dead for, as we have already explained, structured mounds were not exclusively associated with the deceased. Mounds were incorporated because this signalled a clear hijacking of the past: a rewriting or acceleration of earlier land claims. A 'cursus' or 'bank barrow' built over an enclosure increased any symbolic association with the past: the 'cursus' or 'bank barrow' builders were linking them-selves not only to the landscape, but to everything that had previously been enacted there. One does not need to travel along the new linear monuments in a great and organised procession to appreciate what is being said here.

The 'cursus' would serve as a monumental reminder, not only of who owned the land, but the extent of topographic and geographic variation covered by that claim. It linked the 'cursus' builders with the past by demonstrating how emphatically they could reorder and rewrite earlier architectural forms to their own ends. By designing specific 'cursus' monuments to include certain, basic astronomical events, the most important of which would be the movement of the sun and moon during the longest and shortest days of the year, the 'cursus' builders were tying their existence into not just the land, but also the heavens. Specific human communities were demonstrating their position at the centre of all things. Now they could order, predict and control the natural world, the past and the future, both at ground zero and in the skies overhead. A new level of domination had begun.

71 *Woodhenge: the distinctive shape of the circular, single-entranced, internal ditch of the 'henge' is visible in the top left corner of this aerial photograph taken in the early 1920s, as are some of the internal postholes which, when excavated, provided the nickname 'Woodhenge'. Other circular structures are evident as crop marks to the bottom right of the shot.* Sussex Archaeological Society: Holleyman Collection

Secondary circular

The circular ditched enclosures and structured mounds of the later Neolithic and Early Bronze Age are, after the stone circle, probably the most discussed of all prehistoric monument types. These are the 'henge' monuments and 'round barrows'. The inappropriate use of the term 'barrow' has already been discussed in relation to the structured mounds of the Early Neolithic. It is proposed to avoid the term again in the discussion of monument types that follows, given that human burial does not always appear to have been the major defining feature of such circular earthworks.

Circular structured mounds appear in certain parts of Britain from the Early Neolithic and, as already discussed, often represent an acceptable and comparable form of linear forms found elsewhere. From around 2500 BC, the circular structured mounds represent the dominant form of community marker constructed within the British Isles. The internal composition and basic form of these mounds takes on a new coherence and human remains, where encountered, progressively appear as single deposits of fully articulated individuals.

'Henges' represent a new component in the archaeological record for Britain. The word 'henge' is derived from the most famous prehistoric site in Britain: Stonehenge. The origin of the name 'Stonehenge' itself is unclear, though it has been suggested that it came from the belief that the lintelled stones at the Wiltshire site were a form of ancient gallows or hanging place. When a series of large postholes was identified from within a ditched enclosure to the north-east of Stonehenge in the mid-1920s, this site was dubbed 'Woodhenge' (**71**), in the belief it represented the timber fore-runner of the stone structure. Since 1932, when T.D. Kendrick and C.F.C. Hawkes first outlined a particular class of Neolithic circular earthwork, in the book *Archaeology in England and Wales*, the name 'henge' has been applied specifically to a type of prehistoric earthwork and not to any timber or stone uprights found within.

Today the main criterion of the term 'henge' is that the circular ditched enclosure in question must possess an external bank (**colour plate 22**). This is, of course, an inversion of the usual rampart sequence which, as Tim Darvill noted in 1987, makes 'henges'

> useless as defensive works unless the idea was simply to provide a barrier or to keep things in rather than out.

In this definition, Stonehenge itself cannot any longer be classified as a 'henge', for its bank is clearly internal (aside from dating concerns for phase 1 of the site as high-lighted above). The diverse nature of Later Neolithic enclosure circuits, in terms of scale, dimensions and internal features, has prompted the creation of all manner of 'henge' sub-species; hence 'henge-esque', 'henge-related', 'henge-like' and the execrable 'hengi-form'. Despite all this, it is the presence of the external bank that still best defines the categorisation.

'Henges', probable and possible, have been identified over a wide area of the British Isles, from the extreme south-west in Cornwall and Devon, to the Orkney Islands in the north. Identification of discrete regional monument groups, some of which display distinct forms of internal activity and associations (especially with stone circles), have, however, increasingly blurred their supposed defining characteristics. Few sites have been fully investigated and little is known about the presence or absence of internal features. Most internal features, if they exist, often relate to a secondary phase of remodelling, such as the construction of a stone or timber 'circle'.

The most comprehensive reclassification of 'henge' enclosures was conducted by Anthony Harding and G.E. Lee in 1987. In this, Harding and Lee identified a 'classic-henge' as a circular or oval enclosure which possessed an internal, usually segmented ditch, with a width in excess of 2.5m, enclosing an area with an internal diameter of over 14m (anything less is classified as a 'mini-henge'). 'Henges' can vary considerably in scale. One of the smallest, for example, is that recorded from Billown (**72**) which possessed an internal diameter of no more than 1.8m. Considerably larger 'henges' are known from sites like Avebury (**73**), Marden and Durrington Walls, which possess internal diameters of over 400m and cover areas in excess of 12 hectares.

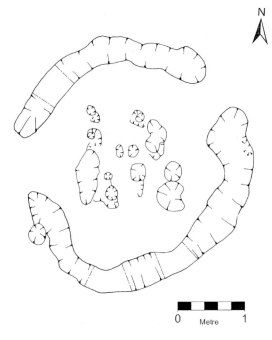

N *72 Billown: plan of the small 'henge'
revealed during excavations in 1996.*
Redrawn from Darvill 1997

*73 Avebury: an oblique aerial photograph, taken in the early 1920s, of the large 'henge'
which partially encloses the modern village of Avebury.* Sussex Archaeological
Society: Curwen Collection

'Henges' possess either a single entrance or two opposed points of entrance. Single entrance sites are orientated in the main towards the north or north-east, whilst those with two entrances appear to prefer a south-east/north-west orientation. Two entrance sites are markedly asymmetrical in plan, whilst single entranced enclosures are more circular in design. Most sites are situated in low-lying positions close to rivers or streams. Current radiocarbon determinations for 'henges' suggest that the main phase of constructional activity was between 2800 and 2000 BC, the majority dating from after 2400 BC (dating evidence being obtained from primary ditch silt accumulation).

The meaning of secondary circulars

The main issue of concern with regard to 'henges' is: why were they were built with an internal ditch/external bank? When William Stukeley first commented upon the 'henge' known as King Arthur's Round Table in his 1776 *Itinerarium Curisom*, he suggested that the bank was

> intended for sports . . . the vallum on the outside lies sloping inward with
> a very gradual declivity on purpose for spectators to stand around it.

The external banks at the site would, in Stukeley's view, have accommodated something in the region of 10,000 spectators. Unfortunately he does not guess at the type of sport being watched.

Today, our understanding of 'henges' has not advanced a great deal from Stukeley's day, other than to note that these are 'enigmatic' sites and that a full understanding of their intended purpose will probably always remain elusive. Recent authors, particularly Anthony Harding (in 1987) and Julian Thomas (in 1991 and 1999) have stressed that patterns of visibility and concealment were essential to the orientation of 'henges'. The interior of most sites would, for example, only have been visible to those approaching along the central entrance-axis of the monument, whilst, once inside, the view of everything outside would have been restricted by the prominent external banks. In such ways an observer's line of sight may have been directed through the rampart to activities taking place at the centre of the enclosure, or out towards a particular landscape feature beyond.

In some cases a basic astronomical alignment (especially solar or lunar) may have been considered important in the construction of a 'henge' monument. The presence of stone or timber uprights has, for example, been noted at a number of sites, and these were usually set within one of the main entrance gaps (**74**). In this context, single stone or timber uprights may plausibly be viewed as a form of 'focusing-device'; something set on the central axis of the monument to aid in the view of a specific landscape feature or astronomical event. Something akin to a gun sight, pinpointing a specific area of the immediate horizon. Such 'focussing devices', if real, would underline the importance of site orientation and alignment to the 'henge'. Alignment, situation and association may have been further emphasised by

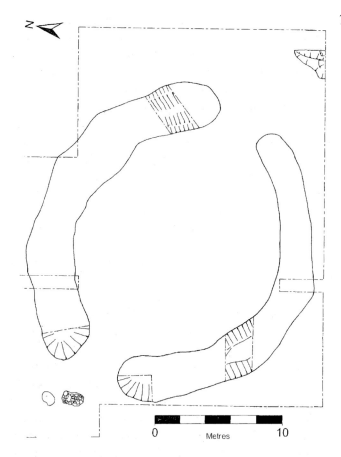

74 Yeavering: plan of the double entrance 'henge' showing two pits placed upon the central axis to the south-west of the monument. Redrawn from Harding 1981

0   Metres   10

the placing of 'henges' on or around earlier forms of Neolithic architecture, sites at Maxey and Thornborough for example overlying sections of 'cursus'.

Richard Bradley, in his 1998 book *The Significance of Monuments*, wondered whether the need to incorporate larger amounts of audiences or active participants within specific activities may, in the Later Neolithic, have prompted certain aspects of 'henge' design. Bradley, like Stukeley before him, wondered if Neolithic audiences may have sat upon the prominent external banks, like those watching events staged in later Roman amphitheatres. Any audience of activities occurring at floor level of a 'henge' would, in such an example, have been kept safely out of harm's reach by the internal ditch; the effect being not dissimilar to the kind of anti-hooligan devices set up within most modern sporting arenas. The positioning of banks, ditches and entrance gaps would, in Bradley's view, originally have generated a threefold division of space: some people could directly access the interior of a 'henge' through the entrance(s); others would look down from the bank; the remainder would be kept away, being only able to speculate as to what was really going on inside (**colour plate 21**).

The key to the interpretation of henges presumably lies in the obvious inversion of the rampart sequence. Most writers, as already noted, have commented on this purely from the point of view of audience participation, as if 'henges' were an early form of arena or amphitheatre. Positioning of the bank and ditch may, however, have more to do with the way in which Neolithic communities perceived their world, than with the physical necessity of protecting and housing an audience. If we view the 'henge' from the same perspective as the 'cursus', the enclosure, the shaft and the structured mound, then we may come to a different perspective.

The first forms of monumental architecture in Britain underlined, emphasised and accelerated the processes of domination and control by human communities of their natural environment. If the 'henge' is, as seems likely, part of this architectural process, then the inversion of rampart sequence may actually be more to do with the clear demarcation of what was and what was not under human control. In a normal enclosure, the rampart sequence is designed to keep things out; be they aggressive animal predators or irate human neighbours. Everything outside the rampart is therefore potentially hostile, whilst everything inside is familiar and comforting. The ditch and bank defines what is wild, dangerous and to be feared, and what is domestic, safe and to be protected.

The deliberate inversion of the henge rampart sequence appears, in physical terms, to make no sense unless, as Darvill has noted, it is to 'keep things in'. What if those 'things' were philosophical or ideological rather than tangible; ideas rather than animals or people? In these terms, the inverted rampart sequence of the 'henge', which completely surrounds a small and easily manageable space, may make more sense. If everything perceived to be wild or untamed is usually kept outside the ditch, then, in the context of a 'henge', the wild and untamed has been totally surrounded; it is held captive; it can be controlled and managed. Ideologically, the human communities building the 'henge' may have wished to demonstrate their near total domination of nature. Certain spaces demarcated by the 'henge' were, in conceptual terms, designed to represent the natural order, the wild, the undomesticated. The human communities had created an architectural form that not only explained and underlined their perceived mastery of nature, it also structured it and made it controllable. The interior of a 'henge' was the natural world in microcosm.

The diverse structural form and internal composition of circular mounds throughout the Later Neolithic and Early Bronze Age, has, at times, caused problems with interpretation. Some mounds possess external ditches, others do not. Some have obvious points of entrance and approach, others appear to have been completely closed. For a time both articulated and disarticulated human remains were deposited. Sometimes the human bone was cremated prior to incorporation. Sometimes animal bone, especially that of the ox, predominated. Sometimes there were no deposits of human bone to speak of.

It is possible that any difference between the deposition of complete human bodies and disarticulated body parts, cremated bone and animal bone, may represent the differing belief systems of varied human communities drawn to particular flint extraction areas or places of good prospective farmland. Alternatively, it may be that, as with earlier linear mounds, problems surrounding the interpretation of 'barrows' may stem from the automatic assumption that such structures were primarily burial

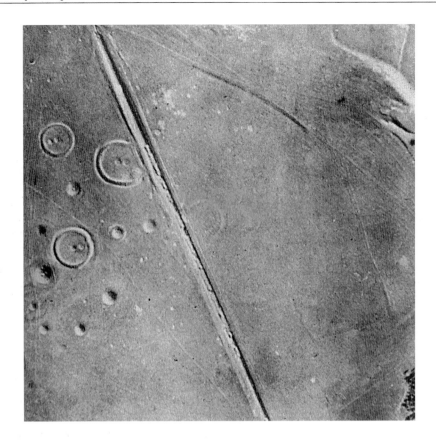

75 *Oakley Down: a compact group of Bronze Age circular structured mounds and ditches cut by Ackling Dyke, a well preserved section of Roman road.* Sussex Archaeological Society: Curwen Collection

mounds; therefore any artefact found within must relate in some way to the deposition of human bodies. Human bone, where discovered, is evidence for primary or secondary burial, animal bone becomes 'evidence for feasting', whilst flint tools and other artefacts become 'grave goods'.

The transformation from linear to circular mounds from the Earlier to the Later Neolithic and Early Bronze Age is furthermore taken as being indicative of a developing social stratification: the rise of the individual within society. Unfortunately, the excavation of linear mounds has demonstrated that the disposal of human remains did not always constitute the primary motive for their construction. Sometimes the importance of the mound appears to have lain with its construction and composition, rather than with any specific association with the human dead. If the linear mounds cannot be viewed as 'burial monuments' *per se*, then the origins, evolution and development of circular mounds, and also the deposition of single, articulated (and therefore presumably largely fleshed) human bodies may also require more careful reconsideration.

76 Silbury Hill: the largest circular structured mound in Europe. Miles Russell

It is possible that the move from linear to circular built forms may represent the deliberate abandonment of the Early Neolithic community archive or community marker, in which the material essence of a particular human group was stored as a form of land claim or to provide an accessible form of social archive. The fact that the circular form of mound (**75**) was being adopted at a time when circular domestic structures are becoming more archaeologically apparent, may however suggest that the concept of mound as symbolic 'house', containing a series of representative community identifiers, actually continued beyond the Early Neolithic. The development of round mounds, with human bodies placed at the centre of the structure, the area of a house normally occupied by the hearth (the centre of community more than just a provider of heat and light), may further add weight to this theory.

Furthermore, the observation that circular mounds became the focus for additional placed deposits, including human remains, throughout the Bronze Age may imply that such structures continued to possess an archival function for the wider community. In this model, the arrival of single, fully articulated bodies in the archaeological record may suggest that the nature of society had altered to the point that individuals could now, at death, act for the whole community. Individual burials, sometimes placed with singular dress items, including daggers, hair braids, archery equipment and so on, had by the Later Neolithic, become the main way of imprinting social identity into the landscape.

The need to establish a clear identity within, and ownership of, specific areas of land may have gained in importance throughout the Late Neolithic and Early Bronze Age as social pressures on territory from competing human groups increased. Silbury Hill, the largest humanly constructed mound in Europe (**76**) may, in this respect, represent the ultimate in community mound. Built in stages, commencing at some time between 2800 – 2500 BC, the feature comprised primary turf and gravel mound, replaced by successively greater mounds of chalk rubble. Excavations have, to date, yet to locate any evidence of human burial, but this should not surprise us. Silbury is unlikely to have been the Neolithic equivalent of an Egyptian pyramid, complete with members of a royal dynasty buried with all their finery, but the final word in 'mound as symbolic house' architecture. It was designed to dominate a restricted part of the landscape, the heartland, perhaps, of a community that devoted much of its time to the construction of monumental forms of architecture, for this is also the home of the Avebury 'super-henge' and the immense palisaded enclosures of West Kennet.

At other times, and in other areas of Britain, communities may have felt the need to hijack the monuments of earlier periods, such as the enclosure and linear mound of the Early Neolithic, in order to strengthen or legitimise their tenure on the land. Such deliberate expropriation of sites could have manifested itself through the incorporation of later pottery types (such as the Beaker), flintwork or, at times, a contemporary, and complete, member of society, deep into a backfilling ditch or weathering mound. As suggested for the body parts found within Early Neolithic linear mounds, such remains need not represent the bodies of the religious leaders, the politically powerful or the financially successful; rather, these individuals may have been chosen due to the fact that they were perceived as being representative elements of society.

In these respects, the 'henge' and the circular structured mounds are a logical extension of the 'cursus', for, whilst the 'cursus' emphasised the extent of topographic and geographic variation covered by a specific land claim, the 'henge' and mound emphasised claim over all natural things. They also took associations with earlier monumental forms, such as the linear structured mound and enclosure, in order to demonstrate how the new order could effectively rewrite the past for its own ends. As with the 'cursus', discrete astronomical alignments appear to have been deliberately incorporated into the construction of 'henges', helping human communities pinpoint specific celestial events such as the summer or winter solstice. The placement of focussing devices within the new circular monuments, which drew the human view line along the central axis, meant that communities could extend their control over celestial activity. The movement of the heavens could now be predicted, sequenced and ordered through the 'natural/wild' space encircled by the inverted 'henge' ramparts. Human groups, by bringing a sense of order to the terrestrial and extraterrestrial, were reaching the logical conclusion of their attempts to tame the nature through the provision of monumental architecture.

Uprights of timber and stone

The final stage of Neolithic architectural innovation is characterised by a monument form that, to the bulk of the population, probably best defines the period of 'prehistory': the stone circle. There have been many investigations of stone circles in the last 100 years and much has been written, not all of it particularly useful. Recent work has, however, stressed not only the longevity of sites, but also their close association with a less visible or archaeologically tangible form of monument: the timber circle.

Stone circles appear in the British archaeological record from at least 2800 BC, though timber circles may have been constructed earlier, perhaps just before 3000 BC. It goes without saying that the dating is, as with other Neolithic monumental forms, far from precise. Timbers, if they survive, can provide useful material for radiocarbon analysis; stones do not. The chronology, such as it is, appears to suggest that the earliest timber upright settings were free-standing, relatively small scale structures such as that established at Arminghall between 3650 and 2650 BC.

At Arminghall and Milfield North, timber circles would appear to pre-date the construction of a 'henge' monument, whereas at other sites, a timber circle seems to represent an addition to the interior of an established 'henge'. Primary timber settings have, at times, been clearly replaced in stone. Alex Gibson, in his book *Stonehenge and timber circles*, refers to such a process as 'lithicisation', noting its occurrence at Balfarg, Cairnpapple, Moncrieffe and, most spectacularly, at Stonehenge. Stone circles also can be demonstrated to represent additions to existing 'henges', though a significant number represent free standing monuments in their own right (**77**). Artefactual associations, as well as relationships with other pieces of architecture, suggest that the practice of building timber and stone circles continued beyond the traditional 'end date' of the Neolithic (as devised by archaeologists), and well into the Middle Bronze Age, so that uprights were still being installed by at least 1500 BC.

Many of the earliest stone settings along the north and western seaboard of Britain possess closely placed uprights and a clear point of entrance, sometimes marked by two independent stones of differing dimensions to the main circle such as at Castlerigg and Swinside. Similar 'entrance points' or façades have been detected for timber circles, notably Durrington South Circle and Sarn-y-bryn-caled (**78**). Additional standing stones or 'outliers' have frequently been observed at a distance to the main circle of uprights. These may have served as a form of focussing device, as per the single stones sometimes recorded from within 'henges', guiding lines of sight to a particular horizon point or landscape feature, or they may have served as a form of marker, directing the movement of people towards the monument (**colour plate 23**).

By 2500 BC, at the end of the Neolithic, the practice of erecting circles and ovals of stone and timber appears more widespread across the British Isles, especially eastern Scotland and south-western England. Most sites were modest in size, measuring on average 20-30m in internal diameter, though larger examples, such as the Ring of Brodgar, Stanton Drew and Avebury (76m, 104m and 410m respectively) are known.

The meaning of timber and stone uprights

More has been written on the nature and possible interpretation of stone circles than probably any other form of archaeological monument in Britain. Unfortunately, as already noted, little of what has been said is particularly helpful; there is much at what

77 *The Ring of Brodgar: a circular arrangement of stone uprights.* Sussex Archaeological Society: Holleyman Collection

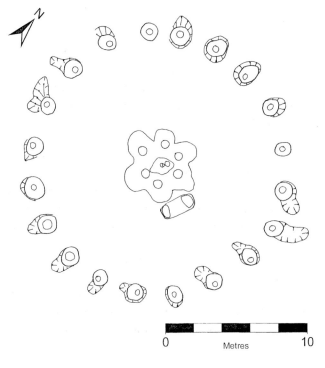

78 *Sarn-y-bryn-caled: plan of the timber structure showing the inner setting (with façade) and outer circle.* Redrawn from Gibson 1994

archaeologists refer to as the 'fringes' of rational debate that serves only to cloud the issue. There have, for example, been many published works that confidently interpret the stone circle as a form of hi-tech observation platform, which charted the cosmos in intricate detail, or as a Stone Age computer, which, through intricate use of geometry and sophisticated mathematics, precisely mapped out the world. There is no evidence for this.

It is clear, however, that, as with the 'henge' and 'cursus', significant astronomical or seasonal events were sometimes recorded within the stone and timber circle through the deliberate alignment of uprights and the placing of certain architectural features. This should occasion little surprise, for not only were human societies, by the Later Neolithic, increasingly reliant upon the agricultural cycle, but also they were exercising their control over nature in ever new and more daring ways. Alignment with the midsummer sunrise does not suggest that Neolithic communities were receiving aid from extraterrestrial beings (this is not an episode of the *X Files*) but that they were attempting to chart and predict changes in the seasons and regulate the timing of important events and activities.

Aubrey Burl produced the first detailed synthesis of stone uprights in his 1976 book *The Stone Circles of the British Isles*, whilst timber circles first received significant analysis in Alex Gibson's *Stonehenge and Timber Circles* published in 1998. Most authors have, as with those writing on 'henge' monuments, stressed patterns of visibility and alignment. Some have suggested that stone and timber circles may have acted as trade or ceremonial centres for local communities. In 1998, Richard Bradley discussed the possible interpretation of stone circles on the basis of activities and potential audiences. When compared to 'henge' monuments, Bradley noted, circles of stone uprights possessed a very different relationship to the surrounding landscape in that:

> a continuous earthwork masks much of that landscape, concealing the surrounding area from view and also restricting visual access to the events taking place within these sites. A stone circle, however, is entirely permeable and its construction can be used to form explicit links between a central enclosure and points in the wider terrain.

In other words, the stone or timber circle was more open, allowing a potential audience fairly unrestricted views of activities occurring within, whilst at the same time permitting those within the bounded space better observation of the immediate topography. It still does not explain what, if anything, was going on within the space enclosed by the circle, but it may go some way to explaining the form of architecture chosen.

Perhaps the key to the understanding of upright circles has been provided by recent work on the bluestone and sarsen circles at Stonehenge. Here, the techniques of joinery between lintels and uprights (**79, colour plates 25 and 26**), especially with regard to mortice and tenon and tongue groove joints, suggest very strongly a timber prototype for the monument. In fact, as Alex Gibson observed in 1998,

79 Stonehenge: techniques of joinery displayed here between lintels and uprights, strongly suggest a timber prototype for the monument. Sussex Archaeological Society: Holleyman Collection

the design of the final monument appears to be much closer to the original wooden sites than do the majority of other 'lithicisations'. It is argued here, therefore, that Stonehenge is not a stone circle – a class of monument in which no direct parallels can be found – but in fact a timber circle, though made unusually in stone.

Gibson has further argued that the uprights which form the core of the majority of timber circles were not originally free-standing, unconnected entities, but were in all probability joined at the top by a lintel. A full scale reconstruction of the Sarn-y-bryn-caled timber circle was duly made by Gibson and observed both with and without connecting lintels. Whilst there is no conclusive proof, as nothing of Neolithic timber circles today survives above ground level, it was interesting to note that with the free-standing posts in position

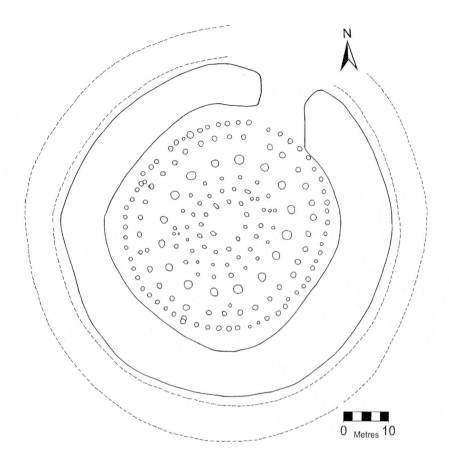

80 Woodhenge: feature plan showing the internally ditched 'henge' enclosure, entrance pointing north-north-east, and internal setting of large timber posts. Redrawn from Cunnington 1929

the circularity of the monument was not at all obvious. Instead, the reconstruction appeared, from ground level, to be a jumble of posts emanating from a base whose ground plan was not at all obvious. Lintels were added and at once the circularity of the monument was obvious.

A similar feeling of confused uprights may be gauged, albeit on a vastly smaller scale, by the modern visitor to the site at Woodhenge. Here the positions of the Neolithic posts (**80**) have today been marked at ground level by small concrete pillars. There is no attempt to join the pillars or to indicate the circularity of the posthole plan, other than to use different width posts and paint the tops different colours, all of which does little than provide the feeling of walking around a surreal modern sculpture park. The circular form of the post-plan would only become apparent here if the pillars, or replacement posts, were joined with lintels as at the sarsen ring at Stonehenge.

135

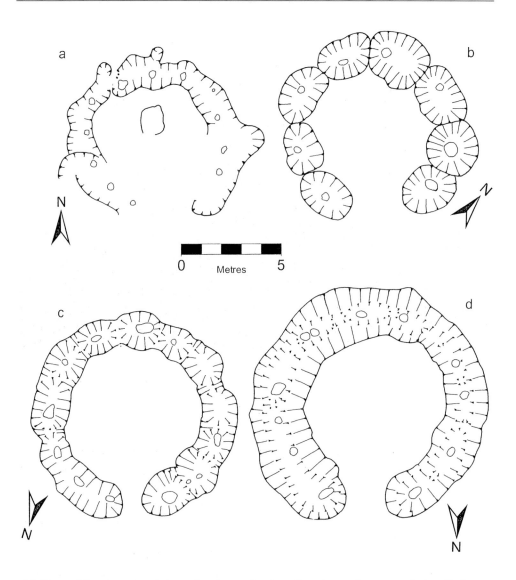

81 Plans of four Late Neolithic palisade trenches/small timber circles: a = Itford Hill; b = Dorchester-on-Thames iv; c = Dorchester-on-Thames v; d = Dorchester-on-Thames vi. Redrawn from Russell 1996

Even if most post circles as well as the main structural phases of Stonehenge were linked thus, so what? What does it tell us about other stone circles which clearly comprised uprights without lintels? What does it tell us about how the timber and stone circles may originally have been used and what they were meant to represent? Well, quite a lot actually. Stonehenge in its final phases has the appearance of a house structure, not a finished, fully roofed building, but the very core of a standard Late Neolithic and Early Bronze Age roundhouse; namely the ring-beam.

82 Bournemouth University: a lintelled structure open to the elements; a house without walls or roof. Miles Russell

The ring-beam was the primary foundation of the house. It defined the circularity and dimensions of the structure as well as performing the essential task of providing a support for the roof. Stonehenge could therefore be viewed in basic terms as a house without walls or a roof. It is open to the sky and to the landscape around. It is a house made monumental. Timber circles like Sarn-y-bryn-caled, Woodhenge and Durrington Walls South and the post-in-palisade slots of Dorchester-on-Thames and Itford Hill (**81**), could well have been the same. They do not make sense as roofed buildings (though many have tried to make them thus in reconstructions). They do, however, make sense as lintelled structures open to the elements (**82**), exactly as in the final stages of Stonehenge (**83**).

What we are left with in the joined circles, therefore, is the last piece of Neolithic monumental building, the final act in a long sequence of domination and control through the provision of architecture: the house. The house as the centre of life. The house as centre of daily activities. The house as ultimate symbol of domestication. Stone circles, even without a linking set of lintels, as suggested for their timber cousins, would represent further monumentalisation of the concept of the house 'skeleton'. Here one has the essential core of a building, with an obvious series of connections to the past, present, future and the heavens, made evident through alignment and association. Stone or timber circles placed within 'henges' could perhaps have further demonstrated a desire by human communities to symbolise the

83 Stonehenge: a lintelled structure open to the elements; a house without walls or roof.
Sussex Archaeological Society: Holleyman Collection

domestication of the wild; the creation of a symbolic settlement structure within a symbolic creation of the untamed or natural world.

In this respect, Stonehenge and other circles represent, not semi-mystical pieces of Stone Age architecture, nor prehistoric computers, but the ultimate attempt to convey human domination over nature: brutal pieces of domestication and control **(colour plates 25 & 26)**. Stonehenge is the final word in Neolithic architecture; it gets no clearer than this.

7 Case studies

We have spent long enough looking at the specifics of Britain's earliest monumental architecture. Now I would like to develop the arguments set out in the previous chapters by examining how Neolithic architecture impacted upon the wild landscapes of Britain. Thus far we have dealt with Neolithic monuments as if they were isolated in time and space; divorced from their social and topographic context. This is not altogether healthy.

When attempting to study patterns of human behaviour, such as the evolution of society through the development of architecture, it is important to examine areas of well-defined space; using blocks of land as a form of laboratory. To this end, any chosen area must possess good geological or geographical constraints. It must possess a reality within the landscape, rather than representing a random piece of land cut into fairly meaningless segments by modern political boundaries. The areas selected for analysis here conform to these particular constraints in that they all possess good natural, geological and topographical borders. Furthermore, each area possesses a clear and distinctive form of Neolithic monumental architecture; each represents an example of how the basic concept and meaning of structural form was modified and applied within different parts of the British Isles. The three areas I have chosen to illustrate these arguments form a block of land bordering the south-eastern coast of England, an island to the north-west of England, and an archipelago to the north-east of Scotland: the South Downs; the Isle of Man; and Orkney (**84**).

THE SOUTH DOWNS

The landscape of central south-eastern Britain is dominated by the chalk ridge of the South Downs. Chalk, a white, permeable rock, supports no surface water. All major river systems flow southwards to the English Channel, the rivers Cuckmere, Ouse, Adur, Arun, Lavant, Meon and Itchen dividing the chalk into a series of discrete blocks. The River Test, draining out into Southampton Water and the Solent, marks the western geographical limit of the Downs, though geologically the chalk continues further west into Wessex and north-eastwards, as the North Downs, into Surrey and Kent. The eastern limit of the South Downs is marked by a series of cliffs, ending at Beachy Head just to the west of Eastbourne. The northern limit of the Downs is characterised by a steep escarpment, rising to a maximum height of 242m above sea level, and faces the sands, sandstones and clays of the Weald, whilst to the south the downs merge gently into the coastal plain. Within the chalk there are seams of nodular and tabular flint, whilst patches of clay-with-flint occasionally occur on the surface.

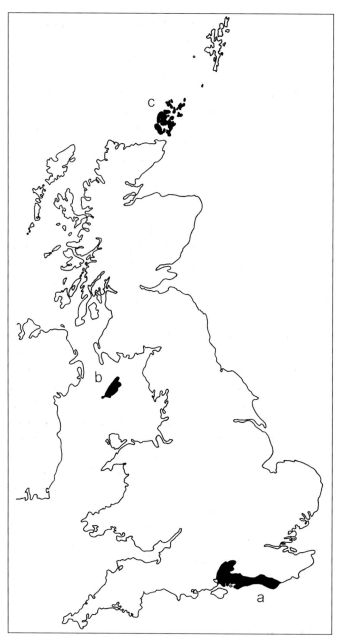

84 Location of the three cases studies examined within chapter 7: a = South Downs; b = Isle of Man; c = Orkney.

Forms of monumental architecture

All the recorded monuments of the Neolithic in central south-eastern Britain (East Sussex, West Sussex and Hampshire) concentrate upon the chalk. These monuments comprise enclosures, linear structured mounds and shafts. There is some evidence for the construction of 'henges', circular structured mounds and timber uprights in the Later Neolithic and Early Bronze Age. The evidence for stone uprights is at best ambiguous.

Some 11 sites have been identified as potential enclosures. Of these, eight are definite, two are probable and one is possible. The definite sites comprise Barkhale, Bury Hill, Combe Hill, Court Hill I, Halnaker Hill, Offham, the Trundle and Whitehawk. The list of probable Neolithic circuits (probable in that there is no certainty that either were ever continuous) comprises Belle Tout A and Court Hill II. The only possible enclosure identified from the South Downs is the, as yet undated, circuit of ditch recorded from an aerial photograph of Cockroost Hill.

A total of 13 sites have been identified as areas of Neolithic shafts. Of these, six may be defined as definite, one as probable and six as possible. The definite sites comprise Blackpatch, Church Hill, Cissbury, Harrow Hill, Long Down and Stoke Down, where extensive periods of excavation and survey have revealed a considerable amount of Neolithic data. The only site listed as an area of probable shafts is Nore Down where two strips of cut almost certainly indicate a zone of Neolithic excavation. Possible areas comprise the plough-disrupted sites of High Salvington and Mount Carvey, with possible extensions to known areas existing at Myrtlegrove (near Blackpatch), West Stoke (near Stoke Down), Roger's Farm (near Church Hill) and the possible quarry site disturbed by later digging activity at Tolmere (close to Church Hill).

Some 41 sites have been identified as potential linear structured mounds from the South Downs. Of these, 17 would appear definite, eight are probable and 16 are possible. The definite sites comprise Alfriston, Bevis' Grave, Bevis' Thumb, Hunter's Burgh, Lamborough, Long Burgh, Moody's Down SE, Moody's Down NW, Moody's Down W, North Marden, Preston Candover, South Wonston N, South Wonston W, Stoughton I, Stoughton II, Upper Cranbourne Farm and Windover Hill. The list of probable Neolithic linear mounds consists of Beacon Hill I, the Camel's Humps, Firle Beacon, Giant's Grave, Lavant Down, Money Burgh, Salt Hill and Warren Farm. Possible long mounds comprise the severely plough damaged earthworks first detected through aerial photography or limited ground survey at Beacon Hill II, Chilbolton Down, Exceat, Great Down, Old Winchester Hill, Welldown, earthworks of disturbed or disputed form such as Burnt Wood II, Glynde, Littlington I, Longwood, Plumpton Plain, South Wonston E, Whitehawk and Woodmancott, or sites that have now been completely destroyed without detailed analysis, such as Portsdown and Preston Drove.

Primary phase (4500-3500 BC)

The radiocarbon chronology for Neolithic architecture on the South Downs is fragmentary to say the least, but it is suggested that the first structures to appear were built between 4500-3500 BC (**85**). These comprise the phase 1 enclosure circuits of the Trundle, Court Hill I and possibly Whitehawk and Offham, radiocarbon determinations for initial phases of construction at the Trundle, Court Hill I and Offham being 4400-3700 BC, 4750-3800 BC, and 3960-3610 BC respectively. The first shafts at Blackpatch, Church Hill, Harrow Hill and Long Down were also dug at this

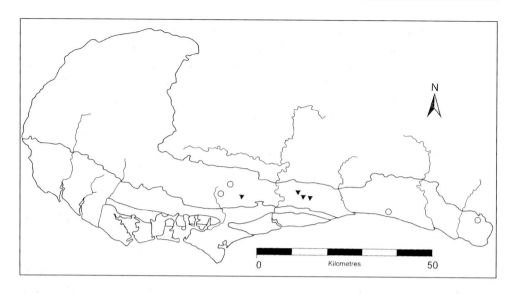

85 South Downs: primary phase (4500-3500 BC); solid triangles = shafts; open circles = enclosures.

time or shortly afterwards, radiocarbon dates for the sites suggesting initial excavation was conducted between 4350-3500 BC, 4500-3700 BC, 4550-3500, and 4250-3600 BC respectively. These architectural forms appear to represent the initial movement of communities away from the coastal plain and Weald and onto the higher ridge of the Downs.

On the Downs, both the Trundle and Whitehawk enclosures dominated significant areas of the chalk ridge, though their primary area of visibility may have been towards the coastal plain. The early phases of Church Hill, Blackpatch and Long Down appear to have possessed similar, if slightly more restricted sight lines towards the coastal plain and southern sections of the Downs. Offham was primarily orientated towards the Weald and the northern scarp of the chalk. With the exception of Court Hill I and the Trundle, none of these early monuments are intervisible. Each may therefore have been designed to open up and claim specific areas of the chalk ridge, whilst looking out and back towards the main areas of earlier hunter-gatherer activity.

How the additional and, as yet largely undated, monuments fitted into this primary phase is unknown. Enclosures like Barkhale and Halnaker Hill, for example, may well have formed part of the earliest form of significant land modification. Halnaker Hill possesses a clear view of the eastern side of the Trundle, and of the Long Down shafts to the south-east. Barkhale is hidden from all three of these sites, though it too possesses a clear and extensive view of the coastal plain and sections of the southern facing dip slope of the Downs. A possible primary phase at Combe Hill may, like Offham, from which Combe Hill is hidden, have been designed to dominate the view from the Weald, an anchor point for progress onto the chalk for those social groups to the north.

The enclosures may have represented a form of seasonal or temporary safe zone, imprinted with the identity of the varied social groups involved in their construction. Here the dispersed and relatively mobile human population could engage in communal activity and settlement within a defined and enclosed area of land. These enclosures seem to represent a broad translation of the strongly defined enclosure circuits identified from earlier contexts across central Europe.

Shafts were not cut from a purely economic necessity, for the generation of flint for trade, though certain prestige items were certainly manufactured from the distinctive subterranean stone. As with enclosures, shafts were seasonal anchor points, drawing dispersed elements of the human population together to engage in specific communal activities. The major difference with the shafts, as compared to the enclosures, would appear to be that they involved a physical (and not just psychological) dislocation from the real and familiar world.

Enclosures and shafts were probably built, used and maintained by a diverse set of human groups. Both types of site may have been established at the margins of a number of existing social boundaries or they may represent centre points of new, more dominant ideologies. Selected material derived from settlement waste, considered representative of each social group, was deliberately incorporated within ditch and shaft backfill, together with additional items that best characterised the group involved. Such material, at times, constituted: flint worked by a particular unit; pottery made or used by the group; geological materials common to the area; animals that lived within the territory and were predated upon; parts of the social group itself in the form of disassembled human bodies. All these elements would have helped emergent Neolithic society to imprint its own specific social identity into the landscape and help establish an ideological control beyond the level of specific monuments.

Secondary phase (3500–2500 BC)

The secondary phase of monument construction on the South Downs (**86**) is marked by the development of new circuits of enclosure at Whitehawk, the Trundle and possibly at Offham and Combe Hill and the establishment of additional enclosures such as Bury Hill and possibly Belle Tout A. The radiocarbon determinations for secondary circuit definition are 3800–3000 BC for Whitehawk and 3650–3000 BC for the primary phase at Bury Hill.

With the exception of Court Hill I/the Trundle and Halnaker Hill/the Trundle, enclosure sites remained invisible from one another. This may have been due to the establishment of defined and discrete territories. Alternatively it may represent a continuation of the desire to impose order on the Downs by establishing a frame of reference extending across a number of interlinked, if not intervisible, enclosures. Bury Hill is positioned, like Offham, to take in a portion of the northern scarp of the Downs and the Weald beyond. Belle Tout, which may, due to its recorded form, also have belonged to this period, enclosed an entire headland and presumably dominated a large section of the coastal plain, now lost through coastal erosion.

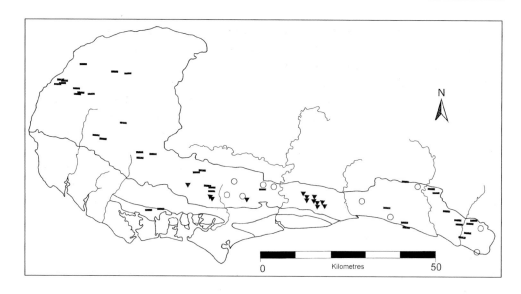

86 South Downs: secondary phase (3500-2500 BC); solid triangles = shafts; open circles = enclosures; solid rectangles = linear structured mounds.

The elaboration of ditch circuits at the Trundle, Whitehawk and possibly Offham and Combe Hill may relate to an increased number of people starting to use the enclosures. Alternatively it may reflect a desire to re-emphasise and re-dramatise particular monuments, increasing their perceived importance and dominance over the landscape and extending their view across the Weald, Downs or coastal plain. Remodification of enclosures, by cutting new circuits, was also important if the visual impact of chalk rubble banks was to be re-established. Simple recutting of backfilled ditches would not have the same effect, for this would have resulted in the dragging up of dark silt, as well as being likely to disrupt earlier forms of community identifier, such as human bone and pottery, already contained within ditch fill.

Modification of, and addition to, enclosure circuits would also result in new ways of approaching and entering the monument in question, which could have empha-sised the importance of particular social groups within the landscape. The creation of more formalised points of entrance is especially clear at Whitehawk and possibly also the Trundle, as is the addition of palisades to dramatise earthwork circuits. Certain areas of the outermost ditch at Whitehawk also appear to have been recut to a more continuous design.

The building of new circuits of bank and ditch may have emphasised the involve-ment of new human communities, and would therefore have to include new forms of social identifier. Particular forms of social marker continue throughout this later period, though articulated human and animal bodies seem to predominate, suggesting that certain individuals were beginning to stand for the wider community. The addition of complete bodies into older segments of enclosure construct may reflect the desire of later communities to dominate, through the addition of a contemporary community member, earlier cultural assemblages and to change the overall configuration of established social markers.

Shafts begin to proliferate in this secondary phase of architectural construction. The cutting of shafts appears to have commenced at Cissbury for the first time, radiocarbon determinations suggesting a date range of between 3800-3000 BC for the initial phases. The Cissbury shafts appear to have been placed so as to face the earlier shaft series of Church Hill. A similar feature also occurs at Harrow Hill, where the new shafts face out across a dry valley towards the earlier shafts of Blackpatch. New shafts at Cissbury and Harrow Hill, like those cut before, remain invisible to the Chalkland enclosure groups to the immediate east and west. The proliferation of shaft cutting at Stoke Down and Long down may also belong to this secondary phase of activity.

The major new component in the Neolithic architectural repertoire, occurring from around 3500 cal BC, is the structured linear mound. Radiocarbon determinations for Alfriston, Bevis' Thumb and North Marden suggest construction dates of between 3340-2615 BC, 3600-2900 BC and 3800-3100 BC respectively. These buildings were not designed as burial monuments or tombs. These were earthworks, which deliberately echo the structural form of continental long houses. They were monuments which were intended to act as visible containers of social identity, imprinting new areas of land with the cultural attributes of a particular human group. As before, these attributes included worked flint, pottery, animal bone, geological material and occasional pieces of human bone. Linear structured mounds may therefore be viewed as a form of cultural archive, designed to place (or increase) a permanent claim over a specific part of land.

The comparative proliferation of linear mounds across the Downs at this stage of social development may indicate the increased numbers of people laying claim to specific areas of the chalk. Alternatively their construction may reflect the desire to increase the fertility of the human group and of the land they inhabited. The majority of linear mounds possessed limited view lines, dominating restricted space within dry valleys or river systems. Few are intervisible, suggesting that human communities were gradually becoming more sedentary within specific sections of the landscape. Some linear mounds, such as Hunter's Burgh and Portsdown, possessed more wide-ranging views, and their positions, at the peripheries of chalkland ridges, may have been important for those wishing to progress onto the Downs via certain proscribed routes. Alternatively they may be interpreted as a form of unwelcome sign such as: 'This territory is ours. Keep away'.

Final phase (2500–1500 BC)

The final period of Neolithic architectural evolution on the South Downs is characterised by the failure to develop additional phases of large scale enclosure circuit and the proliferation of new small scale circular monumental forms. The development of structured round mounds may reflect the continuation of the concept of mound as symbolic house containing the cultural attributes of a particular human group. Rights of land ownership could presumably be legitimised by the inclusion of contemporary community members within such forms. Gradually the nature of individual deposition seems to have become more elaborate, but the concept of mound as a community archive may have continued, with later generations inserting their dead into these earthworks.

Gradually the cutting of vertical shafts into specific areas of the chalk comes to an end. The final phases at Blackpatch, and possibly Church Hill, are marked with an elaborate series of flint and artefact structured mounds. Symbolically–charged flint artefacts do not appear to be in demand and the majority of flint tools in everyday use appear to have been generated from surface flint deposits.

Circular timber settings represent a new addition to the monument repertoire in this final phase of activity, as do the small scale externally embanked enclosures, traditionally termed 'henges'. Examples of new timber upright forms may be seen at Itford Hill and Pyecombe, whilst instances of new circular enclosure circuits can be evidenced at Blackpatch (Barrow 9) and Mile Oak. The appearance of smaller, more diverse forms of structure across the chalk presumably reflects the fact that, ideologically speaking, the wild had been conquered. It may also reflect the more fragmented nature of human society, which by this stage was no longer largely composed of relatively mobile communities requiring defined anchor points, but a series of more sedentary, small scale groups whose subsistence base was relying ever more upon agricultural forms of production. The battle for the South Downs was effectively over. Nature had been domesticated.

ISLE OF MAN

The Isle of Man covers an area of around 570 square kilometres and comprises three major topographic zones, namely the upland massifs centred upon Snaefell, South Barrule and Mull Hill, the lowland coastal strip of the west, south and east, and the northern plain. The upland massifs dominate the island landscape, Snaefell rising to a height of 621m above sea level and South Barrule rising to 483m.

The massifs comprise mostly of slates and greywackes. The northern plain, a rough triangle of land representing around a third of the island's land mass, is broadly flat and composed of Pleistocene deposits. The western coastal zone comprises a low, gently undulating strip of land, comprising mostly of sands and gravels, around three kilometres in width. This strip extends considerably along the southern edge of the island (to around eight kilometres in width), but is discontinuous along the eastern fringe.

Forms of monumental architecture

The Neolithic monumental architecture of the Isle of Man is dominated by what are traditionally interpreted as tombs or burial monuments. These structures have

*87 King Orry's Grave I and II:
plan of the linear structured
mounds and their proposed
relationships.* Redrawn
from Darvill 1997

a

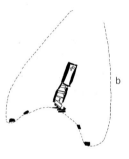

b

0   Metres   10

variously been classified and categorised as court tombs, chambered tombs and long
barrows, all defined here as linear structured mounds, and passage tombs or passage
graves, all defined here as circular structured mounds.

   Some five sites have been identified as potential Neolithic linear structured
mounds from the Isle of Man. Of these, two would appear definite, one is probable
and two are possible. The definite sites comprise Cashtal yn Ard and King Orry's
Grave I. A probable Neolithic linear mound exists at Ballafayle. Possible linear
mounds comprise the chambers of King Orry's Grave II and the badly damaged
structure Cloven Stones. King Orry's Grave II, the western of the two chambered
areas recorded from the site, presumably represents a discrete mound built close to,
but distinct from, King Orry's Grave I to the immediate east (**87**), though the possibility that it could represent the western part of a doubled-ended linear mound
(similar to Audleystown in Ireland or Tulloch of Assery in Scotland), should not at
this stage be discounted. The list of seven potential circular structured mounds
comprises: the definite, if anomalous, site at Mull Hill (**88**) and the chambered cairn
at Ballakelly; the probable site of Giant's Grave at Kew, and the possible sites at
Balleterson Cronk, Ballaharra, Corvalley and Cronk ny Arrey.

147

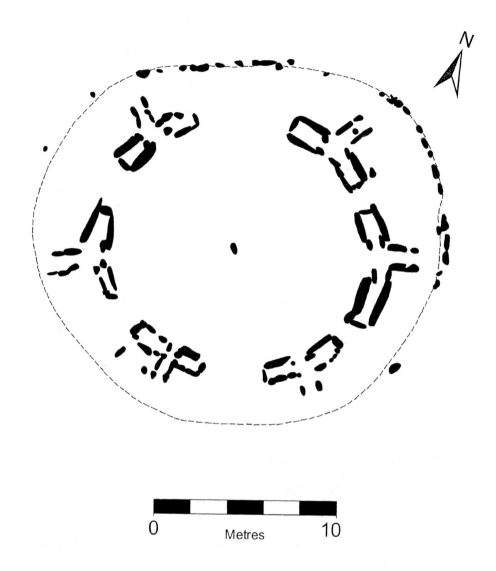

88 Mull Hill: plan of the circular stone-structured (chambered) mound. Redrawn from Darvill 1995

A series of Early Neolithic pits and shafts and traces of at least two discrete, if over-lapping, enclosure circuits has recently been excavated on the south of the island at Billown. The larger of the two enclosures appears to have been overlain by a Neolithic secondary linear structure (a 'cursus' or 'bank barrow'). Multiple stone uprights, at least two possible stone circles and a number of potential 'henges' (or secondary phase enclosures) have also been suggested for the later Neolithic of Man.

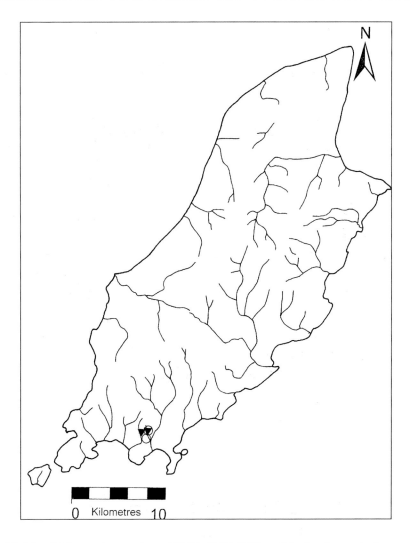

89 Isle of Man: primary phase (4700-4000 BC); solid triangles = shafts; open circle = enclosures.

Primary phase (4700-4000 BC)

The radiocarbon chronology for the Manx Neolithic is unfortunately limited, with less than 10 determinations having been processed prior to 1995. This situation is now changing, the excavation and fieldwork programme developing at Billown by Manx National Heritage and Bournemouth University providing a range of contexts and dating samples. The increasing suite of dates, when combined with the new excavation and survey data from projects directed by Tim Darvill and Stephen Burrow, may suggest a tentative chronology for the development and evolution of architectural form on Man (**89**).

a

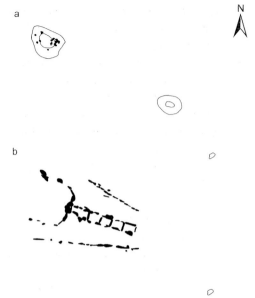

90 Cashtal yn Ard: suggested three phase plan of the linear mound: a = phase 1 small irregular mound with stone chamber, oval mound with overlying burnt stone platform and stone upright; b = phase 2 linear stone-structured mound with forecourt and five celled chamber; c = phase 3 doubling of size to linear mound. Redrawn from Darvill 2000

b

c

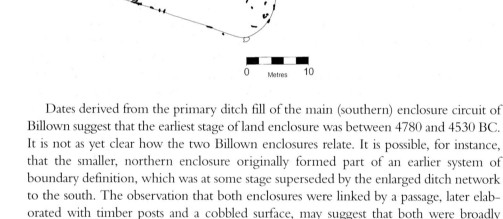

0   Metres   10

Dates derived from the primary ditch fill of the main (southern) enclosure circuit of Billown suggest that the earliest stage of land enclosure was between 4780 and 4530 BC. It is not as yet clear how the two Billown enclosures relate. It is possible, for instance, that the smaller, northern enclosure originally formed part of an earlier system of boundary definition, which was at some stage superseded by the enlarged ditch network to the south. The observation that both enclosures were linked by a passage, later elaborated with timber posts and a cobbled surface, may suggest that both were broadly contemporary, the northern perhaps representing a form of annexe. Until the full plan of both sites is determined (difficult considering the extent of post medieval quarrying), a clear understanding of chronology and phasing may prove elusive.

Timber recovered from the upper fill of at least one shaft at Billown has provided a date of around 4900-4600 BC, suggesting the possibility that the cutting of shafts represents the earliest form of Neolithic land alteration on Man. Other shafts and pits at Billown appear to date from roughly the same period as the construction of the first enclosure circuits. The majority of shafts, of which at least 70 have now been recorded from a geophysical survey, cluster to the west of the northern enclosure, and could originally have been accessed via the main entrance to the enclosure and its associated hollow way. The recorded cuts would not appear to have possessed an economic function (that is for the generation of stone for tool manufacture or trade), and they may represent a form of seasonal anchor point or area of social dislocation/initiation, as suggested for certain shafts on the southern English chalk.

How the additional and, as yet largely undated, monuments of Man fitted into this primary building phase is as yet unclear. At Cashtal yn Ard, a possible stone platform recorded beneath the linear structured mound may represent an early phase of monument definition (**90**), whilst Darvill has argued that the stone chamber from Ballaharra may be an early variant of the 'portal dolmen'. The only useful date yet generated from the Manx linear structured mounds is that of the forecourt structure at King Orry's Grave I, and this suggests a creation date somewhere in the mid- to late fourth millennium, or secondary phase Neolithic. Circular, 'passage grave' structured mounds may derive from the earliest phases of Neolithic building activity on Man, but without secure dating evidence, it may be safer to view these as also belonging to the secondary Neolithic.

The Billown enclosures and shaft series occupy the upper, south and south-west facing slopes of a low, gently rounded hilltop, and would originally have dominated the view towards a significant portion of the south-western coastal plain. The main entrance points for both enclosure sites appear to have been along their broader, slightly concave, western perimeters. Together, these observations may suggest the initial movement of human settlement away from the coastal plain, and onto the higher ridges of the interior. The Billown enclosures could therefore have represented a form of seasonal settlement or temporary safe zone, established either at the margins of pre-established social boundaries or at the centre of a new one.

Ditches were imprinted with the identity of the varied social groups involved in their construction. Pottery, burnt timbers, worked flint and other geological materials (especially quartz pebbles) represent the major forms of artefact deposition within ditch fill, especially during later phases. Unfortunately, the largely acidic soil conditions across the site are not conducive to the survival of bone, so it remains unknown whether disassembled human or animal bodies were also originally incorporated. As with the sites of the South Downs, these artefactual elements would have helped emergent Neolithic societies imprint their own social identity into the landscape and help establish an ideological control beyond the level of the monument. The landscape of the southern coastal plain was no longer totally wild; places were being altered and their significance and meaning rewritten in new and more permanent ways.

Secondary phase (4000-3000 BC)

The secondary phase of monumental construction across the Isle of Man (**91**) is marked by a major new component in the architectural repertoire: the structured mound. As noted above, there are as yet few useful radiocarbon dates for these built forms, other than a single determination of 3360-2920 BC for a feature in the

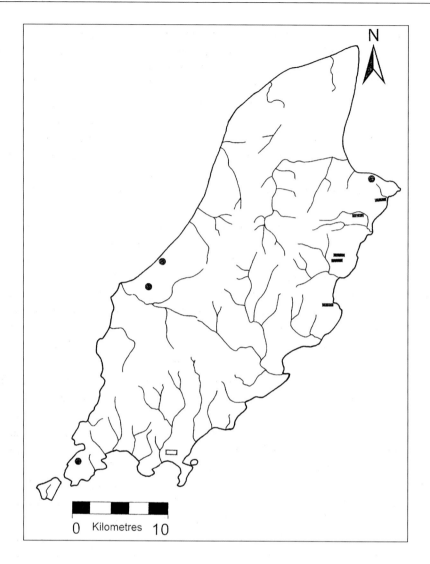

91 Isle of Man: secondary phase (4000-3000 BC); closed circles = circular structured mounds; closed rectangles = linear structured mounds; open rectangle = 'bank barrow' / 'cursus'.

forecourt structure of King Orry's Grave I. This date, when combined with the limited artefactual associations observed within mound structures, may suggest that, as with the South Downs, structured mounds represent a secondary architectural development, perhaps associated with an accelerated form of Neolithic land claim.

The Manx structures, both circular and linear, were not primarily designed as burial monuments or tombs. These were buildings of earth, stone and timber, which externally echoed the form of long and roundhouses. These were monuments which acted as prominent, visible and accessible containers of social identity, designed to imprint new areas of land with the cultural attributes, including the tools, pottery, stone and bone (both animal and human) of particular human communities. As such, both linear and circular forms may be viewed as cultural archives, placing a permanent and inarguable claim over a specific part of land.

The full extent of archival community data stored within structured mounds is unfortunately unknown, the combination of acidic soils and the disturbance generated by antiquarian investigators and earlier 'tomb raiders' having been fairly destructive. Evidence for human bone has, however, been recorded beneath the paving of a chamber at Ballaharra, whilst a small amount of human bone was found in the primary chamber of King Orry's Grave I and bone, including fragments of skull, has been observed from the chambers of Cashtal yn Ard. Pieces of cremated human bone also appear to have derived from some of the chambers investigated at Mull Hill. Animal bone, including the teeth of sheep and cattle, has been found at Ballaharra, whilst Middle Neolithic pottery, flint and other stone including quartz has been retrieved from the sites of Ballaharra, Cashtal yn Ard, King Orry's Grave I and Mull Hill.

The Manx structured mounds were, unlike those of the South Downs, clearly accessible. Any information stored within these buildings could therefore have been reordered, reclassified, reinterpreted and added to at various times through a number of different generations. The position of constricting stones at the entrance to a number of Manx chambers, most notably within the forecourt of King Orry's Grave I, and Cashtal yn Ard, would have served to restrict or limit access to the interior. This may suggest that consultation, reading and reordering of the community archive was purely for those of the slight of build, possibly the immatures within society who were approaching adulthood.

The comparative proliferation of structured mounds across Man at this stage of social development may indicate the increased numbers of people laying claim to specific areas of the more fertile island fringes. Alternatively, as with the chalkland mounds, their construction may reflect the desire to increase both the fertility of the land and of the human group that inhabited it. The majority of linear mounds possess relatively limited view lines, dominating restricted spaces along the coastal fringe of Man, away from the upland massifs. None are intervisible, suggesting that either social groups were gradually becoming more sedentary or they were at least attempting to lay a permanent psychological claim over specific sections of the land. The cutting of shafts and pits at Billown seems to have continued within this secondary phase of monumental architecture, radiocarbon determinations suggesting that most of the archaeologically investigated examples were dug between 3500 and 3100 BC

The development of the Billown enclosure systems appears to have continued during the secondary Neolithic, though the extent and nature of remodelling must, in the light of the limited areas so far exposed, remain unclear. The entrance passage linking the northern and southern circuits was, as noted above, remodelled on a number of occasions, the final stages involving the realignment of ditches, erection of timber posts and laying down of a cobbled surface. Modification of the entranceway also appears to have been accompanied by the construction of a palisade slot just inside the ditch of the southern circuit, possibly to strengthen or better stabilise an existing rampart. The interrupted ditch, where archaeologically examined, would appear to have been recut on at least three occasions, the final phase involving the insertion of upright slabs of local stone.

The elaboration of ditch and rampart circuits may relate to an increase in the number of people using the enclosures. Alternatively it may reflect a desire to re-emphasise and re-dramatise the sites, thus increasing their dominance over the landscape and extending their view across the coastal plain. The recutting of ditches may have been designed, not only to provide sufficient material to increase the height of the banks, but also to rewrite and reorder earlier forms of community identifier already contained within ditch fill. Building of new circuits may have emphasised the involvement of new human communities, and would therefore have to include new forms of social identifier, such as the quartz pebbles noted more commonly from the final phases of site use. Modification of enclosure circuits would also result in new ways of approaching and entering the monument, something that the re-dramatised timber entranceways and palisaded rampart would help to enforce.

The sheer quantity of leaf-shaped flint arrowheads recorded from upper ditch fills of the Billown enclosures, as well as from within areas enclosed, may suggest that at least one phase of the monument came to a violent end. Such an ending may, as suggested for the enclosures of Carn Brae, Crickley Hill and Hambledon Hill, where similar quantities of projectile points have been recorded, have been both abrupt and complete, involving the slighting of rampart circuitry.

A major new architectural component may also have been established on Man within this secondary phase of monument definition, namely the possible secondary Neolithic linear noted from geophysical survey at Billown. The feature, comprising two roughly parallel ditches aligned for a distance of over 120m, has to date only been partially examined, though preliminary results would seem to indicate that it certainly predates the Later Bronze Age. The feature appears to have been designed to overlie a significant portion of the larger, southern enclosure at Billown, in a way reminiscent of the 'cursus' and 'bank barrow' linears sealing deposits at Maiden Castle, Etton, Fornham All Saints and Crickley Hill. If so, and only further excavation will demonstrate this, the Billown linear could represent a further example of the deliberate erasure and rewriting of primary phase Neolithic monumental form.

Final phase (3000–2500 BC)

The final period of Manx Neolithic architectural development is characterised by the decline of enclosure building, shaft cutting and structured linear mounds, most of which appear to have fallen out of use by at least 3000-2500 BC. Circular structured mounds appear to have continued to some degree, though few have been archaeologically examined and so the full sequence and chronology can only be guessed at. Other circular forms of monument are also only hinted at from the archaeological record. A 'henge' of exceptionally small dimensions has been observed from Billown, placed within an entrance break in the former line of the northern early Neolithic enclosure circuit. Other circular interrupted enclosure circuits, hinted at through geophysics and air photographic survey, may also have existed within the immediate vicinity at Billown, Billown Beg and Manammon's chair.

At least two settings of stone uprights may have existed as elliptical circles, one at Billown House, the other at the Braaid. Both sites have been heavily disrupted, Billown in the course of building an ornamental garden and the Braaid by a Norse settlement. The remaining stone uprights, most of which are of quartz and concentrate more across the southern half of Man, are of uncertain origin and chronology, though most are likely to date from this final phase of Neolithic monumental building. For what purpose these were set up, and whether they acted originally as sight lines, orientation guides, pathfinders, parts of larger structures (now destroyed), or whether they even remain in their original setting or position, is, in the majority of cases, unknown.

Major features of the final phases of non-domestic Neolithic activity on Man are the so-called 'flat cemeteries' containing scatters of small pits, some of which contain pottery ('earth fast jars'), and cremated bone (presumably human). Good examples of these 'flat cemeteries' are represented by sites at Ballateare, Killeaba, Ballaharra and possibly also at Billown (**colour plate 24**). Carbon preserved on the outside of pottery at Ballateare has provided radiocarbon determinations of between 2700-2200 BC, whilst dates from Ballaharra suggest a range between 2930-2600 BC. Though such sites are predominantly viewed as cemeteries, they could, in the sometimes significant absence of human burial, perhaps more plausibly be viewed as a form of Later Neolithic cultural archive. It may be that by the third millennium BC, the main way that human society imprinted the land with a specific identity was through the placing of 'earth fast jars', some containing bone. There was no longer the need for costly (or time consuming) pieces of monumental architecture.

The decline of Neolithic monumental architecture on Man coincides with the appearance, in the archaeological record, of significant areas of semi-permanent settlement. By this stage human society does not appear to have required defined anchor points or obvious symbols of dominance within their landscape. Perhaps there had been a significant shift in thinking or perhaps an absence of major migration into the island in some way ensured that monumental architecture was unnecessary. Whatever the case, from the third millennium BC we see more evidence of well-dispersed, relatively small scale, sedentary communities, relying ever more upon agricultural and industrial forms of production. The ideological battle between humans and the wild was over; the natural world had been domesticated.

ORKNEY

The Orkney archipelago consists of around 40 individual islands and over 20 islets covering 969 square kilometres. The main 13 islands that comprise Orkney are Rousay, Westray, Papa Westray, North Ronaldsay, Eday, Sanday, Stronsay, Shapinsay, Burray, South Ronaldsay, Flotta, Hoy and the Mainland. Much of the Orcadian visible land mass comprises Red Sandstone covered with boulder clay. The lower beds of the Sandstone produce grey flagstones, an exceptionally high quality building material.

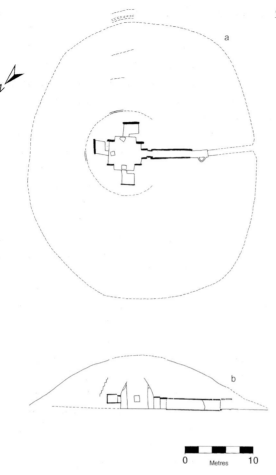

92 Maes Howe: plan (a) and section (b) through the circular stone-structured mound that has given its name to the 'Maes Howe group'. Redrawn from Davidson and Henshall 1989

0   Metres   10

Much of the local topography is fairly low lying, hills seldom rising over 200m above sea level, though the high points of Hoy attain a maximum height of 480m. Spectacular cliffs exist along the western edges of Hoy, Mainland and Westray, whilst the northern island series possesses elongated sandy beaches. Flint occurs both within some of the boulder clays and as beach pebbles.

Forms of monumental architecture

The Neolithic monumental architecture of Orkney is, like that of Man, dominated by what are traditionally interpreted as tombs or burial monuments. These structures have variously been classified and categorised as chambered tombs, stalled tombs, long cairns, rectangular cairns, round cairns, short-horn cairns, Orkney-Cromarty-type chambered cairns, Bookan type tombs and Maes Howe type tombs. For the purpose of this discussion two broad categories of mound structure only will be discussed; linear and circular/oval.

These distinctions are usually clear from the outside of a particular structure, but are unfortunately sometimes less obvious once the interior has been revealed. The oval cairn at Isbister, for example, contains a stalled chamber with side cells, whilst the compartmentalised side chambers of Bookan appear almost as an evolutionary mid-point between cells and stalls (hence occasional use of the phrase 'Bookan-style'). Linear forms usually possess a single, elongated chamber, divided into compartments by the use of multiple stone uprights set along the main axis of the chamber, often referred to as 'stalled'. Circular or oval cairns on Orkney can possess stalled or 'Bookan-style' chambers, though a more distinctive form in larger examples is the more complex internal arrangement, with central chamber and side cells, approached by a single passage of restricted dimensions. These are often referred to as being of 'Maes Howe' type (**92**).

Some 79 sites have been identified as potential Neolithic structured mounds from Orkney. A total of 46 mounds are circular (of which 12 are of 'Maes Howe' type, four are of 'Bookan' type and 26 are stalled), 23 are linear (19 possessing stalled chambers) and 10 are of uncertain affiliation or date. The definite circular or oval cairn structures comprise Bigland Round, Bookan, Burgar, Calf of Eday NW, Calf of Eday SE, Cubbie Roo's Burden, Cuween Hill, Eday Church, Eday Manse, Fara, Faraclett Head East, Faraclett Head West, Fitty Hill, Grice Ness, Helliar Holm, Head of Work 2, Hesta Head, Holm of Papa Westray Centre, Holm of Papa Westray South, Holy Kirk, the Howe, Hoxa Hill, Huntersquoy, Iphs, Isbister, Kierfea Hill, Knowe of Craie, Knucker Hill, Lamb Ness, Maes Howe, Mount Maesry, Nev Hill, Newan, Onziebist, Pierowall, Powdykes, Quanterness, Quoyness, Quoys, Sandhill Smithy, Swona, Taverseoe Tuick, Unstan, Vere Point, Vinquoy Hill and Wideford Hill.

Definite rectangular, or linear, cairn structures comprise Bigland Long, Blackhammer, Braeside, Burray, Calf of Eday Long, Duncan's Geo, Earl's Knoll, Hacksness, Head of Work 1, Holm of Papa Westray North, Kelsburgh, Knowe of Lairo, Knowe of Lingro, Knowe of Ramsay, Knowe of Rowiegar, Knowe of Yarso, Korkquoy, Midhowe, Point of Cott, Redland North, Redland South, Staney Hill and Tres Ness. Sites of uncertain form comprise Holm of Huip, Linkataing, Rose Ness, Stebb Hill, Stones of Via, Tofts Ness, Trenabie, Vestra Fiold, Wart of Kirbister and Withebeir. The so-called 'rock cut tomb' of Dwarfie Stane, generally cited as a Neolithic monument, is not considered here as there is as yet no positive proof that it dates from this period. With the exception of the monumental 'domestic' structures, such as those recorded from Skara Brae which are discussed below, Neolithic architecture on Orkney is confined to the secondary phase monuments such as stone uprights and 'henges'.

Primary phase (3600–3000 BC)

As with the radiocarbon chronologies derived for the South Downs and the Isle of Man, that generated for the Orcadian Neolithic is unfortunately only fragmentary. There remains, furthermore, a significant question mark over the reliability of a

93 Orkney: primary phase (3600-3000 BC); closed circles = circular structured mounds; closed rectangles = linear structured mounds.

number of dates generated before the 1980s, when sampling strategies were somewhat unfocused. Much work, especially that conducted by the Orkney Archaeological Institute, has however been undertaken in recent years to resolve dating issues, and it is hoped that a clearer picture of Orcadian chronology will soon emerge.

The primary stage of architectural development on Orkney (**93**) would, from radiocarbon determinations, appear to have been the linear stalled cairn. Survey and excavation on Orkney has yet to produce evidence of alternative Early Neolithic structural form such as the enclosure or shaft. Furthermore, radiocarbon determinations produced from within linear stone-structured mounds suggest a date range that is broadly comparable with the construction of the earliest linear forms on Man and across the South Downs, suggesting that the primary phase Orcadian Neolithic was contemporary with the secondary developments in these areas. Further excavation and examination may of course disprove this observation, but the comparatively late establishment of Neolithic architecture on Orkney may well have affected the way in which monument form developed here, a point we shall return to below.

Human bone, recovered from the chambers within the Point of Cott, Papa Westray North and Isbister, has provided dates of 3630-3570 BC, 3340-3220 BC, and 3370-2920 BC respectively, for the earliest phases of human bone deposition within these mounds. How the additional and, as yet, largely undated, linear stone-structured mounds fitted into this primary phase, is unclear. The recorded artefactual evidence, however, small though it undoubtedly is, does seem to indicate that most linear cairns, especially those with stalled chambers, were also constructed on Orkney within the time period 3600-3000 BC.

The placing and repositioning of skeletal material within mounds may have continued for some significant time over many generations. The final determinations for human bone recovered from Papa Westray North and Isbister, for example, are 2880-2470 BC and 2460-2000 BC respectively. These dates would, if taken at face value, imply either that significant access to chambers was provided for almost 1,000 years, or the earliest deposition of bone in the mounds included material that had already been curated for some significant time. We may never know the answer to this conundrum, though the artefactual evidence recovered, especially the flint and pottery, seems to suggest that the earlier dates are more reflective of the initial phases of activity.

The basic design of the 'stalled tomb', as many have already noted, is clearly linked to the design and construction of other Orcadian Neolithic buildings. The house structure from the Knap of Howar is a particular case in point, being rectangular with rounded corners, the internal space divided into three segments by paired slabs of upright stone and approached by two short passageways. The usual interpretation of these similarities in basic constructional form is that 'the tomb' represented 'a house for the dead'. It may be more profitable, however, to view the linear stone-chambered mound as deliberately reflecting more domestic forms of architecture precisely because it was designed to house the community archive and not simply because it was a type of family vault or tomb.

Orcadian social identity, unlike that recorded from lowland Britain, appears to have centred predominantly upon the human component. Thus, although we see animal, bird and fish bone, pottery, flint and other geological material occurring within chambers, the human element appears to have been fundamental. This may have been due to a different ideological perspective to that of the South Downs or Man, either on behalf of the indigenous hunter-gatherer population or of new colonising groups. Alternatively, it may be a reflection of the comparatively late date for the inception of Neolithic monumental architecture on Orkney.

It has already been noted that the first Neolithic structures on the archipelago appear to date from 3600-3000 BC, a time when secondary elements were impacting upon the landscapes of the South Downs and Man. Perhaps the absence of an earlier Orcadian Neolithic meant that any new colonising groups had no previous or ancestral monument framework on which to hang their new architecture. There had been no previous attempt to domesticate the natural world, therefore the Neolithic equivalent of Year Zero commenced with the structured mound. Absence of earlier forms of social archive may have meant that the new community markers, necessary if the untamed Orcadian landscapes were to be imprinted with the identifiable seed of the new group, had to emphasise the human component. Increased reliance on the actual bodies and body parts of the new order could have strengthened the potency of land claim, ensuring that the wild could successfully (and speedily) be tamed.

Such a theory could also serve to explain the density of stone-structured mounds across Orkney, especially across Westray, Eday, Stronsay and Rousay. Hoy (with the removal of the anomalous 'Dwarfie Stane') is the only major island within the Orcadian archipelago that does not possess any form of structured mound. This may be a reflection of its distinctive landform, as today Hoy is the highest and most barren of the island group, comprised almost entirely of moorland, or it may just be that the focus of Neolithic monumental construction and domestication was, for whatever reason, concentrated elsewhere.

The majority of passageways into Orcadian stone-structured mounds faced out in a south-easterly direction. Such an orientation may well have been due to the deliberate attempt to focus attention towards the midwinter solstice, a point after which the length of daylight hours steadily begins to increase. J. Davidson and A. Henshall note that the solstice was understandably important for 'agrarian communities in northern latitudes', marking as it does a turning point in the yearly cycle and a vital time for those concerned with the organised production of food.

Many of the stone-structured mounds of Orkney possess a topographical placement similar to those of the South Downs and Man in that they appear to have been sited to appear impressive within a comparatively restricted block of land. Iphs and Fitty Hill, for example, are positioned on hill spurs, below the crest of high points, whilst the mounds of Cuween Hill and Kierfea Hill occur upon particularly steep sections of the landscape. Large numbers of sites are positioned close to the sea (which admittedly may not be too significant for an island group), though many, including Blackhammer, Grice Ness, Knowe of Lairo and Knowe of Rowiegar, possess outstanding prominence only if viewed from the sea or from a neighbouring island. In this respect, structured mounds may have been important markers for those wishing to progress from the sea via certain proscribed routes, or they may have possessed a more basic purpose as a monumental sign of land ownership and authority.

Final phase (3000-2000 BC)

The final phase of Neolithic architectural development across Orkney (**94**) was marked by a new type of large and structurally complex form of circular mound. Such structures are, as already noted, often referred to as being of 'Maes Howe type',

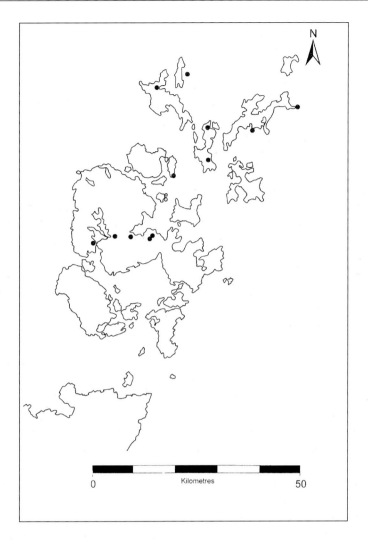

94 Orkney: final phase (3000-2000 BC); closed circles = circular structured mounds.

after the most famous monument of its class investigated on the Mainland. The radiocarbon chronology is somewhat sparse, though reliable determinations of 3020–2710 BC and 3040–2860 BC have been made for human bone recovered from sites at Quanterness and Quoyness.

'Maes Howe' style stone-structured mounds (**95**) appear unique to Orkney. Their positioning, across the centre of Mainland and on, or at, the margins of, Westray, Holm of Papa Westray (west of Papa Westray), Egilsay (west of Rousay), Eday and Sanday, to the north, may indicate an intensification of land claim at certain key points. The most significant aspect of the 'Maes Howe' style of circular stone-structured mound would appear to lie in the elaborate way in which internal space was organised and manipulated. Colin Richards, in particular, has commented upon how

161

95 Maes Howe: the great circular stone-structured mound. Derek Russell

progress through the restricted passageways of Maes Howe affects the way in which the central chamber, 'quite probably the highest enclosed space ever experienced by Neolithic Orcadians', may be appreciated.

The passage linking central chamber with the outside world represents the clearest (and indeed most emphatic) way in which Neolithic society could remove itself from the real and comforting; the ultimate development in the process of isolation and separation as evidenced within the shafts and stone-structured mounds of the South Downs and Man. The length of the 'Maes Howe' type passages, as with the galleries extending from shafts and flint mines could, in Richard's words, mark 'a single prolonged period of liminality'. Those entering the chambers of a 'Maes Howe' type round mound were making a significant move away from the familiar and into the unknown. They were about to access the community database; the collective store of everything that made them who they were and legitimised their tenure of the land. They were moving from one world to another; from immaturity to adulthood. This was a rite of passage in every sense of the word.

The type of separation evident at Maes Howe is not just restricted to the structured mound, but is also clear at another site on Orkney, namely Skara Brae (**96**). Skara Brae has, since its excavation, been treated as a simple, two-phase domestic settlement. As a cluster of stone built structures, broadly contemporary in date with the building of the Maes Howe style structured mounds, there are however a number of significant parallels between the two types of site. There is of course the basic similarity of structural form, with both sites possessing rounded exteriors and square interiors. There are the side cells (**97**) leading from the single, central space. There are the low entrance points and restricted linking passageways.

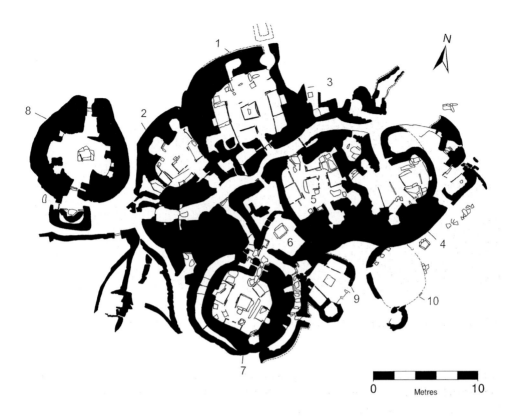

96 Skara Brae: plan of 'huts' 1-10 as exposed through excavation. Structures 1, 3, 4 and 5 represent the primary phase; 2, 6, 7 and 8, secondary additions. Compare this plan with the basal gallery plan for the Cissbury shafts. Redrawn from Childe 1931

There are other aspects of construction and artefact deposition within the Skara Brae site that make the simple interpretation of 'settlement' somewhat difficult to sustain. Hut 7, for example, is approached by a long passage of restricted dimension, whilst access through the door of the 'hut' appears to have been controlled from the outside. Whatever was originally contained within this structure could be locked in: an arrangement quite unlike any other house at Skara Brae. The passage leading to the 'hut', as well as a number of stones within the walls of the building, carried a distinct series of linear incisions. The bodies of two, fully articulated, adult females were furthermore found beneath the western stone 'bed' of the 'hut', whilst a mass of artefacts, including the skull of a bull, pottery and stone tools, was also recorded.

The density of artefacts recovered from hut 7 far exceeds that found elsewhere on site (though a large amount of flint was noted from within Hut 8). This material assemblage was interpreted by the excavator as a 'morass of filth . . . that the inhabitants were too lazy to remove'. Alternatively, and perhaps more plausibly given the form and layout of hut 7, the assemblage may be viewed as a form of structured cultural archive akin to those recovered from mounds, shafts and enclosure ditches.

Even if the rest of the Skara Brae site was originally a settlement in the conventional sense (something which is by no means certain), access to the hut 7 archive, through a restricted and highly decorated passage and externally re-sealable door slab, would have emphasised isolation and separation as effectively as the chambered mound or shaft gallery. The linear incisions found within the hut 7 passage, and over the entrance points to chambers and side cells (**98**), may suggest a further link to another type of Neolithic feature associated with dislocation from the familiar: the subterranean galleries of shafts. Similar patterns of lines, chevrons and lozenges have already been noted occupying broadly similar positions, close to or over gallery openings, at the flint mine sites Cissbury, Harrow Hill and Grimes Graves. In fact the plan of Skara Brae phases 1 and 2, with circular spaces linked by a network of tunnels, does not look dissimilar to the interconnected shafts already noted from Cissbury and may well have performed a broadly similar role within Neolithic society with regard

98 Skara Brae: a series of linear incisions recorded from above the SE cell within 'hut' 7. Compare this (both in basic format and general position) with the linears recorded from above the basal galleries of shafts at Cissbury, Harrow Hill and Grimes Graves. Redrawn from Ritchie 2000

to the movement through liminal space. It may be unwise to speculate further at this stage, though it is evident that Skara Brae requires a full and complete reassessment for a simple, 'domestic settlement' it clearly is not.

Another, no less important, series of components within the architectural repertoire of Later Neolithic Orkney is the 'henge' and circle of stone uprights recorded at Stenness (**99**) and the circle of stones comprising the Ring of Brodgar. A single radiocarbon date obtained from the ditch of the Stenness 'henge' suggests a constructional range of between 3300 and 2650 BC for the monument which, although quite early for the 'henge' class as interpreted by modern archaeologists, appears in keeping with structural development elsewhere in northern Scotland.

The Stenness 'henge' was built upon ground which today is a peninsula on Mainland, between the Loch of Harray and the Loch of Stenness, whilst the Ring of Brodgar exists to the immediate north-west on the Ness of Brodgar. Today the Stenness peninsula and the Ness of Brodgar are separated by a short section of water, but in Neolithic times it is probable that there was a land bridge connecting the two. It is this area of land at the 'heart' of Mainland, flanked on either side by water and framed by the surrounding hills (of both Mainland and Hoy to the south west), that archaeologists have referred to as 'the ceremonial centre of Orkney'. The earliest periods of construction in the area relate to the structured mounds of the primary

99 The Stones of Stenness: the fully restored stone upright group. Derek Russell

phase Neolithic, such as Bookan, Unstan and Staney Hill, but from 3000 BC the construction of Maes Howe, Brodgar and Stenness seems to emphasise further the significance of place, reinforcing themes of domestication and control.

Stenness, with its inverted rampart sequence, represents the natural world in microcosm; the wild and untamed held captive and controlled. Internal stone uprights monumentalise the ring-beam, the primary foundation of a round house. In these terms, the Stones of Stennes and the Ring of Brodgar represent, in basic terms, the symbolic skeleton of a house; the house being important as centre of human life and the community, focus of daily activities and ultimate symbol of domestication. Here, connections to the past, present, future and the heavens above are made evident through architecture, alignment with key astronomical events and association with earlier structural form. Their construction marks the climax of the ideological struggle between human society on Orkney and the natural order of things. As with the land-scapes of Stonehenge and Avebury, the monuments at the centre of the Orcadian Mainland represent the final stages of domestication; control of nature made evident through the brutal and unyielding application of monumental architecture.

8 Conclusions: structuring the land

As noted at the very beginning of this book, the switch from a lifestyle dependent upon the hunting and gathering of foodstuffs to one reliant upon a single harvest is neither a given evolutionary path for humankind, nor an easy one. Quite why human populations made that crucial and all embracing sociological change is a question that has dogged antiquarians, archaeologists, anthropologists and historians for some considerable time, without, it would seem, ever reaching a satisfactory conclusion.

In the early years of the twentieth century, interpretation of the Neolithic appeared easy: farming arrived because it was brought by colonists arriving with ploughs, domesticated cereals, cattle and sheep, new artefacts and a thoroughly new outlook on life. How these postulated migratory bands of farmers were viewed by modern science depended on the political climate of the time. Sometimes they were seen as enlightened missionaries, bringing the word of farming to poor impoverished Mesolithic hunters. At other times, they were seen as an aggressive group of invaders, stamping out or enslaving the inadequately armed indigenous hunter-gatherer population.

The invasion hypothesis was popular in the years leading up to the Second World War. At this time, across Europe, there was a very tangible fear of invasion and with it a feeling of mistrust or suspicion of all that was considered alien, strange or foreign. Maps drawn throughout the 1930s, purporting to show the spread of agriculture across Europe, look instead as if they are plotting carefully planned military advances. Directional arrows become the march of armoured regiments. Artefacts are weapons. Site names become battlefields.

Distinct objects and discrete forms of archaeological site were also, at this time, credited to specific cultures. Thus we read of 'the Windmill Hill Culture' for a particular kind of Early Neolithic society, or 'Beaker culture' for the end of the Neolithic or 'La Tène Culture' for the Early Iron Age. Using a very traditional approach to archaeological artefacts and sites, it is easy to argue that each defined 'culture' is the manifestation of a specific ethnic group. Most early archaeological attempts at explaining change within defined cultures interpreted the arrival of new material forms in terms of invasion or folk migration. After all, did not Julius Caesar, arguably the first useful historical source for north-western Europe, talk in great terms of the mass folk migrations of the mid-late first century BC across late Iron Age Gaul? If migrations were commonplace then, why not 4000 years earlier?

This view of enforced acculturation, or aggressive cultural change, has, since the 1960s, undergone a gradual and significant revision. The New Archaeologies that evolved during that period and into the 1970s stepped away from the invasion hypothesis, which appeared to provide a rather simplistic take on the evidence, and progressively replaced it with more subtle concepts. The advent of the Neolithic, it was argued, was due to a more permissive form of cultural and ideological change. People changed their lifestyles for a whole variety of different reasons and at different times through choice, not because they were forced to.

Change occurred through social interaction, be it from co-existence, emulation, competition, invention, religion, the transmission of ideas, the ceremonial exchange of valuable goods or the flow of commodities through trade. There was no need to explain the Neolithic in terms of war, migration or conquest. An example of how fixed the new view has become within archaeological literature may be seen in the most recent review of Neolithic Sussex provided by Peter Drewett in 2001:

> It is now widely accepted that there was no major immigration of agri-
> cultural peoples into Britain and that certain Neolithic elements were
> adopted by indigenous Mesolithic peoples more readily than others,
> including perhaps, the full adoption of agriculture based on the central
> European model.

The archaeological evidence, as it is presently interpreted, would imply a passive change on behalf of the indigenous Mesolithic population. The hunter-gatherers dropped their spears and picked up ploughs. Unfortunately we are still no closer to understanding why.

Perhaps everyone has been looking at the problem from the wrong angle. In the last few years there has been an increased awareness within archaeological circles that the Neolithic was not just about the arrival of farming; it was also about architecture. In fact, as argued at the beginning of this book, though monuments are often viewed as being secondary to farming (as if without the new form of food production monuments would not exist), doubts have already been expressed with regard to the timing of architecture and agriculture in Britain. Richard Bradley, for example, observed in 1993 that:

> We talk about farming, as if monument building was only a side-effect of
> agriculture. We may have asked why monuments were built: we are told
> how their building was financed

The Neolithic was a time when monuments were necessary; a time when certain humans were trying to dominate and control the natural world. To ask which came first, agriculture then monuments or agriculture after monuments (perhaps to feed those actively engaged in their construction and upkeep) seems, on the face of it, ultimately pointless, for both are bound together. They are both part of the same process of domination and domestication.

So where does this leave the 'invasion versus migration of ideas' hypotheses? So far the arguments have tended to fluctuate between two extremes:

1 The introduction of the Neolithic through invasion and the complete replacement of hunter-gatherer society by an aggressive group of monument-building farmers.
2 The introduction of farming and monument building as ideas which were gradually incorporated into the lifestyle of hunter-gatherers through passive acculturation.

What if it were neither?

Recently, the study of human genetic material, our DNA, has come under scrutiny to see if it may provide answers to the why, how and wither of the Neolithic in Britain. The study is still in its early days, but the work of Bryan Sykes and his colleagues at the University of Oxford upon mitochondrial DNA has produced some interesting preliminary results. The data, it would appear, assuming that one was looking for clear signs of the migration of farming/monument building groups into Europe from the Middle East, suggests that though there were new arrivals at exactly the right time 'it was not an overwhelming replacement'. In other words, the DNA evidence seems to be implying that the Neolithic was a combination of some new people AND some new ideas and not explicitly one or the other.

Is this is a cop out?

Not necessarily. Mesolithic society is often viewed as being distinct from that of the Neolithic in that hunter-gatherers were essentially mobile, tracking animals and searching for foodstuffs along seasonal paths through the landscape. Neolithic society is usually thought of as being sedentary: fixed groups at fixed points in the land tending crops, building monuments and watching over their herd. To some extent this is basically true having established a farm one is hardly likely to leave it for any length of time but the observation masks a more subtle social pattern.

Unlike hunters, farmers colonise. This is a point that often overlooked by archaeologists and historians, but not anthropologists. Hugh Brody in his essay on hunter-gatherer society *The Other Side of Eden* makes the observation that

> Farmers appear to be settled, and hunters to be wanderers. Yet a look at how ways of life take shape across many generations reveals that it is the agriculturalists, with their commitment to specific farms and large numbers of children, who are forced to keep moving, resettling, colonising new lands. Hunter-gatherers, with their reliance on a single area, are profoundly settled. As a system, over time, it is farming, not hunting, that generated 'nomadism'.

Hunter-gatherer societies rely on the natural resources of the lands they occupy. They may modify these lands to some extent, through the construction of traps, shelters and houses and the removal of trees through selective burning, but they do not generate the changes of the sort made by the farmer. They do not cut down large swathes of forest. They do not break up the soil for planting. They do not keep large herds of animals. They do not create permanent boundaries. They do not have large numbers of children.

169

It is possibly the last point, that of family size, that is the most crucial from the perspective of hunter-gatherer success and survival. Hunter-gatherers do not need large families, in fact great numbers of children can be a positive hindrance for social groups that are constantly on the move within a specific landscape. Availability of natural resources may also affect the size of hunting groups and anthropological studies seem to agree that most groups do not desire more than two children at any one time. Farming groups, on the other hand, do not have such a limit. More children means more help in running the farm; more people to keep nature firmly under control. There is a biological reason for this population increase too, as Bryan Sykes has observed, in his book *the Seven Daughters of Eve*

> This was partly due to a more consistent source of nutrition, but also because the new cereals, high in carbohydrates, removed the hormonal check on ovulation during lactation that had ensured a long gap between children.

More children eventually results in further colonisation. As the descendants of the first farmers grow into adulthood, they can either stay put and share the land, thus stretching the resource base, or they can move on and establish farms of their own. Brody refers to this inevitability as 'the curses of Genesis' noting that

> In the history of European civilisation, as in the history of agricultural cultures, the combination of settlement, large families and movement has resulted in a more or less relentless colonial frontier. An agricultural people can never rest – as farming families, as a lineage – in one place. They love home, but they also love the leaving of it. They celebrate stability and security, and yet they are committed to movement.

Hunter-gatherers, once established in a given area, do not tend to stray far. To leave one's territory is to risk one's very existence. In a war of colonisation and survival, then, it is the farmers, with their ever-increasing population and desire for land, who will consistently emerge triumphant.

I would like to suggest here that the change from Mesolithic to Neolithic, from hunter-gatherer to architecturalist/agriculturalist, was indeed one of folk migration and invasion, but not in the traditional sense. Invasions are, by their very nature, emotive issues, implying the movement of peoples and death on a large scale. Historically we can chart many such dramatic events across Europe. Unfortunately, from the perspective of interpretation, invasions do not, on the whole, involve the sudden and complete replacement of one population by another. So, although they often accelerate the process of cultural change within a given area, invasions are themselves archaeologically ephemeral.

Even the most dramatic of conquests, for example that of the Britain by Rome in AD 43, has left no conclusive trace as a specific event within the archaeological record. Without the benefit of (near) contemporary written sources stating that 'in a particular year, a few thousand heavily armoured psychopaths landed in Britain and set about killing everyone', we would not know that there ever had been direct military contact between Britain and Rome. Archaeological evidence is just not that precise.

The problem is that, in our chosen example of AD 43, certain elements of Iron Age society in Britain had already been infected by Roman culture before the Roman military attempted to make conquest a reality. In other words, though archaeology can tell us that different people in Britain were being Romanized, at different times, coins appearing by the early first century BC, new pottery forms by the mid-first century BC, wine by the late first century BC, forts by the early first century AD, towns by the mid-first century AD and villas by the late first century and early second century AD, it can never tell us why. Neither is it very useful at explaining why so many people, particularly those in western and northern Britain, remained wholly unaffected by the process.

We also possess problems when trying to explain what the term 'Roman' actually means in the context of invasion: 'conquered by' or 'influenced by' Rome? Similarly, what does the term 'British' actually mean within the Late Iron Age? This problem is compounded by the fact that there was no such thing as a single 'British Culture' prior to the industrial revolution. The diverse geographies of Britain, when combined with issues of communication and trade, probably meant that throughout prehistory, parts of Britain had more in common with neighbouring areas of France, Belgium and the Netherlands than with other parts of the same island. If we define the terms 'Roman' and 'Briton' to mean things that were more common to the Roman Empire or to Britain then we hit the problem that some Britons, or at least those who could afford to, were drinking wine, eating Mediterranean fish sauce, using olive oil, eating from Gaulish tableware, decorating their homes with German marble and, for all we know, cutting their hair short, shaving, wearing togas and speaking Latin, well before the magic date of AD 43.

The basic problem is that when we hear the word 'invasion', whether it is associated with events occurring in 55 BC, 54 BC, AD 43, AD 367, AD 410, AD 793, or AD 1066, there is an obvious implication of mass population replacement: that one set of people conquered and exterminated the former inhabitants of a given territory, totally replacing the indigenous culture with their own. War and conquest, loathsome though they undoubtedly are, in the great modern scheme of things are invariably followed by something far worse: genocide. The total eradication of a people, their cultural traits, their traditions and ways of life, euphemistically referred to today as 'ethnic cleansing' was, thankfully, rarely achievable within ancient society. The army of Rome invaded Britain in AD 43 and killed a large number of Britons in the process, but no there was no attempt to replace British society with one born and bred in the Mediterranean.

For most people living in southern Britain in the mid-first century AD, if there were not unfortunate enough to get in the way of the advancing Roman army, then life immediately post invasion would have continued pretty much the same way as before. Crops were grown, livestock fed, metals worked, taxes paid. Admittedly, taxes may now have been paid to a new style of administrator (possibly the old tribal chief in a different dress), but the basic rhythms of life would have been the same. Sudden change, following any invasion, is reserved for those who hold power. Following the Roman, Saxon, Viking or Norman Conquest, it was the indigenous ruling elite, be they Kings, Queens, Dukes, Generals or Earls, who were most affected. They either died on the battlefield, or they modified their beliefs so as to find their place within the new order. For the bulk of the population, change was a more gradual process.

Immediately following the Roman military invasion, the Briton on his or her farm may have decided that the best way to succeed was to adopt the customs and fashions of the conquerors; the new social elite. Gradually more togas were worn and more dinner parties hosted. Hair was cut short, swords discarded, and new houses, with frankly bizarre forms of internal decoration, constructed. Children were given nice new Latin names. Gradually any previous cultural distinctiveness would fade. Archaeologically, these people were no longer Iron Age Britons, they were Roman, or Romano-Britons.

Similar forms of cultural change may be detected around the time the collapse of the Roman administration in Britain during the fourth and fifth centuries AD. This is a time of de-Romanization. There were less trade items originating from the Mediterranean, coin supply decreased, there was an end to buildings of stone and mortar, town life decreased in importance, villas came to an end, Roman-style art-forms diminished, and there is a move away from official forms of Christianity. At the same time, the eastern seaboard of Britain became gradually more 'Germanized'. More Germanic style artefacts appeared in settlements and in graves, there was a greater use of cremation in burial, and the arrival of new Germanic forms of religion, fashion and language. The western seaboard of Britain, less affected by trade with Germany, Denmark and Scandinavia, appears to have been more dominated by contact with Ireland and western France. In other words, it became progressively 'Celticized' (an ugly word, but useful). There were more Celtic-style artefacts appearing in settlements and graves, a greater emphasis on fortified enclosures, a greater use of inhumation in burial, and the re-emergence of Celtic forms of religion, fashion and language.

During the fourth and fifth centuries AD, so history tells us, Britain was invaded by the Angles, Saxons, Jutes, Scots and Picts. These migrant groups gave their name to those areas that they settled and dominated. Hence the Angles gave us East Anglia and England, the Scots Scotland and the Saxons Sussex, Essex and Wessex. During these times of invasion, neither in the eastern nor the western areas of Britain do we possess archaeological evidence for mass population displacement, or for the brutal extermination of previous life patterns by the newcomer. It may well have happened, but archaeology alone cannot provide the necessary evidence. We do however possess significant archaeological evidence for gradual cultural replacement; Britons previously infected with Roman culture slowly began to adopt new and different forms of popular fashion. Archaeologically they ceased to be Romano-Britons and instead became either Germanic or Celtic-Britons.

So, if it is true in the absence of written sources, we would see the events of AD 43 and 410 as part of a gradual process of passive acculturation, the Britons slowly adopting Mediterranean, German and 'Celtic' traits, and not part of a direct military assault, what then of earlier periods in *pre*-history? Could we explain, say, the arrival of metals, of Beaker pottery, of henges and, rather more crucially, of agriculture and architecture, as part of a great invasion? I do not wish here to hark back to the ideas of early twentieth-century archaeologists, whose theories compare the arrival of farming to a complex agricultural blitzkrieg, but I do not feel that the idea of a folk migration should be totally rejected.

If the Neolithic were a process of domination, of land and of nature, would it not seem plausible that the instigators of that domination were newcomers; part of a new social elite? In such a model, there would be no wiping out of backward hunter-gatherers by progressive farmers, but the attempt to dominate new lands, by way of ploughing fields, domesticating animals and building architecture, by a small group of new people. As has always been the case, the bulk of the population base may have remained unchanged from the Mesolithic, but those seeking to control the landscape were beginning to visualise and modify the land around them in strange and varied new ways.

The architectural forms that seem to explode into Britain during the late fifth and early fourth millennia BC are part of this desire to reorder and dominate the land. As such they may be viewed as the product of colonisation, a new social elite, a new order. This is not the attempted conquest of Britain, say in the sense that Claudius or William the Bastard would have understood, but the gradual accumulation of new lands and the definition of fledgling territories. Part of this colonisation was undoubtedly the product of a migration across the Channel, not by a marauding army of heavily armoured, well-disciplined fighting farmers, nor a roaming band of architectural evangelists bring the word of building to the pagan, but a gradual influx of small groups of settlers looking for new landscapes to inhabit, control and call their own.

Some of these social groups may have been well connected by ties of family, others were not. Some of their new ideas may have been taken up and redesigned by indigenous hunting groups keen to bring their own identity and sense of order to the land. Other groups continued as before. The introduction of new ideas and new products (such as pottery, querns, domesticated animals and plants) into Britain and the development and evolution of farming and of monumental architecture took many generations and was neither planned nor uniform in its application. As a system, over time, however, the 'relentless colonial frontier' of the Neolithic continued to develop natural landscapes on an incremental, though undeniably dramatic, basis. Humans were making their presence felt.

The monuments that define the Earliest Neolithic are clearly part of this desire to dominate and domesticate. The structured mound was easily the most widespread of architectural forms. Most mounds were not built to be seen across vast swathes of land, as many modern monuments are. These were structures designed to dominate a more restricted view line: a valley, river system or plain. These buildings laid claim to a particular block of previously wild land. They took elements of the social group staking that claim, and imprinted them into the ground for eternity. These were symbolic house structures built to hold, or to mark permanently, the very essence of the new community. These were symbols of conquest.

The diverse external form, internal structure and artefactual contents of structured mounds undoubtedly reflects the length of time during which these structures were designed and built and the ways in which particular concepts of domination were transmitted or evolved across the British Isles. Some structures were linear, perhaps because their form had originally evolved in central Europe where timber long houses were far more common than in Britain. Some early structures were circular, possibly reflecting the no doubt different building styles and traditions across Britain. All were designed as the monumental representation of a house. Some mounds were designed to be continually accessible, possibly so that the archive could continually be reordered, re-catalogued and added to. Some mounds, particularly those of lowland Britain, were designed to cover and emphatically seal earlier forms of archive, marking their position in the land for the next generation.

A common feature for all forms of archive was the concept of detachment and isolation from the world of the everyday. The contents of the community database were stored either within a single timber chamber, sometimes subdivided into discrete sections, or multiple stone chambers connected by a passage way. Chambers in both were accessed via an often restricted entrance, marked by an elaborate series of posts or stones. Once in the chamber, whoever was attempting to modify, view or access the archive, would find themselves in a place that was alien, unsettling and strange. It was a world of the super or hyper natural where all the senses were distorted and one could easily become disorientated and confused.

Detachment and isolation are also common features of the shaft. Not all shafts were cut for purely economic gain and, as has already been noted, many involved the movement of people away from the familiar and into a world that, as with the chamber, was dark, unsettling and strange. Galleries were accessed through restricted entrance points. Narrow tunnels often expanded into chambers from which stone could be detached and removed and community markers left to imprint space with the identity of those engaged in the work or staking claim to the land. This combination of restricted space, isolation and the placing of identifiers appears elsewhere in Neolithic Britain, most notably at Skara Brae, a site sometimes interpreted as a 'normal' domestic settlement.

Community identifiers also feature strongly in the ditch cuts of the earliest enclosure systems. These enclosures mark the main settlements, safe zones or central places of the colonising unit. Ramparts were designed to break up and divide the land, creating a space that could be accessed along well defined points of entrance, some of which were marked by elaborate façades and timber posts. Ditch cuts provided the spoil for the ramparts and the space in which to place the pots, bones, flints and other materials that defined and best represented the new community, imprinting their essence deep into the ground. Later circuits of ditch contained new forms of identifier and new ideological ways of expressing the self.

New peoples and new ideas brought different ways of visualising and controlling the land throughout the Neolithic. The ways in which people moved through the territory slowly became more important. View lines to particular landscape features, horizon points or basic astronomical features required better forms of control. A community that could dominate both the worlds of the terrestrial and extra terrestrial was one which could wield all sorts of political, religious, economic and social power. Heavenly cycles (such as sunrise and sunset at key points in the year) and particular annual events (such as the harvest) could now be catalogued, controlled, ordered and recorded. Monuments were redefined and modified, their significance rewritten.

Through the Neolithic, and towards the arrival of the first forms of metal production, the house, the enclosed space and the community marker all remained important features. Subsequent communities continued to place artefacts that were important to them or which best signalled their presence (such as Beaker or Grooved Ware pottery) into the later fill of ditch or shaft cuts. New enclosure forms inverted the sequence of bank and ditch, creating a space that was both 'wild' and 'outside' the community, but which was surrounded and could easily be controlled by it. Through these spaces, view lines and key seasonal or astronomical events could further be manipulated and controlled.

Round mounds gradually overtook linear mounds as the built form of choice at the same time that round houses appeared in the archaeological record. The deposition of important objects that best mark the community (single human skeletons, pottery, flint and, later, metals such as gold and copper) was set at the central hearth point of these new ceremonial forms of house. Other forms of symbolic house structure were generated, most notably the house skeleton or ring beam, made monumental through the use of immense timbers or stone. Through these sites, society could continually manipulate the natural world whilst further monumentalising their achievements and claim to the land and sky (**100**).

Postscript

The Neolithic is today sometimes treated as if it were a great, quasi-spiritual period. Publications or media reports on the archaeological 'fringe' sometimes imply that this was a time of mysticism and astrology; crystals and healing; ley lines and incense. A time when human kind was somehow more in tune with nature and the heavens. A time when humans understood and were a part of the natural order of things.

It was not.

The Neolithic was in fact a time of significant change. It marked the first stages in the control, reordering and domination of nature. It signified the origins of the modern world. Imposing a different order upon the land, through building and the imprinting of human identity, was new and alien. The linear mound, the enclosure and the shaft may look harmonious, mysterious, idyllic and tranquil to us, but to our ancestors these structures were as intrusive and as psychologically shocking as the motorway, airport and nuclear power plant are today. The new buildings created massive scars upon the land; new ideas caused profound shifts in

100 Wiltshire: the landscapes of Britain have now been totally reshaped and reordered by human society. Fields, fences, houses and monuments have, since the Neolithic, systematically eradicated nature to the point that the land is no longer wild. Miles Russell

ideology and human social organisation. Architecture, building projects, large areas of urban settlement, over population, mass deforestation, agriculture, ecological disaster, industrial production, organised religion, pollution, malnutrition, epidemics, war and genocide: the Neolithic is where it all began. Who knows where it will end?

Further reading

The list of publications that follows is not an authoritative bibliography for the British Neolithic. Instead, it provides a summary of the more comprehensive and useful texts for the period and for the themes of monumental architecture developed within this particular work. The list is highly selective, but I feel that it represents a body of work which best reflects the subject under discussion. In an attempt to introduce clarity, I have indicated which publications represent the most useful starting point for those unfamiliar with the subject matter.

PREHISTORY

Recommended introduction

Cunliffe, B. 1993 *Wessex to AD 1000*. Longman. London.

Darvill, T. 1987 *Prehistoric Britain*. Batsford. London.

Hunter, J and Ralston, I. (eds) 1999 *The archaeology of Britain: An introduction from the Upper Palaeolithic to the Industrial Revolution*. Routledge. London.

Megaw, J and Simpson, D. 1988 *Introduction to British Prehistory* (4th edition). Leicester University Press.

Other texts

Barrett, J., Bradley, R. and Green, M. 1991 *Landscapes, Monuments and Society: The prehistory of Cranborne Chase*. Cambridge University Press.

Bradley, R. 1978 *The Prehistoric Settlement of Britain*. Routledge and Kegan Paul. London.

Bradley, R. 1984 *The social foundations of prehistoric Britain*. Longman. London.

Bradley, R. 1993 *Altering the Earth*. Society of Antiquaries of Scotland Monograph 8. Edinburgh.

Bradley, R. 2000 *An Archaeology of Natural Places*. Routledge. London.

Castleden, R. 1983 *The Wilmington Giant: the quest for a lost myth*. Turnstone Press. Wellingborough.

Clark, G. 1953 *Prehistoric England*. The Country Book Club. London.

Crawford, O., and Keiller, A. 1928 *Wessex from the air*. Clarendon Press. Oxford.

Curwen, E. 1954 *The Archaeology of Sussex*. Methuen. London.

Drewett, P., Rudling, D., and Gardiner, M. 1988 *The south-east to AD 1000*. Longman. London.

Darvill, T. 1987 *Prehistoric Gloucestershire*. Alan Sutton. Gloucester.

Darvill, T. 1996 *Prehistoric Britain from the air: a study of space, time and society*. Cambridge University Press.

Higham, N. 1986 *The northern counties to AD 1000*. Longman. London and New York.

Kendrick, T. and Hawkes, C. 1932 *Archaeology in England and Wales 1914-31*. Society of Antiquaries. London.

Reece, R. 1988 *My Roman Britain*. Cotswold Studies. Cirencester.

Ritchie, A. 1995 *Prehistoric Orkney*. Historic Scotland. Batsford.

Sykes, B. 2001 *The Seven Daughters of Eve*. Bantam Press. London.

Taylor, T. 1996 *The prehistory of sex: four million years of human sexual culture*. Fourth Estate. London.

Wickham Jones, C. 1994 *Scotland's First Settlers*. Historic Scotland. Batsford.

THE NEOLITHIC

Recommended introduction

Bradley, R. 1998 *The significance of monuments*. Routledge. London.

Brody, H. 2001 *The Other Side of Eden: Hunter-gatherers, Farmers and the Shaping of the World*. Faber and Faber. London.

Edmonds, M. 1999 *Ancestral geographies of the Neolithic: landscapes, monuments and memory*. Routledge. London.

Pollard, J. 1997 *Neolithic Britain*. Shire. Princes Risborough.

Thomas, J. 1999 *Understanding the Neolithic*. Routledge. London.

Whittle, A. 1996 *Europe in the Neolithic : the creation of new worlds*. Cambridge University Press.

Other texts

Ashmore, P. 1996 *Neolithic and Bronze Age Scotland*. Historic Scotland. Batsford.

Bradley, R., and Edmonds, M. 1993 *Interpreting the axe trade*. Cambridge University Press.

Barrett, J. 1994 *Fragments from Antiquity*. Blackwells. Oxford

Barrett, J. and Kinnes, I. 1988 (eds) *The archaeology of context in the Neolithic and Bronze Age: Recent trends*. University of Sheffield.

Bradley, R., and Gardiner, J. 1984 *Neolithic Studies*. British Archaeological Report 133.

Brodie, N. 1994 *The Neolithic-Bronze Age Transition in Britain: A Critical Review of some Archaeological and Craniological Concepts*. British Archaeological Report 238.

Burgess, C. and Miket, R. (eds) *Settlement and economy in the third and second millennia*. British Archaeological Report 33.

Burrow, S. 1997 *The Neolithic Culture of the Isle of Man: A Study of Sites and Pottery*. British Archaeological Report 263.

Case, H. 1969 Neolithic explanations. *Antiquity* 43, 176-86.

Castleden, R. 1987 *The Stonehenge people*. Routledge. London.

Cooney, G. 2000 *Landscapes of Neolithic Ireland*. Routledge. London.

Childe, G. 1949 The origin of Neolithic culture in Northern Europe. *Antiquity* 23, 129-35.

Darvill, T. and Thomas, J. 1996 (eds) *Neolithic houses in Northwest Europe and beyond*. Oxbow Monograph 57. Oxford.

Edmonds, M. 1995 *Stone tools and society: working stone in Neolithic and Bronze Age Britain*. Batsford. London.

Edmonds, M. and Richards, C. (eds) 1998 *Understanding the Neolithic of north western Europe*. Cruithne Press. Glasgow.

Fraser, D. 1983 *Land and Society in Neolithic Orkney*. British Archaeological Report 117.

Gibson, A., and Simpson, D. (eds) 1998 *Prehistoric ritual and religion: essays in honour of Aubrey Burl*. Sutton Publishing. Stroud.

Hodder, I. 1990 *The domestication of Europe*. Blackwell. Oxford.

Kendall, H. 1917 More about Windmill Hill, Avebury and Grime's Graves. *Proceedings of the Prehistoric Society of East Anglia* 2, 563-75.

Parker Pearson, M, and Richards, C. (eds) 1994 *Architecture and order*. Blackwell. Oxford.

Piggott, S. 1954 *The Neolithic cultures of the British Isles*. Cambridge University Press.

Pitts, M. 2000 *Hengeworld*. Arrow. London.

Ritchie, A. 2000 *Neolithic Orkney in its European Context*. Macdonald Institute Monograph. Cambridge.

Ruggles, C., and Whittle, A. (eds). 1981 *Astronomy and society during the period 4000-1500 BC*. Oxford. British Archaeological Report.

Russell, M. 2001 *The Early Neolithic Architecture of the South Downs*. British Archaeological Report 321.

Sharples, N., and Sheridan, A. 1992 *Vessels for the Ancestors: Essays on the Neolithic of Britain and Ireland*. Edinburgh University Press.

Simpson, D. 1971 *Economy and settlement in Neolithic and Early Bronze Age Britain and Europe*. Leicester University Press.

Thomas, J. 1991 *Rethinking the Neolithic*. Cambridge University Press.

Thomas, J. 1996 *Time, culture and identity: an interpretative archaeology*. Routledge. London.

Tilley, C. 1994 *The phenomenology of landscape: paths, places and monuments*. Berg. Oxford.

Topping, P. (ed) 1997 *Neolithic Landscapes*. Neolithic Studies Group Seminar Papers 2. Oxbow. Oxford.

Whittle, A. 1977 *The Earlier Neolithic of Southern England and its Continental Background*. British Archaeological Report 35.

Whittle, A. 1985 *Neolithic Europe: a survey*. Cambridge University Press.

Whittle, A. 1988 *Problems in Neolithic archaeology*. Cambridge University Press.

STRUCTURED MOUNDS

Recommended introduction

Ashbee, P. 1970 *The earthen long barrow in Britain*. Dent. London.

Hedges, J. 1984 *Tomb of the Eagles: A Window on Stone Age Tribal Britain*. Tempvs Repartvm. Oxford

Kinnes, I. 1992 *Non-Megalithic Long Barrows and Allied Structures in the British Neolithic*. British Museum Occasional Paper.

Royal Commission on the Historical Monuments of England 1979 *Long Barrows in Hampshire and the Isle of Wight*. Her Majesty's Stationery Office: London.

Woodward, A. 2000 *British Barrows: A matter of Life and Death*. Tempus. Stroud.

Other texts

Ashbee, P. 1966 The Fussell's Lodge long barrow excavations 1957. *Archaeologia* 100, 1–80.

Ashbee, P, Smith, I., and Evans, J. 1979 Excavations of three long barrows near Avebury, Wiltshire. *Proceedings of the Prehistoric Society* 45, 207–300.

Barber, J. 1997 *The Excavation of a Stalled Cairn at the Point of Cott, Westray, Orkney*. Scottish Trust for Archaeological Research. Edinburgh.

Bradley, R. 1992 The excavation of an oval barrow beside the Abingdon causewayed enclosure, Oxfordshire. *Proceedings of the Prehistoric Society* 58, 127–42.

Buckley, D., Major, H., and Milton, B. 1988 Excavation of a possible Neolithic long barrow or mortuary enclosure at Rivenhall, Essex, 1986. *Proceedings of the Prehistoric Society* 54, 77–92.

Coombs, D. 1976 Callis Wold round barrow, Humberside. *Antiquity* 50, 130–1.

Crawford, O. 1925 *The long barrows of the Cotswolds*. Gloucester. John Bellows.

Daniel, G. 1950 *The prehistoric chamber tombs of England and Wales*. Cambridge University Press.

Darvill, T. 1982 *The megalithic chambered tombs of the Cotswold-Severn region*. Vorda. Highworth.

Davidson, J., and Henshall, A. 1989 *The Chambered Cairns of Orkney*. Edinburgh University Press.

Drew, C., and Piggott, S. 1936 The excavation of long barrow 163a on Thickthorn Down, Dorset. *Proceedings of the Prehistoric Society* 2, 77–96.

Drewett, P. 1975 The excavation of an oval burial mound of the third millennium BC at Alfriston, East Sussex, 1974. *Proceedings of the Prehistoric Society* 41, 119–52.

Drewett, P. 1986 The excavation of a Neolithic oval barrow at North Marden, West Sussex, 1982. *Proceedings of the Prehistoric Society* 52, 31–51.

Harding, P., and Gingell, C. 1986 The excavation of two long barrows by F. de M and H.F.W.L. Vatcher. *Wiltshire Archaeological Magazine* 80, 7–22.

Henshall, A. 1963 *The chambered tombs of Scotland, 1*. Edinburgh University Press.

Henshall, A. 1972 *The chambered tombs of Scotland 2*. Edinburgh University Press.

Herity, M. 1974 *Irish passage graves-Neolithic tomb builders in Ireland and Britain 2500 BC*. Irish University Press. Dublin.

Hodder, I. 1994 Architecture and meaning: the example of Neolithic houses and tombs. IN. M. Parker Pearson and C. Richards (eds), 73-86.

Hodder, I. 1998 The domus: some problems reconsidered. IN. M. Edmonds and C. Richards (eds), 84-101.

Hodder, I, and Shand, P. 1988 The Haddenham long barrow: an interim statement. *Antiquity* 62, 349-53.

Kinnes, I., 1979 *Round Barrows and Ring Ditches in the British Neolithic*. British Museum Occasional Paper.

Masters, L. 1973 The Lochill long cairn. *Antiquity* 47, 96-100.

Morgan, F. 1959 The excavation of a long barrow at Nutbane, Hants. *Proceedings of the Prehistoric Society* 25, 15-51.

Phillips, C. 1936 The excavation of the Giant's Hills long barrow, Skendleby, Lincolnshire. *Archaeologia* 85, 37-106.

Piggott, S. 1937 The excavation of a long barrow in Holdenhurst parish, near Christchurch, Hants. (No. 183 of Neolithic Wessex Map). *Proceedings of the Prehistoric Society* 3, 1-14.

Piggott, S. 1962 *The West Kennet Long Barrow*. Her Majesty's Stationery Office. London.

Piggott, S. 1967 'Unchambered' long barrows in Neolithic Britain. *Palaeohistoria* 12, 381-93.

Pitt-Rivers, A. 1898 *Excavations in Cranborne Chase iv*. Privately Printed.

Saville, A. 1990 *Hazleton North, Gloucestershire, 1979-82: The excavation of a Neolithic long cairn of the Cotswold-Severn group*. English Heritage Archaeological Report 13.

Stone, J. and Gray Hill, J. 1940 A round barrow on Stockbridge Down, Hampshire. *Antiquaries Journal* 20, 39-51.

Thurnam, J. 1868 On ancient British barrows, especially those of Wiltshire and the adjoining counties (part 1-long barrows). *Archaeologia* 42, 161-243.

Thurnam, J. 1872 On long barrows and round barrows. *Wiltshire Archaeological Magazine* 13, 339-43.

Vyner, B. 1984 The excavation of a Neolithic cairn at Street House, Loftus, Cleveland. *Proceedings of the Prehistoric Society* 50, 151-95.

Whittle, A. 1991 Wayland's Smithy, Oxfordshire: excavations at the Neolithic tomb in 1962-63 by R.J.C. Atkinson and S. Piggott. *Proceedings of the Prehistoric Society* 57 (2), 61-102.

Wymer, J. 1966 Excavations of the Lambourn long barrow, 1964. *Berkshire Archaeological Journal* 62, 1-16.

ENCLOSURES

Recommended introduction

Darvill, T., and Thomas, J. 2001. *Neolithic Enclosures in Atlantic Northwest Europe*. Oxbow. Oxford.

Mercer, R. 1980 *Hambledon Hill: A Neolithic Landscape*. Edinburgh University Press.

Mercer, R. 1990 *Causewayed enclosures*. Princes Risborough. Shire.

Oswald, A., Dyer, C., and Barber, M. 2001 *The Creation of Monuments: Neolithic Causewayed Enclosures in the British Isles*. English Heritage. Swindon.

Other texts

Andersen, N. 1997 *The Sarup Enclosures. Sarup volume 1*. Jutland Archaeological Society Publications. Aarhus University Press.

Avery, M. 1982 The Neolithic causewayed enclosure, Abingdon. IN. H.Case and A.Whittle (eds), *Settlement Patterns in the Oxford Region*. Council for British Archaeology Research Report 4, 10–50.

Bamford, H. 1985 *Briar Hill. Excavation 1974-1978*. Northamptonshire Development Corporation Archaeological Monograph 3.

Barker, G. and Webley, D. 1978 Causewayed camps and Earlier Neolithic economies in central southern England. *Proceedings of the Prehistoric Society* 44, 161–85.

Bedwin, O. 1981 Excavations at the Neolithic Enclosure on Bury Hill, Houghton, West Sussex. *Proceedings of the Prehistoric Society* 47, 69–86.

Bedwin, O. 1984 The excavation of a small hilltop enclosure on Court Hill, Singleton, West Sussex, 1982. *Sussex Archaeological Collections* 122, 13–22.

Burgess, C. Topping, P., Mordant, C., and Maddison, M. 1988 *Enclosures and Defences in the Neolithic of Western Europe*. British Archaeological Report 403.

Connah, G. 1965 Excavations at Knap Hill, Alton Priors, 1961. *Wiltshire Archaeological Magazine* 60, 1–23.

Crawford, O. 1937 Causeway settlements. *Antiquity* 11, 210–12.

Cunnington, M. 1912 Knap Hill Camp. *Wiltshire Archaeological and Natural History Magazine* 37, 42–65.

Curwen, E.C. 1929 Excavations in the Trundle, Goodwood, 1928. *Sussex Archaeological Collections* 70, 33–85.

Curwen, E.C. 1930 Neolithic camps. *Antiquity* 4, 22–54.

Curwen, E.C. 1931 Excavations in the Trundle, Second Season, 1930. *Sussex Archaeological Collections* 72, 100–50.

Curwen, E.C. 1934 Excavations in Whitehawk Neolithic camp, Brighton, 1932–3. *The Antiquaries Journal* 14, 99–133.

Curwen, E.C. 1936 Excavations in Whitehawk camp, third season, 1935. *Sussex Archaeological Collections* 77, 60–92.

Darvill, T. 1996 *The Billown Neolithic landscape project, Isle of Man 1995.* Bournemouth University. School of Conservation Sciences Research Report 1.

Darvill, T. 1997 *The Billown Neolithic landscape project, Isle of Man 1996.* Bournemouth University. School of Conservation Sciences Research Report 3.

Dixon, P. 1972 Excavations at Crickley Hill. *Antiquity* 46, 49-52.

Drewett, P. 1977 The Excavation of a Neolithic Causewayed Enclosure on Offham Hill, East Sussex, 1976. *Proceedings of the Prehistoric Society* 43, 201-41

Drewett, P. 1994 Dr V. Seton Williams' excavations at Combe Hill, 1962 and the role of Neolithic causewayed enclosures in Sussex. *Sussex Archaeological Collections* 132, 7-24.

Edmonds, M. 1993 Interpreting causewayed enclosures in the past and present. IN. C.Tilley (ed), *Interpretative archaeology.* Berg. Oxford, 99-142.

Evans, C. 1988 Acts of Enclosure: A Consideration of Concentrically-Organised Causewayed Enclosures. IN J. Barrett and I. Kinnes (eds), 85-96.

Evans, C. 1988 Monuments and analogy: the interpretation of causewayed enclosures. IN C.Burgess *et al.* 1988, 47-74.

Evans, C, 1988 Excavations at Haddenham, Cambridgeshire: a 'Planned' Enclosure and its Regional Affinities. In C. Burgess *et al.* (eds), 127-45.

Hedges, J. and Buckley, D. 1978 Excavations at a Neolithic causewayed enclosure, Orsett, Essex, 1975. *Proceedings of the Prehistoric Society* 44, 219-308.

Leeds, E. 1928 A Neolithic site at Abingdon, Berks. *Antiquaries Journal* 8, 461-77.

Mercer, R. 1981 *Excavations at Carn Brae, Illogan, Cornwall, 1970-73.* Cornish Archaeological Society Monograph.

Pryor, F. 1998 *Etton: Excavations at a Neolithic Causewayed Enclosure near Maxey, Cambridgeshire, 1982-7.* English Heritage. London.

Robertson-Mackay, R. 1987 The Neolithic Causewayed Enclosure at Staines, Surrey: Excavations 1961-63. *Proceedings of the Prehistoric Society* 53, 23-128.

Russell, M and Rudling, D. 1996 Excavations at Whitehawk Neolithic enclosure, Brighton, East Sussex: 1991-93. *Sussex Archaeological Collections* 134, 39-61.

Smith, I. 1965 *Windmill Hill and Avebury, excavations by Alexander Keiller.* Clarendon. Oxford.

Wheeler, M. 1943 *Maiden Castle, Dorset.* Society of Antiquaries. London.

Whittle, A. 1977 Earlier Neolithic enclosures in north west Europe. *Proceedings of the Prehistoric Society* 43, 329-48.

Whittle, A., Pollard, J. and Grigson, C. 1999 *The Harmony of Symbols: The Windmill Hill Causewayed Enclosure.* Oxbow. Oxford.

Williamson, R. 1930 Excavations in Whitehawk Neolithic camp, near Brighton. *Sussex Archaeological Collections* 71, 57-96.

SHAFTS

Recommended introduction

Barber, M., Field, D. and Topping P. 1999 *The Neolithic Flint Mines of England.* English Heritage and the Royal Commission on the Historical Monuments of England. London.

Holgate, R. 1991 *Prehistoric flint mines.* Shire. Princes Risborough.

Russell, M. 2000 *Flint Mines in Neolithic Britain.* Tempus. Stroud

Other texts

Armstrong, A. 1926 The Grime's Graves problem in the light of recent researches. *Proceedings of the Prehistoric Society of East Anglia* 5, 91–136.

Armstrong, A. 1934 The Percy Sladen Trust excavations, Grimes Graves, Norfolk: interim report 1927–1932. *Proceedings of the Prehistoric Society of East Anglia* 7, 57–61.

Ashbee, P., Bell, M., and Proudfoot, E. 1989 *Wilsford Shaft: Excavations 1960-62.* English Heritage Archaeological Report 11.

Booth, A., and Stone, J. 1952 A trial flint mine at Durrington, Wilts. *Wiltshire Archaeological and Natural History Magazine* 54, 381–8.

Bradley, R. 1974 A Chalk-cut Shaft at Belle Tout. *Sussex Archaeological Collections* 112, 156.

Clarke, W. (ed) 1915 *Report on the excavations at Grime's Graves, Weeting, Norfolk, March – May 1914.* H.K. Lewis. London.

Crawford, H. (ed) 1979 *Subterranean Britain: Aspects of underground archaeology.* John Baker. London.

Curwen, E. and Curwen, E. C. 1926 Harrow Hill Flint Mine Excavation 1924–5. *Sussex Archaeological Collections* 67, 103–38.

Goodman, C., Frost, M., Curwen, E., and Curwen, E.C. 1924 Blackpatch Flint Mine Excavation 1922. *Sussex Archaeological Collections* 65, 69–111.

Green, M. 2000 *A Landscape Revealed: 10,000 Years on a Chalkland Farm.* Tempus. Stroud.

Greenwell, W. 1870 On the opening of Grime's Graves in Norfolk. *Journal of the Ethnological Society of London* 2, 419–39.

Harrison, J. 1877 On marks found upon chalk at Cissbury. *Journal of the Royal Anthropological Institute* 6, 263–71.

Harrison, J. 1878 Additional discoveries at Cissbury. *Journal of the Royal Anthropological Institute* 7, 412–433.

Holleyman, G. 1937 Harrow Hill excavations, 1936. *Sussex Archaeological Collections* 78, 230–51.

Irving, G. 1857 On the camps at Cissbury, Sussex. *Journal of the British Archaeological Association* 13, 274–94.

Lane Fox, A. 1869 Further remarks on the hillforts of Sussex, being an account of the excavations at Cissbury and Highdown. *Archaeologia* 42, 27–52.

Lane Fox, A. 1875 Excavations in Cissbury camp; being a report of the exploration committee of the Anthropological Institute for the year 1875. *Journal of the Anthropological Institute* 5, 357-90.

Longworth, I., and Varndell, G. 1996 *Excavations at Grimes Graves Norfolk 1972-1976. Fasicule 5: Mining in the deep mines.* British Museum Press.

Mercer, R. 1981 *Grimes Graves, Norfolk. Excavations 1971-72: Volume 1.* Department of the Environment Archaeological Report 11.

Pull, J. 1932 *The Flint Miners of Blackpatch.* Williams and Norgate. London.

Russell, M. 2001 *Rough Quarries, Rocks and Hills: John Pull and the Neolithic Flint Mines of Sussex.* Oxbow. Oxford.

Saville, A. 1995 Prehistoric exploitation of flint from the Buchan Ridge Gravels, Grampian Region, north-east Scotland. *Archaeologia Polona* 33, 353-68.

Shepherd, R. 1980 *Prehistoric mining and allied industries.* Academic Press. London.

Sieveking, G. de G. 1979 Grime's Graves and Prehistoric European Flint Mining. IN Crawford, H. (ed) *Subterranean Britain: Aspects of Underground Archaeology.* John Baker. London, 1-43.

Stone, J. 1932 Easton Down, Winterslow, South Wiltshire, flint mine excavation, 1930. *Wiltshire Archaeological and Natural History Magazine* 45, 350-65.

Stone, J. 1935 Excavations at Easton Down, Winterslow, 1933-4. *Wiltshire Archaeological and Natural History Magazine* 47, 68-80.

Turner, E. 1850 On the military earthworks of the South Downs, with a more enlarged account of Cissbury, one of the principal of them. *Sussex Archaeological Collections* 3, 173-84.

Willett, E. 1880 On flint workings at Cissbury, Sussex. *Archaeologia* 45, 337-48.

SECONDARY ELEMENTS

Recommended introduction

Barclay, A., and Harding, J. (eds) 1999 *Pathways and Ceremonies: The Cursus Monuments of Britain and Ireland.* Oxbow. Oxford.

Burl, A. 1991 *Prehistoric Henges.* Shire. Princes Risborough.

Burl, A. 2001 *Prehistoric Stone Circles.* Shire. Princes Risborough.

Harding, A. and Lee, G. 1987 *Henge Monuments and Related Sites of Great Britain.* British Archaeological Reports 175.

Malone, C. 1989 *Avebury.* English Heritage. Batsford.

Wainwright, G., 1989 *The Henge Monuments – Ceremony and Society in Prehistoric Britain.* Thames and Hudson. London.

Other texts

Atkinson, R., Piggott, C., and Sanders, N., 1951 *Excavations at Dorchester, Oxon: First Report.* Ashmolean Museum. Oxford.

Barclay, G. 1989 Henge monuments: reappraisal or reductionism? *Proceedings of the Prehistoric Society* 55, 260–2.

Barclay, G., and Maxwell, G. 1998 *The Cleaven Dyke and Littleour.* Society of Antiquaries of Scotland Monograph. Edinburgh.

Bradley, R., and Chambers, R. 1988 A new study of the Cursus complex at Dorchester on Thames. *Oxford Journal of Archaeology* 7, 271–90.

Burl, A. 1969 Henges: Internal structures and regional groups. *Archaeological Journal* 126, 1–28.

Catherall, P. 1971 Henges in perspective. *Archaeological Journal* 128, 147–53.

Childe, G. 1931 *Skara Brae: A Pictish Village in Orkney.* Kegan Paul, Trench, Trubner and Co. London.

Clare, T. 1986 Towards a reappraisal of henge monuments. *Proceedings of the Prehistoric Society* 52, 281–316.

Clare, T. 1987 Towards a reappraisal of henge monuments: Origins, evolutions and hierarchies. *Proceedings of the Prehistoric Society* 53, 457–77.

Clark, J. 1936 The timber monument at Arminghall and its affinities. *Proceedings of the Prehistoric Society* 2, 1–52.

Cleal, R., Walker, K., and Montague, R. 1995 *Stonehenge in its landscape: 20th century excavations.* English Heritage Archaeology Report 10.

Cope, J. 1998 *The Modern Antiquarian.* Harper Collins. London.

Cunnington, M. 1929 *Woodhenge.* Simpson. Devizes.

Darvill, T. 2000 *Billown Neolithic Landscape Project, Isle of Man: Fifth Report 1999.* Bournemouth University School of Conservation Sciences Research Report 7.

Gibson, A. 1994 Excavations at the Sarn-y-bryn-caled cursus complex, Welshpool, Powys, and the timber circles of Great Britain and Ireland. *Proceedings of the Prehistoric Society* 60, 143–223.

Gibson, A. 1998 *Stonehenge and timber circles.* Tempus. Stroud.

Harding, A, 1981 Excavations in the Prehistoric Ritual Complex near Milfield, Northumberland. *Proceedings of the Prehistoric Society* 47, 87–135.

Hedges, J., and Buckley, D. 1981 *The Springfield Cursus and the Cursus Problem.* Essex County Council.

Miket, R., 1985 Ritual Enclosures at Whitton Hill, Northumberland. *Proceedings of the Prehistoric Society* 51, 137–48.

Piggott, S. and Piggott, C. 1939 Stone and earth circles in Dorset. *Antiquity* 38, 218–9.

Richards, J. 1990 *The Stonehenge Environs Project.* English Heritage Archaeological Report 16.

Ritchie, J. 1978 The stones of Stennes, Orkney. *Proceedings of the Society of Antiquaries Scotland* 107, 1–60.

Russell, M. 1996 *A reassessment of the Bronze Age cemetery-barrow on Itford Hill, East Sussex, and its place in the prehistory of southeast England.* Bournemouth University: School of Conservation Sciences Research Report 2.

Tratman, E. 1967 The Priddy Circles, Mendip, Somerset, henge monuments. *Proceedings of the University of Bristol Spelaeological Society* 11, 97–125.

Vyner, B. 1988 The Street House Wossit: the excavation of a Late Neolithic and Early Bronze Age palisaded ritual monument at Street House, Loftus, Cleveland. *Proceedings of the Prehistoric Society* 54, 173-202.

Wainwright, G., 1969 A Review of Henge Monuments in the Light of Recent Research. *Proceedings of the Prehistoric Society* 35, 112-33.

Wainwright, G. 1979 *Mount Pleasant, Dorset: Excavations 1970-1971.* Society of Antiquaries Research Report 37. London.

Wainwright, G., and Longworth, I. 1971 *Durrington Walls: Excavations 1966-1968.* Society of Antiquaries, London.

Whittle, A., Atkinson, R., Chambers, R., and Thomas, N. 1992 Excavations in the Neolithic and Bronze Age complex at Dorchester-on-Thames, Oxfordshire, 1947-52 and 1981. *Proceedings of the Prehistoric Society* 58, 143-202.

Whittle, A. 1997 *Sacred Mound, Holy Rings: Silbury Hill and the West Kennet Palisade Enclosures – A Later Neolithic Complex in North Wiltshire.* Oxbow. Oxford.

Index